Daily

INCOME TAX

1993–94

Daily Mail

INCOME TAX

1993–94

For the year April 6th, 1993 to April 5th, 1994 in accordance with the Budget proposals of March 1993

EDITED BY

KENNETH R. TINGLEY

Chapmans

Chapmans Publishers
A division of The Orion Publishing Group Ltd
Orion House
5 Upper St Martin's Lane
London WC2H 9EA

First published by Chapmans for Associated Newspapers Ltd 1993

ISBN 1–85592–737–3

Photoset in Linotron Melior by
MC Typeset Ltd, Wouldham, Rochester, Kent
Printed and bound in Great Britain by
Benham & Co Ltd, Colchester, Essex

Contents

RATES AND ALLOWANCES	vii
THE TAX SYSTEM	1
INDEPENDENT TAXATION	3
LIABILITY TO INCOME TAX	6
ALLOWANCES	8
HOW TO OBTAIN ALLOWANCES	25
PENSION CONTRIBUTIONS	26
INTEREST PAID	36
HOW TO OBTAIN RELIEF FOR INTEREST PAID	44
NATIONAL INSURANCE CONTRIBUTIONS	50
BUSINESS EXPANSION SCHEME	51
LIFE ASSURANCE PREMIUMS	55
MEDICAL INSURANCE PREMIUMS	55
VOCATIONAL TRAINING	56
EMPLOYMENTS	58
BENEFITS IN KIND	72
REDUNDANCY PAYMENTS	87
BUSINESSES AND PROFESSIONS	90
CAPITAL EXPENDITURE	104
PROPERTY INCOME	115
INVESTMENT INCOME	122
SOCIAL SECURITY BENEFITS	136
DEEDS OF COVENANT	138
CHARITABLE BODIES	143
MARRIAGE	148
DEATH OF SPOUSE	150
DIVORCE AND SEPARATION	152
REPAYMENT OF TAX	158
SCHEDULES AND CASES	161
DATE TAX PAYABLE	162
HOW TO APPEAL	166
RATES OF TAX FOR EARLIER YEARS	167
CAPITAL GAINS TAX	168
MAKING THE ANNUAL RETURN	183
COMPANIES	187
VALUE ADDED TAX	192
INHERITANCE TAX	197
INDEPENDENT TAXATION – PRACTICAL CONSIDERATIONS	207
HINTS ON SAVING TAX	212
ACTION BEFORE APRIL 6th, 1994	222
TABLES	
READY RECKONER	224
GROSSING-UP TABLES	228
TAX ON SPECIMEN INCOMES	230
INDEX	231

Rates of Income Tax 1993–94

ANY ALLOWANCES to which an individual may be entitled are subtracted from total income to establish the amount of income chargeable to income tax. Should the allowances exceed total income there can be no liability. Where, however, a surplus of income remains this will be chargeable to income tax at the following rates for 1993–94:

Lower rate	20 per cent on first £2,500
Basic rate	25 per cent on next £21,200
Higher rate	40 per cent on the remainder

In addition to allowances there are other deductions which may be made when calculating total income and these will affect the amount of income chargeable to income tax.

The rates of tax may require some modification where income includes dividends received from companies.

It is the intention that the lower rate 20 per cent band should be increased from £2,500 to £3,000 for 1994–95, but this increase will have no application for the year ending on April 5th, 1994.

Allowances 1993–94

Additional personal allowance for children	**£1,720**
Blind person's allowance	**£1,080**
Married couple's allowance:	
age of elder spouse:	
below 65	**£1,720**
65 to 74	**£2,465**
75 and over	**£2,505**
Personal allowance:	
Taxpayer's age:	
below 65	**£3,445**
65 to 74	**£4,200**
75 and over	**£4,370**
Widow's bereavement allowance	**£1,720**

The tax system

THE BUDGET

DURING THE SPRING of each year successive Chancellors of the Exchequer have traditionally delivered their main Budget Statement outlining proposals for amending the system of both direct and indirect taxation. These proposals are subsequently recorded in a Finance Bill, which is subjected to Parliamentary debate and further amendment before becoming part of the law of the United Kingdom. The present Chancellor, Mr Norman Lamont, followed tradition on Tuesday, March 16th, 1993, by announcing a wide range of proposed changes. These proposals are discussed on the following pages and numerous examples illustrate the calculation of liability to taxation. As the proposals must be debated in Parliament it will not be overlooked that further amendments may be introduced at some later time before Royal Assent is eventually forthcoming shortly before August 5th, 1993.

The Budget Statement of March 1993 will be the last delivered in the spring. In future, Budget Day is being moved to a date falling near the end of November. This change is considered advisable to create a unified Budget including both the Government's spending proposals, announced in the autumn, and the tax-raising proposals previously announced in the spring.

The first November Budget will be delivered in November 1993, with Royal Assent given not later than May 5th in the following year. To achieve a smooth transition from the old to the new there will be two Budget Statements in the calendar year 1993, namely one already delivered on March 16th and the other due at the end of November.

THE PERSONAL TAX SYSTEM

The system of personal taxation imposed in the United Kingdom for the year of assessment 1993–94, which commences on April 6th, 1993, and ends on April 5th, 1994, fully incorporates the independent taxation of husband and wife. Any allowances and other deductions available to individuals must be set against income chargeable to tax. Where the deductions exceed chargeable income there will be no liability. If surplus income remains, the first £2,500 will be charged at the lower rate of 20 per cent and the next £21,200 charged at the basic rate of 25 per cent. Should chargeable income exceed £23,700 the excess is taxed at the higher rate of 40 per cent. These rates apply generally to both earned and investment income but some adjustment may be required where a taxpayer's income includes dividends or other distributions from a company.

PAYE tax deductions made from earnings extend to income charged at all three rates, where earnings are sufficiently substantial. Tax at these rates will be collected simultaneously where business and professional profits, rents and other receipts are assessed directly on the taxpayer. Where income is received, or is treated as received, after deduction of income tax, any further liability at the higher rate will be collected by direct assessment on the taxpayer.

Tax relief on many, but not all, payments of mortgage interest is given under the MIRAS scheme by deducting income tax at the basic rate of 25 per cent from each payment. Similar relief may be available on other payments made after deduction of income tax. This deduction procedure is merely a method of providing relief and has little effect on the net income tax liability eventually borne.

The unified personal tax system, incorporating tax payable at all three rates, is administered by Inspectors of Taxes and their staff.

THE FUTURE

In his March, 1993, Budget Statement the Chancellor announced a number of proposed changes which will not come into operation until a later date. These included raising the 20 per cent rate band from £2,500 to £3,000 in 1994–95. However, relief for the married couple's allowance, the additional personal allowance, the widow's bereavement allowance and payments of maintenance to a divorced or separated spouse will be limited to 20 per cent in 1994–95 and future years. Relief at this reduced level will extend also to payments of mortgage interest in 1994–95 and future years.

A further significant and far-reaching proposed change will not be introduced until April 1996. This will abolish the "preceding year" basis of assessment which applies to self-employed individuals. It may also be possible for many taxpayers to adopt a system of self-assessment, although there will be no compulsion to proceed in this manner.

A brief note of the proposed future changes appears under the appropriate heading in the Guide.

Independent taxation

THE OLD SYSTEM

BEFORE THE INTRODUCTION of independent taxation on April 6th, 1990, the income of a married woman "living with" her husband was usually assessable to tax in the husband's name. This did not apply in the year of marriage and in a limited range of other situations it was possible for the wife to be separately assessed. These exceptions apart, the husband was responsible for completing an income tax return recording the income of both himself and his wife and was required to discharge any tax due. This latter obligation was not particularly onerous as many items of income were received after deduction of income tax at the basic rate or through the PAYE deduction scheme.

A similar approach applied when imposing capital gains tax on capital gains and only one combined annual exemption could be obtained by the couple.

In contrast to income tax and capital gains tax, the system of inheritance tax and its predecessor, capital transfer tax, did not draw any distinction between husband and wife "living together" and those living apart. Each spouse was consistently required to satisfy his or her own inheritance tax liability, with the benefit of separate reliefs and nil rate bands when determining the amount of tax due. It was also possible for assets to be transferred between most husbands and wives, whether living together or living apart, without incurring any commitment to inheritance tax.

The anomaly between a system of inheritance tax which recognised independent taxation and a system of income tax and capital gains tax which did not, created considerable adverse criticism. This led to the introduction of independent taxation on April 6th, 1990, which is now a well-established feature of the United Kingdom tax code.

INDEPENDENT TAXATION

It is a feature of independent taxation that all individuals, whether married or single, are independently assessed to income tax. In the case of a married couple "living together" each spouse is responsible for submitting his or her tax returns, satisfying compliance requirements and discharging the amount of income tax due.

All individuals receive a basic personal allowance, which may be increased for those aged 65 or over and further increased for those who have celebrated their 75th birthday. The amount of the increased allowance may be reduced where the individual's income exceeds stated limits. With the exception of special transitional reliefs, any unused personal allowance of one spouse cannot be transferred to the other.

A married man whose wife is "living with" him qualifies for a married couple's allowance. Before April 6th, 1993, this allowance had to be used by the husband if his income was sufficient. Where a deficiency of income arose the unused married couple's allowance could be transferred to the wife. On and after April 6th, 1993, different rules may apply for sharing the allowance between husband and wife.

The amount of the married couple's allowance may be increased where either husband or wife is 65 years or over, or further increased where one party has celebrated his or her 75th birthday. Some reduction in these increased allowances may be necessary where the income of the husband exceeds a stated limit. Here also some special transitional relief may be due for the purpose of ensuring that the introduction of independent taxation has not resulted in any loss of aggregate allowances.

Apart from the personal allowance and the married couple's allowance, the only remaining allowances comprise:

a An additional personal allowance, for children

b A widow's bereavement allowance

c A blind person's allowance

Of these three allowances, only the blind person's allowance can be transferred from one spouse to the other where it cannot be fully absorbed by the qualifying spouse.

TRANSITIONAL ALLOWANCES

Three groups of special transitional allowances have been made available to ensure that the level of aggregate allowances granted after April 5th, 1990 does not fall by reason only of the introduction of independent taxation. These special allowances may be available where:

a A husband has insufficient income to absorb his personal allowance. The unused allowance may then be transferred to his wife, if she is living with her husband.

b A husband and wife fall into different age groups. If an increased allowance was available for 1989–90 by reason only of the wife's age, an increased allowance may be available in future years.

c A separated husband is maintaining his wife without obtaining any tax relief for the cost of maintenance. The husband may qualify for the married couple's allowance, notwithstanding that he is not "living with" his wife.

CAPITAL GAINS TAX

Capital gains tax is also subject to independent taxation, with all individuals being separately assessed. It is unnecessary to restrict the annual exemption to the combined gains of a husband and his wife, as each may obtain his or her separate exemption. However, it remains possible for assets to be transferred between husband and wife "living together" without incurring capital gains tax commitments.

THE APPROACH

When approaching the independent taxation of husband and wife the following steps are of great importance:

a The allowances which are available to each individual must be identified;

b The reliefs which each individual may obtain for outgoings must be established;

c The income of each individual must be accurately determined; and

d The capital gains and capital losses realised by each individual must be separately calculated.

Where a husband and wife are "living together" there may be an opportunity for allocating income and outgoings between the spouses to obtain the most beneficial tax result.

Comments made on the following pages analyse the effect of independent taxation in detail. A separate chapter commencing on page 207 discusses many practical matters and considerations which may arise as a result of independent taxation.

Liability to income tax

PERSONS LIABLE TO PAY TAX

ALL INDIVIDUALS whose incomes exceed £3,445 may be liable to income tax for 1993–94, but there are increased exemption limits for persons aged 65 or over. Most forms of income are assessable to income tax but there are a number of exceptions. The following lists illustrate income which is, and that which is not, liable to tax. The lists are not intended to be exhaustive but provide an indication of the approach applied to many items of income experienced by a large number of taxpayers.

INCOME ASSESSABLE TO INCOME TAX

Annuities excluding the "capital" portion of certain purchased life annuities.

Bank interest arising on deposits.

Benefits in kind made available to most directors of companies, and to employees earning £8,500 per annum or more. Certain benefits enjoyed by employees earning less than this sum may also be assessable.

Building society interest on deposits.

Christmas boxes to employees.

Dividends from companies.

Furnished letting receipts (net profits after expenses).

Pensions, whether voluntary or received under the terms of employment and whether received in respect of the recipient's services or those of another person.

Premiums from letting premises for periods which do not exceed fifty years (part only may be assessable).

Profits from businesses and professions.

Rents and other income from land and property.

Rent-free accommodation occupied by certain employees (income assessed by reference to a notional value).

Salaries, wages, bonuses, commission, and all other earnings from offices and employments. Voluntary payments made at the end of an employment and payments of compensation for loss of office are usually taxable, but liability may be limited to the excess of the aggregate sum received over £30,000.

Social security benefits. A list of those benefits which are taxable appears on page 136.

Tips received in connection with a business or employment.

INCOME NOT ASSESSABLE

Annuities paid to holders of the Victoria Cross, George Cross, Albert Medal, Edward Medal and certain other gallantry awards.

Bounty payments to members of the armed forces who voluntarily extend their service.

Compensation for loss of office and **redundancy** payments for loss of office, but where the aggregate receipts exceed £30,000 the excess is taxable.

Covenanted payments made under a voluntary non-charitable deed of covenant executed after March 14th, 1988.

Dividends arising under Personal Equity Plans.

Interest on contractual savings under the Save As You Earn scheme.

Interest on National Savings Certificates and Children's Bonus Bonds.

Interest arising under TESSA deposit schemes.

Maintenance payments under most Court Orders or agreements, although liability remains for payments under older arrangements.

National Savings Bank Interest. The first £70 of interest received on ordinary deposits with the National Savings Bank is exempt, but the excess will be taxable. This exemption does not extend to interest on investment deposits.

Payments in kind (where not convertible into cash or money's worth), except where received by most directors or by an employee earning £8,500 per annum or more. Certain benefits received by employees earning less than this sum may also be taxable.

Rent received under the "rent a room" scheme where gross receipts do not exceed £3,250 or perhaps some lower figure.

Scholarship income.

Social security benefits. A list of those benefits which are not taxable appears on page 136.

Travel vouchers, warrants and allowances for members of the armed forces when travelling on leave.

Allowances

HUSBAND AND WIFE LIVING TOGETHER

The nature and amount of the allowances which many individuals can claim may be affected by whether a husband and wife are "living together". This relationship of "living together" will be treated as satisfied unless the couple are:

a separated under an order of a court of competent jurisdiction;

b separated by deed of separation; or

c in fact separated in such circumstances that the separation is likely to be permanent.

PERSONAL ALLOWANCE

For 1993–94 all individuals receive a personal allowance. The amount of this allowance is governed by the individual's age and in some cases by the level of income received.

Individuals below the age of 65 years receive a basic personal allowance of £3,445. The allowance is not affected by the amount of the individual's income.

For those who were 65 years of age or more at any time in the year ended April 5th, 1994, the allowance will be increased to £4,200. A further increase to £4,370 is available to those who are 75 or over in the same year. In both cases the increased allowance will be forthcoming for an individual who died before reaching his or her 65th or 75th birthday if that age would otherwise have been achieved before April 6th, 1994.

The amount of the increased allowance available to older taxpayers will be reduced if the total income of the individual exceeds £14,200 for 1993–94. Where this level is exceeded the increased personal allowance is reduced by one-half of the excess. This process continues until the personal allowance is reduced to the level of the basic allowance of £3,445 when no further reduction will be made. When establishing the total income of an individual for this purpose the income of that individual's spouse, if any, is ignored.

All individuals receive a personal allowance. Therefore both a husband and his wife will independently receive a personal allowance of £3,445, or some increased amount based on age, for 1993–94. Subject to an exception designed to smooth the introduction of independent taxation (see page 19), any unused personal allowance of one spouse cannot be transferred to the other.

The personal allowance is not confined to adults but can also be obtained by children of any age. There are, however, complex rules which prevent tax advantages being obtained by parents who transfer income-producing assets to young children.

1 *BASIC PERSONAL ALLOWANCE*

Sue is 42 years of age and divorced. Her only income for 1993–94 is a salary of £13,000.

	£	
Total income	13,000	
Less Personal allowance	3,445	
Tax chargeable on	£9,555	
Tax payable:		
On first £2,500 at 20 per cent		500.00
On balance of £7,055 at 25 per cent		1,763.75
		£2,263.75

2 *INCREASED PERSONAL ALLOWANCE*

George is a widower aged 78. He receives a social security retirement pension of £2,917 and taxable income from letting properties of £7,200.

Total income:	£	
Retirement pension	2,917	
Letting income	7,200	
	10,117	
Less Personal allowance	4,370	
Tax chargeable on	£5,747	
Tax payable:		
On first £2,500 at 20 per cent		500.00
On balance of £3,247 at 25 per cent		811.75
		£1,311.75

The maximum personal allowance is available as the taxpayer is over the age of 74 years and his income does not exceed £14,200.

MARRIED COUPLE'S ALLOWANCE

A married man whose wife is "living with" him throughout, or during any part of, the year ending on April 6th, 1994, is entitled to a married couple's allowance. The amount of this allowance is also governed by the age of the parties to a marriage and perhaps by the level of the husband's income.

The basic married couple's allowance is £1,720. This may be increased to £2,465 if either the husband or the wife is 65 years or over at any time in the year ending on April 5th, 1994. A further increase to

3 *MARGINAL PERSONAL ALLOWANCE*

Ethel is a widow aged 69. In 1993–94 she receives aggregate income of £10,800 from a social security retirement pension and a company occupational pension scheme administered by her late husband's employers. Interest of £3,900 (gross) is received from a number of deposits.

Total income:		£
Pensions		10,800
Interest		3,900
		14,700
	£	
Less Personal allowance	4,200	
Deduct one-half of excess over £14,200 (£14,700 less £14,200)	250	3,950
Tax chargeable on		£10,750
Tax payable:		
On first £2,500 at 20 per cent		500.00
On balance of £8,250 at 25 per cent		2,062.50
		£2,562.50

Part, or all, of the tax payable will be offset by tax deducted from interest and PAYE deducted from payments made by the previous employer's pension scheme.

4 *LOSS OF MARGINAL PERSONAL ALLOWANCE*

Applying the facts in Example 3, let it be assumed that the investment income was increased to, say, £5,900, thereby increasing total income to £16,700.

The marginal personal allowance would then be calculated as follows:

	£
Maximum allowance	4,200
Deduct one-half of excess over £14,200 (£16,700 less £14,200)	1,250
	£2,950

However, as the figure of £2,950 is less than the basic personal allowance of £3,445, no marginal personal allowance will be granted and the basic allowance will be obtained. The calculation continues:

Total income:	£
Pensions	10,800
Investment income	5,900
	16,700
Less personal allowance	3,445
Tax chargeable on	£13,255
Tax payable:	
On first £2,500 at 20 per cent	500.00
On balance of £10,755 at 25 per cent	2,688.75
	£3,188.75

£2,505 will be forthcoming if either spouse is 75 or over at any time in the year. In the case of a spouse who died during the year but would otherwise have reached the age of 65 or 75 respectively before April 6th, 1994, the appropriate increase will be available.

It has been shown above that the increased personal allowance due to an individual over the age of 64 may be reduced where that individual's total income exceeds £14,200 for 1993–94. A similar restriction may apply when calculating the increased married couple's allowance. The allowance must then be reduced by:

a one-half of the husband's total income (not including any income of the wife) in excess of £14,200, less

b the amount of any reduction made to the husband's increased personal allowance by reason of his income exceeding £14,200.

The reduction under **b** is necessary to ensure that two different allowances are not both reduced by reference to the same amount of excess income. Subject to this, the reduction process continues until the

5 *BASIC MARRIED COUPLE'S ALLOWANCE*

Peter and his wife Katherine are both below the age of 65 and "living together". Peter has earnings of £17,000 in 1993–94. Katherine receives a salary of £9,000 and interest of £250 (gross). No election has been made to transfer any part of the married couple's allowance.

Peter

	£	£
Total income – earnings		17,000
Less Personal allowance	3,445	
Married couple's allowance	1,720	5,165
Tax chargeable on		£11,835

Tax payable:	
On the first £2,500 at 20 per cent	500.00
On the balance of £9,335 at 25 per cent	2,333.75
	£2,833.75

Katherine

	£
Total income:	
Salary	9,000
Interest	250
	9,250
Less Personal allowance	3,445
Tax chargeable on	£5,805

Tax payable:	
On the first £2,500 at 20 per cent	500.00
On the balance of £3,305 at 25 per cent	826.25
	£1,326.25

6 *MARGINAL MARRIED COUPLE'S ALLOWANCE*

Joe and his wife Eileen are both 72 years of age and "living together". Joe's total income for 1993–94 is £16,300. Eileen has a total income of £4,150. No election has been made to transfer any part of the married couple's allowance.

The personal allowance available to Joe will be calculated as follows:

	£
Full increased allowance	4,200
Deduct one-half of excess over £14,200 (£16,300 less £14,200)	1,050
	£3,150

However, the reduced personal allowance cannot fall below the basic personal allowance of £3,445. Therefore the income of Joe has reduced the allowance by £755 (£4,200 less £3,445).

The married couple's allowance will be:

	£	£
Full increased allowance		2,465
Deduct one-half of excess over £14,200 (£16,300 less £14,200)	1,050	
Less Reduction in personal allowance	755	295
Allowance due		£2,170

Joe

	£	£
Total income		16,300
Less Personal allowance	3,445	
Married couple's allowance	2,170	5,615
Tax chargeable on		£10,685

Tax payable:	
On first £2,500 at 20 per cent	500.00
On balance of £8,185 at 25 per cent	2,046.25
	£2,546.25

Eileen

	£
Total income	4,150
Less Personal allowance	4,200
Tax chargeable on	NIL

married couple's allowance has been reduced to the basic allowance of £1,720 when no further reduction will take place.

A man may qualify for only one married couple's allowance for the year 1993–94, notwithstanding that one marriage terminates and a second marriage takes place in the same year.

There is a limitation in the amount of the married couple's allowance for 1993–94 where the marriage takes place after May 5th, 1993. This limitation is discussed on page 148.

7 MARRIED COUPLE'S ALLOWANCE – TRANSFER

For 1993–94 the business profits of Roy were only £4,600. He was "living with" his wife Jane throughout the year and her income comprised a salary of £10,500. Neither spouse had any other income and both were under the age of 65. No election has yet been made to transfer any part of the married couple's allowance.

Roy is entitled to a personal allowance of £3,445 and a married couple's allowance of £1,720. The aggregate of these allowances exceeds his total income of £4,600 and there will be no liability to income tax. Roy may transfer the unused married couple's allowance to his wife. If he agrees, the amount to be transferred is calculated as follows:

	£	£
Married couple's allowance		1,720
Less Total income	4,600	
Deduct personal allowance	3,445	1,155
To be transferred		£565

If total income was reduced to, say, £2,600 the maximum married couple's allowance capable of being transferred could not exceed £1,720, the amount of the allowance. The unused personal allowance cannot be transferred unless the special transitional reliefs discussed on page 19 apply.

Jane

	£	£
Total income		10,500
Less Personal allowance	3,445	
Married couple's allowance transferred	565	4,010
Tax chargeable on		£6,490

Tax payable:

On the first £2,500 at 20 per cent	500.00
On the balance of £3,990 at 25 per cent	997.50
	£1,497.50

As a transitional measure, the married couple's allowance may occasionally be available to a husband who separated from his wife before April 6th, 1990 (see page 23). Further transitional relief may be obtained by elderly persons who would otherwise suffer a disadvantage from the introduction of independent taxation (see page 21).

Allocation of married couple's allowance

For 1992–93 the married couple's allowance was allocated primarily to the husband and not to the wife. If the husband had sufficient income to utilise the allowance fully, no part of that allowance was capable of being transferred to the wife. Where, however, the married couple's allowance exceeded the husband's total income, less allowances and reliefs, the balance of the allowance could be transferred to the wife. When calculating the excess over total income, any business expansion scheme relief had to be ignored. Also disregarded were deductions attributable to payments made under deduction of income tax, including

8 MARRIED COUPLE'S ALLOWANCE – ELECTION

Adapting the facts in Example 5, let it be assumed that an election was made by Katherine to take one half of the married couple's allowance.

Peter

	£	£
Total income – earnings		17,000
Less Personal allowance	3,445	
Married couple's allowance – one half	860	4,305
Tax chargeable on		£12,695
Tax payable:		
On the first £2,500 at 20 per cent		500.00
On the balance of £10,195 at 25 per cent		2,548.75
		£3,048.75

Katherine

		£
Total income:		
Salary		9,000
Interest		250
		9,250
Less Personal allowance	3,445	
Married couple's allowance – one half	860	4,305
Tax chargeable on		£4,945
Tax payable:		
On the first £2,500 at 20 per cent		500.00
On the balance of £2,445 at 25 per cent		611.25
		£1,111.25

MIRAS mortgage contributions, many pension scheme contributions, medical insurance contributions and contributions for vocational training.

For the unused married couple's allowance to be transferred, the husband was required to provide written notice to the Inland Revenue within a period of six years following April 5th, 1993. The husband could not be compelled to provide the required notice and if he failed to do so his wife was unable to obtain the benefit of any unused married couple's allowance.

A different method of allocating the married couple's allowance is available for 1993–94 and future years. This provides married couples with the following options:

a To take no action and continue the treatment shown above, with the married couple's allowance being allocated primarily to the husband.

b For the wife to elect, as of right, to take one-half of the basic allowance of £1,720, leaving the remaining one-half allocated to the husband.

c For the couple to elect jointly that the entire basic married couple's allowance should be given to the wife, with no part of that allowance being absorbed by the husband.

The elections available under **b** and **c** must be restricted to the basic married couple's allowance of £1,720. It is not possible for individuals over the age of 64 years and receiving an increased allowance to include the amount of the increase in any election.

Subject to two exceptions, an election will only be effective for a year of assessment if it is made before the commencement of that year on April 6th. The first exception enables the election to be made not later than May 5th, if H M Inspector of Taxes was notified before the previous April 6th that an election would be forthcoming. The second exception deals with the year of marriage and enables an election to be made at any time in that year.

Once made, an election continues indefinitely for each succeeding year until it is withdrawn. The time limits for withdrawal are similar to those which govern the ability to make an election.

Where a joint election has been submitted under **c** for the wife to take the entire basic married couple's allowance, the husband can subsequently elect to retrieve one-half of that allowance. This election also must be made within the normal time limits.

It is possible that the husband or wife to whom all or part of the basic married couple's allowance has been allocated cannot utilise the entire allowance due to an absence of income. The spouse involved may then give written notice transferring the unabsorbed part to the other spouse. This option is also available to a husband who obtains that part of the married couple's allowance in excess of the basic allowance.

Future relief

For 1994–95 and future years it is proposed that the married couple's allowance will produce relief at the 20 per cent lower rate only. This is in contrast to the relief available for 1993–94 where relief may be available at the basic rate of 25 per cent and also at the higher rate of 40 per cent where taxable income is sufficiently substantial.

To compensate couples over the age of 64 for this restriction the increased married couple's allowance of £2,465 and £2,505 respectively will each be increased by £200.

ADDITIONAL PERSONAL ALLOWANCE

An additional personal allowance of £1,720 may be available to:

a A woman who is not, throughout the year ended April 5th, 1994, married and living with her husband.

b A man who is neither married nor living with his wife for the whole or any part of the year. A man separated from his wife but who may claim the special transitional married couple's allowance discussed on page 23 must be excluded.

c A man who, for the whole or any part of the year, is a married man living with his wife, if the wife is totally incapacitated by physical or mental infirmity throughout the entire year.

9 *ADDITIONAL PERSONAL ALLOWANCE*

Peggy is a divorced mother aged 43, with an eleven-year-old daughter and a nine-year-old son living at home. She has not remarried and earns a salary of £12,000 for 1993–94.

	£	£
Total income		**12,000**
Less **Personal allowance**	**3,445**	
Additional personal allowance	**1,720**	**5,165**
Tax chargeable on		**£6,835**
Tax payable:		
On the first £2,500 at 20 per cent		**500.00**
On the balance of £4,335 at 25 per cent		**1,083.75**
		£1,583.75

To obtain the additional personal allowance the claimant must show that a qualifying child is resident with him or her for the whole or part of the year. Only one allowance of £1,720 is available, notwithstanding the number of qualifying children.

The expression "qualifying child" means a child:

a born during the year ending on April 5th, 1994, or

b under the age of 16 years on April 6th, 1993, or

c over the age of 16 on April 6th, 1993, and either receiving full-time instruction at a university, college, school or other educational establishment or undergoing training for a trade, profession or vocation throughout a minimum two-year period.

It is also necessary to demonstrate that the qualifying child:

a is a child of the claimant, or

b not being a child of the claimant, was either born during the year ended April 5th, 1994, or under the age of 18 years on April 6th, 1993, and maintained for the whole or part of the succeeding twelve-month period by the claimant at his own expense.

"Child" includes a stepchild, an illegitimate child if the parents have subsequently married, and an adopted child under the age of 18 years at the time of the adoption.

A woman may be married and living with her husband during part of the year of assessment. She will only qualify for the additional personal allowance if the qualifying child is resident with her during that part of the year when she was not living with her husband, i.e. following separation.

A man who marries during the year may elect to forgo the married couple's allowance and obtain the additional personal allowance for that year should that allowance otherwise be available; a course of action which would usually be advantageous.

Where a man and woman are unmarried but living together as husband and wife it is not possible for both to obtain the full additional personal allowance for different children. In this situation the claim must be limited to the youngest of the qualifying children only. In those cases where two or more individuals can each claim the allowance for the same child, the allowance can be divided between them in whatever proportions may be agreed.

The additional personal allowance will often be claimed by a separated spouse or divorced former spouse having custody of a child or children. It will also be available to other single persons, including widows, and a married man with an incapacitated wife, if of course there is at least one qualifying child.

An individual who qualifies for the additional personal allowance of £1,720 also receives the lower personal allowance of £3,445 (or perhaps more if the individual is over 64). These two allowances aggregate £5,165, which is identical to the aggregate of the personal allowance and the married couple's allowance available to a married man. It will therefore be apparent that a single parent family is effectively taxed on a basis similar to that of a married man "living with" his wife.

The additional personal allowance cannot be transferred and is available only to the claimant.

The future

For 1994–95 and future years it is proposed that the additional personal allowance will only produce relief at the lower rate of 20 per cent. At present relief is available at all rates, including the higher rate of 40 per cent where income is sufficiently substantial.

WIDOW'S BEREAVEMENT ALLOWANCE

Where a husband and wife are "living together" and the husband dies the widow is entitled to a widow's bereavement allowance. The allowance is available for the year in which death occurs. It will also be available for the following year only, unless the widow remarries in the year of her late husband's death. For 1993–94 the amount of the allowance is £1,720.

A widow entitled to the widow's bereavement allowance of £1,720 for 1993–94 also receives a personal allowance of £3,445 (or perhaps some greater amount if the widow is over 64). The aggregate of these two allowances is £5,165, which is identical to the aggregate of the personal allowance and married couple's allowance available to a married man "living with" his wife. In addition, a widow with a qualifying child or children may also obtain the additional personal allowance of £1,720.

It is a necessary requirement that immediately before the time of his death the husband and wife were "living together". The widow's bereavement allowance will not usually be available if the parties were separated at that time.

The widow's bereavement allowance is available only for the year of assessment in which the husband dies and for the immediately following year and cannot be obtained for future years. The allowance is confined to widows and there is no similar allowance for widowers.

10 *WIDOW'S BEREAVEMENT ALLOWANCE*

John and Margaret were "living together" until September 16th, 1993, when John died. The two children of the marriage, aged fourteen and eleven, continued to reside with their mother. Margaret's total income for 1993–94, comprising a salary, a pension and taxable social security benefits, amounted to £10,100. No part of the married couple's allowance was transferred. The tax payable by Margaret will be calculated as follows:

	£	£
Total income		10,100
Less Personal allowance	3,445	
Widow's bereavement allowance	1,720	
Additional personal allowance	1,720	6,885
Tax chargeable on		£3,215
Tax payable:		
On first £2,500 at 20 per cent		500.00
On balance of £715 at 25 per cent		178.75
		£678.75

Further information governing the liability of parties to a marriage where one spouse dies will be found on page 150.

The widow's bereavement allowance is available to the widow only and cannot be transferred to any other person.

The future

It is proposed that for 1994–95 and future years the widow's bereavement allowance will only produce relief at the lower rate of 20 per cent.

BLIND PERSON'S ALLOWANCE

An individual who, at any time in the year ending on April 5th, 1994, is registered as blind on a register maintained by a local authority may obtain a blind person's allowance of £1,080.

The blind person's allowance available to a husband may exceed the balance of total income remaining after making deductions for other allowances and reliefs. For this purpose there may be disregarded deductions for the married couple's allowance and business expansion scheme relief. Deductions for payments made under deduction of income tax, including interest under the MIRAS scheme, certain pension contributions and medical insurance contributions, may also be disregarded. If the husband is a married man living with his wife any unused excess of the blind person's allowance may be transferred to the wife.

It is possible that the wife cannot use her own blind person's allowance; with the unused excess being calculated as above but excluding any married couple's allowance. The wife may then transfer the unused blind person's allowance to her husband.

A transfer from either spouse to the other will only be effective if it is evidenced by written notice given by the transferor within a period of six years following April 5th, 1994.

Unlike some other allowances, the blind person's allowance is not to be restricted to the 20 per cent lower tax band for 1994–95 and future years.

11 *BLIND PERSON'S RELIEF*

Eric is a single man aged 35 and registered as blind. His only income for 1993–94 is a salary of £6,000.

	£	£
Total income		6,000
Less Personal allowance	3,445	
Blind person's allowance	1,080	4,525
Tax chargeable on		£1,475
Tax payable:		
On £1,475 at 20 per cent		£295.00

TRANSITIONAL RELIEFS

When changing from the old pre April 1990 system of taxing husbands and wives to the present system of independent taxation it was the intention that the change should not result in any increased income tax liability due to the reduction or loss of allowances. There were, however, three situations where a fall in allowances could occur, and special transitional reliefs have been introduced to prevent this. These situations concern:

a Husbands with insufficient income to absorb the personal allowance.

b Husbands with older wives.

c Separated couples.

The transitional reliefs affect only couples who were married before April 6th, 1990, and can have no application to those who marry subsequently.

It must be emphasised that the great majority of taxpayers will not be affected by these special transitional reliefs, which are discussed below.

TRANSITIONAL RELIEF –
Husbands with low incomes

Where the income of a husband is insufficient to absorb the personal allowance it is not normally possible to transfer any unused allowance to his wife. However, it may be possible for the wife to obtain the benefit of the unused allowance where the parties were married before April 6th, 1990. The first step is to establish the amount of the husband's unused personal allowance transferred to the wife in 1990–91. For this purpose a distinction must be made between marriages taking place before April 6th, 1989, and those taking place on or after that date but before April 6th 1990.

Marriage before April 6th, 1989

To obtain the transitional allowance for 1990–91 in the case of marriages taking place before April 6th, 1989, it must be shown that:

a a husband and wife were living together for the whole or part of both 1989–90 and 1990–91;

b no wife's earnings election was in operation for 1989–90; and

c the allowances available to the husband for 1989–90 (including married man's allowance, wife's earned income allowance and blind person's allowance) exceeded the aggregate of:

i the husband's total income for 1990–91, and

ii the allowances available to the wife for 1990–91 (including married couple's allowance and blind person's allowance).

Where these requirements are satisfied and there is such an excess the wife may obtain a special transitional allowance for 1990–91 equal to that excess.

Marriage after April 5th, 1989

To obtain the transitional allowance for 1990–91 in the case of marriages taking place during the year 1989–90 it must be shown that:

a a husband and wife were "living together" for the whole or part of 1990–91; and

b the allowances available to the husband for 1989–90 (disregarding any wife's earned income relief) exceeded his total income for 1990–91.

Where these requirements are satisfied and such an excess arises the wife may obtain a special transitional allowance equal to the amount of that excess. However, if the allowances available to the wife for 1990–91 (including married couple's allowance and blind person's allowance) exceed the lower of:

a the wife's total income for 1989–90, and

b the allowances available to the wife for 1989–90 (excluding any additional personal allowance, widow's bereavement allowance or allowances transferred from the husband),

the transitional allowance must be reduced by the excess, or perhaps eliminated.

When determining total income for the purpose of either calculation there may be disregarded any personal allowance and business expansion scheme relief. In addition, MIRAS interest, pension contributions, medical insurance contributions and other items paid under deduction of income tax may be disregarded.

The transitional allowance will not be available for 1990–91 unless the husband provides written consent on Form 575 within a period of six years after April 5th, 1991. It will also be necessary for the husband to transfer the married couple's allowance and any blind person's allowance to his wife.

The allowance for 1993–94

If the special transitional allowance is to be obtained for 1993–94 it must be shown that:

a the transitional allowance was made to the wife for 1990–91;

b the transitional allowance was also made to the wife for both 1991–92 and 1992–93; and

c the couple are "living together" throughout or during some part of 1993–94.

Where these requirements are satisfied, the transitional allowance capable of being transferred to the wife for 1993–94 will comprise the smaller of:

i the transitional allowance given to the wife in 1992–93, less any increase in the personal allowance and married couple's allowance given to the wife for 1993–94 over that for the previous year;

ii the husband's personal allowance for 1993–94 which he cannot use.

This calculation ensures that once there is a year in which the transitional allowance is not available, or not claimed, no allowance will be forthcoming in any future year.

TRANSITIONAL RELIEF –
Husbands with older wives

For 1989–90, before the introduction of independent taxation, a married man "living with" his wife was entitled to an increased married man's allowance (often referred to as an age allowance) where the older of the two was above the age of 64 years, or perhaps 74 years if relevant. Whilst the age of the older spouse governs the married couple's allowance for 1990–91 and future years, it is only the age of the husband which determines the amount of his personal allowance for those years. The possibility therefore arises that where a husband falls in a lower age group than his wife there could be a loss of allowances as between the old basis and the new. This possibility is removed by providing the husband with a special transitional personal allowance for 1990–91 and future years in place of the personal allowance which would otherwise be available.

To obtain the special personal allowance the husband must show that he qualified for an increased age allowance in 1989–90 because his wife's age fell into a higher age group (over 64 or over 74 years). It must also be demonstrated that the amount of the 1989–90 allowance exceeded the aggregate of the personal allowance and married couple's allowance available to the husband for 1990–91 or a future year. In this situation the husband's personal allowance will be:

a £3,400 if the wife was over 64 but not over 74 in 1989–90, or

b £3,540 if the wife was over 74 in that year.

The amounts of £3,400 and £3,540 comprise the single personal allowance (or age allowance) available for 1989–90 for those in the

12 *TRANSITIONAL ALLOWANCE – HUSBAND WITH LOW INCOME*

Brian and Mary, both under the age of 65, had been married for many years. In 1990–91 Brian was unable to use any part of his married couple's allowance and the entire allowance of £1,720 was transferred to Mary. A claim was also made under the special transitional provisions for part of Brian's personal allowance to be transferred to his wife. As a result, £435 was transferred. Similar claims were made in 1991–92 and 1992–93 which resulted in a transfer of £200 in the earlier year and £50 in the later. The entire married couple's allowance was transferred in each year.

The following information was obtained for 1993–94:

a Brian's total income was £3,225

b Mary's income was £16,000

c The married couple's allowance of £1,720 was transferred by Brian to Mary

The special transitional allowance representing part of Brian's personal allowance which can be transferred to Mary will be the lower figure produced by the following calculations:

	£	£
i Transitional allowance for 1992–93		50
Less Increase in allowances to Mary:		
1993–94 £3,445 + £1,720	5,165	
Deduct 1992–93 £3,445 + £1,720	5,165	NIL
		£50

	£
ii Brian's personal allowance 1993–94	3,445
Less income 1993–94	3,225
	£220

The smaller figure is £50 and this will comprise the special transitional allowance available to Mary for 1993–94.

Brian has no income tax liability for 1993–94 and the tax payable by Mary becomes:

	£	£
Total income		16,000
Less Personal allowance	3,445	
Married couple's allowance	1,720	
Special transitional allowance	50	5,215
Tax chargeable on		£10,785

Tax payable:	
On first £2,500 at 20 per cent	500.00
On balance of £8,285 at 25 per cent	2,071.25
	£2,571.25

Transitional relief will continue for future years until it is overtaken by increases in allowances or Brian's ability to use his personal allowance in full.

appropriate age group and replace the personal allowance which otherwise applies based on the husband's age. The special personal allowance for 1993–94 may be reduced if the husband's income exceeds £14,200.

The special personal allowance will continue for future years until the parties cease living together or the allowances exceed the level of the age allowance for 1989–90. The basic personal allowance has been increased beyond £3,400 to £3,445 for 1992–93 and 1993–94. It follows that relief under **a** can no longer apply. Nor will relief be available under **b** once the husband reaches the age of 65 and can obtain a personal allowance of £4,200. This transitional relief must therefore be confined for 1993–94 to a husband below the age of 65 whose wife is 75 years or more.

The special allowance cannot be obtained if a wife's earnings election was in force for 1989–90.

The special personal allowance can also be obtained by a separated husband maintaining his wife if the requirements outlined on the following page are discharged.

13 *SPECIAL PERSONAL ALLOWANCE*

William will celebrate his 65th birthday on July 4th, 1994. His wife, Anne, was 65 on October 18th, 1989. This enabled William to obtain a married man's age allowance of £5,385 for 1989–90, as there was no restriction due to income exceeding the, then, income limit of £11,400.

The allowances available to William for 1993–94 were:

	£
Personal allowance (below 65)	3,445
Married couple's allowance (wife over 64)	2,465
	£5,910

The aggregate allowances of £5,910 exceed the age allowance of £5,385 for 1989–90. As a result no special transitional allowance will be available.

TRANSITIONAL RELIEF –
Separated couples

For 1989–90 and earlier years an increased married man's personal allowance was available to a husband "living with" his wife, unless a wife's earnings election was in force. Exceptionally, the married man's allowance could be obtained by a husband separated from his wife if she was wholly maintained by him and the husband obtained no tax relief for the cost of providing maintenance. As no married couple's allowance can be obtained for 1990–91 and future years in this situation the separated husband could be at a disadvantage from the introduction of independent taxation. To remove this possibility a special transitional married couple's allowance may be available. This allowance can only be obtained if:

a The couple ceased to live together before April 6th, 1990;

b The couple have remained husband and wife;

c The wife has been wholly maintained by her husband;

d The husband cannot obtain any tax relief for sums paid to his wife as maintenance; and

e The husband was entitled to the married man's personal allowance for 1989–90.

Where these several requirements are satisfied the husband can obtain a special transitional married couple's allowance, based on the age of the older party, for 1993–94. The husband cannot transfer any part of an unused married couple's allowance to his separated wife, the wife cannot claim a special transitional personal allowance where the husband's income is small, and any blind person's allowance cannot be transferred between the parties.

The special transitional married couple's allowance continues for later years until the conditions shown above cease to be satisfied. Once this stage has been reached no further transitional relief will be available.

It is proposed that the married couple's allowance will only produce relief at the lower 20 per cent rate for 1994–95 and future years.

INDEXATION

The tax legislation contains provisions for index-linking the allowances discussed above, with the exception of the blind person's allowance. This is achieved by increasing the allowances in line with changes in the retail prices index. Similar index-linking may be applied to income tax rate bands. However, Parliament may disregard changes in the retail prices index and impose some increased or smaller adjustment, or no adjustment at all.

The allowances and rate bands for 1993–94 were due to be uprated by the increase in the retail prices index for the year to December 31st, 1992. However, no increases of any description have been made.

For 1994–95 and future years, increases in the index for the year to September 30th preceding the commencement of the tax year will be used. This change is required following the transfer of Budget Day from March to November.

How to obtain allowances

IN NORMAL CASES the allowances, shown on the previous pages, are given in arriving at the tax payable, or in fixing the code number used for PAYE purposes. The allowances cannot be granted unless the Inland Revenue are informed of the taxpayer's personal circumstances and for this purpose a proper claim must be made. A suitable form, namely an Income Tax Return, may be obtained from the local office of H.M. Inspector of Taxes, if one has not been received without request. The completion of the claim portion of the form is simple but the information *must* be inserted as follows:

Personal allowance. — All individuals receive a basic personal allowance. Those aged over 64 years should place an "X" in the special box provided. This will enable any increased personal allowance to be calculated. There is a further box for those wishing to claim the special transitional personal allowance.

Married couple's allowance. — A man must insert the full Christian or other forenames of his wife and should indicate the date of marriage, if during the previous income tax year, in order that the allowance may be claimed for that year also. Special boxes require the insertion of an "X" if the increased married couple's allowance is being claimed for older taxpayers or the special transitional allowance is being claimed for those separated before April 6th, 1990. It must be stated whether the couple are "living together". A further box is available for the insertion of an "X" if a transfer notice form is required.

Additional personal allowance. — It is necessary to indicate whether the qualifying child for whom an allowance is claimed resides with the claimant. Details of the child's age and other information should be given, together with a note of any other person claiming for the same child. If the claim is being made by a married man on the grounds that his wife is incapacitated, the nature of the incapacity and whether it is likely to continue throughout the year of claim should be stated.

Blind person's allowance. — The date of registration and the name of the local authority with whom registration was made should be recorded.

Death and superannuation benefits. — The name of the friendly society, union or scheme concerned, the full year's contribution and the part attributable to death benefits.

Note: Many taxpayers arrange to have these matters handled by qualified accountants who are expert in tax affairs and can ensure that allowances are properly claimed and that no more tax is paid than the law requires.

Pension contributions

PENSIONS FROM THE STATE

THE PROVISION of a pension or lump sum payment arising on retirement, disablement or some other event is of considerable importance. Most individuals will qualify for pensions or other social security benefits provided by the State. These may arise in several differing forms but there are two main headings. Firstly, there is a general entitlement to the basic social security retirement pension. Secondly, an additional pension may be due under the State Earnings-Related Pension Scheme (SERPS) which is available to those who have been in employment. The level of the basic retirement pension is determined annually, with increases becoming payable from the beginning of April. In contrast, the additional pension provided by SERPS is governed by the amount of Class 1 national insurance contributions paid within upper and lower limits. The volume of additional pension payments is growing as contributors reach retirement age and in an attempt to reduce the escalating cost the value of this pension (but not the retirement pension) will fall from a future date.

It has long been possible to "contract out" from the SERPS scheme, where a satisfactory alternative pension arrangement was made under a scheme linked with an individual's employment. Previously contracting out implied a reduction in both primary and secondary Class 1 contributions to eliminate the SERPS element of those contributions. With the introduction of personal pension schemes on July 1st, 1988, the ability to contract out has been increased without directly reducing the level of contributions. Contracting out may also be achieved by employees contributing additional voluntary contributions.

There are no particular taxation reliefs or advantages which can be obtained when securing title to the basic retirement pension or the additional pension, or indeed other social security benefits, with the exception of relief for Class 4 contributions paid by the self-employed (see page 51).

However, many individuals will increase the future level of retirement and other benefits by involvement in an employer's occupational pension scheme, a retirement annuity scheme or a personal pension scheme during their working lives.

OCCUPATIONAL PENSION SCHEMES

Many directors and employees pay contributions to an approved occupational pension scheme or superannuation fund. Individual arrangements differ but are designed to provide pensions or other benefits in the event of an individual's death or retirement. The rules of the scheme or fund must be approved by the Inland Revenue before tax relief can be obtained, both by the contributors and by trustees or other persons administering the arrangements.

Maximum annual contributions paid by a director or employee must generally be limited to 15 per cent of earnings. Contributions payable under most occupational pension schemes usually fall below, perhaps substantially below, this limit but it is possible for individuals to make additional voluntary contributions (AVC's) provided the limit of 15 per cent is not exceeded. AVC's may be paid to trustees or others administering an occupational pension scheme. Alternatively, it is possible to make "free standing" AVC's to an insurance company or other qualifying institution of the employee's choice.

Any contributions paid to trustees or others administering an approved occupational pension scheme qualify for tax relief when calculating the liability of the payer. Relief is usually given by deducting the approved contributions from earnings arising from the office or employment. This ensures that the earnings chargeable to income tax are reduced by the amount of the approved contributions and PAYE deductions limited to the net sum. However, where "free standing" AVC's are paid these are usually discharged after deducting income tax at the basic rate of 25 per cent. This provides full relief at that rate but where the contributor is liable to the higher rate of 40 per cent further relief will be forthcoming. The introduction of a 20 per cent income tax band does not affect the ability of a contributor to deduct, and to retain tax at the basic rate from payments of "free standing" AVC's.

Difficulties may sometimes arise in determining whether the amount of contributions to be paid on "free standing" AVC's will exceed the permissible limit. This can only be verified if detailed information is forthcoming on the amount of contributions made to the employer's scheme. However, unless the AVC's exceed £2,400 in any year a check will only be applied when the contributor retires. Any excess contributions will then be returned, subject to a tax charge.

The primary purpose of paying contributions is to provide a pension to the contributor on retirement, or to the spouse or dependants of the contributor following death. For older contributors the pension will usually be limited to two-thirds of final salary. Whilst the two-thirds approach is retained, an earnings cap of £60,000 was placed on the maximum amount of final salary for new schemes introduced after March 13th, 1989, and for individuals joining existing schemes after May 31st in the same year. This indicates a maximum pension of £40,000 per annum for those joining after these dates, although increased amounts apply for earlier entrants.

The ceiling of £60,000 not only applies to determine an individual's final salary but also governs the maximum amount of earnings which can be recognised when calculating contributions capable of being paid.

However, the ceiling may, although not necessarily will, be index-linked to changes in the retail prices index.

The earnings cap was increased in the early years following 1989–90 but no increase was made for 1993–94. The figures are as follows:

Year of assessment	Amount £
1990–91	64,800
1991–92	71,400
1992–93	75,000
1993–94	75,000

It is often possible to take a tax-free lump sum at retirement and a reduced pension subsequently. For those joining after the dates mentioned above the maximum lump sum will be limited to one and a half times the earnings cap.

The maximum pension and other benefits which can be provided by an approved occupational pension scheme may be considered insufficient by the prospective pensioner. However, it is possible for an employer to set up an unapproved "top-up" scheme providing additional pension rights. Contributions to this scheme will not secure tax reliefs and there are other taxation disadvantages, but the existence of an unapproved scheme will not, of itself, affect recognition of a qualifying scheme.

Occupational pension schemes remain unaffected by the introduction of personal pension schemes but it is no longer mandatory for an employee to remain, or indeed to become, a member of an employer's scheme.

RETIREMENT ANNUITIES

Self-employed individuals, together with directors and employees not in pensionable employment, cannot retain membership of an occupational pension scheme. For many years it has been possible for these individuals to secure annuities or lump sums payable on retirement or death under retirement annuity arrangements. Premiums paid to obtain an annuity or lump sum may entitle the payer to tax relief if, but only if, a number of conditions are satisfied. Both the conditions governing relief and the application of that relief are briefly discussed below, but it is not possible to conclude *new* retirement annuity arrangements after July 1st, 1988. Contributions paid after this date in respect of arrangements concluded previously will, however, continue to obtain relief. The inability to conclude new retirement annuity arrangements is explained by the introduction of personal pension schemes, discussed later, which retain most but not all of the features to be found in retirement annuity arrangements.

It is a necessary requirement that the retirement annuity contract or other document is drafted in a form approved by the Inland Revenue but in general the contract will:

a provide the taxpayer with a life annuity in retirement;

b provide an annuity for the spouse of the taxpayer or for one or more dependants of that individual; or

c provide a lump sum on the death of the individual before he or she attains the age of 75.

Where these requirements are satisfied, any premiums paid qualify for relief in calculating liability to income tax. Premiums paid in a year of assessment are primarily allocated to that year. However, the taxpayer may elect to treat the payments as having been made in the previous year, or in a year falling two years before the year of payment if there were no net relevant earnings in the previous year. Individuals deriving relevant earnings from Lloyd's underwriting activities may relate premiums paid back to even earlier years.

Relief for premiums paid, or treated as paid, in a year of assessment is not to exceed 17.5 per cent of the contributor's net relevant earnings for that year. This percentage may be increased to the levels shown by the following table for 1993–94 for those over the age of 50 on April 6th, 1993.

Age on April 6th, 1993	Percentage
51 to 55	20
56 to 60	22.5
61 and above	27.5

"Net relevant earnings" comprise the taxpayer's earned income, after subtracting capital allowances and losses. Personal outgoings, such as mortgage interest, may be ignored. The earnings cap of £75,000 which applies to restrict the amount of earnings on which personal pension scheme contributions can be based has no direct application to retirement annuity premiums.

Where the premiums relate to a contract falling under **b** or **c** above, the allowable premiums are limited to 5 per cent of the individual's net relevant earnings for the year of assessment. However, the figure of 17.5 per cent, suitably increased for older taxpayers, represents the maximum relief which can be obtained for all premiums falling under **a**, **b** and **c** paid by the claimant. This maximum figure cannot be further increased by the addition of premiums falling within the 5 per cent restriction.

It is possible that the full potential relief for a year of assessment has not been obtained, due to an absence of sufficient premiums paid. This unused relief may be carried forward for a maximum period of 6 years and applied to relieve premiums paid which exceed the 17.5 per cent (or higher) limitation in future years. The relief is given for the year of assessment in which premiums are paid, or treated as having been paid, and not for the year in which the unused relief arose. Once the six-year period has expired the unused relief can no longer be carried forward and will be lost.

Unused retirement annuity relief can be carried forward in this manner and set against future excess contributions paid under personal pension schemes.

PERSONAL PENSION SCHEMES

On July 1st, 1988, personal pension schemes were introduced in place of retirement annuity contracts. Personal pension schemes do not replace occupational pension schemes, which continue largely undisturbed. Overlapping is avoided by ensuring that earnings from a pensionable employment carrying membership of an occupational pension scheme cannot be taken into account when calculating relief under personal pension scheme arrangements. Thus an individual whose sole source of income arises from an employment, and who is a member of the employer's occupational pension scheme, cannot contribute to a personal pension scheme unless he ceases membership of the employer's scheme. An individual who receives earnings supporting membership of an occupational pension scheme and who also receives non-pensionable earnings from a different source may incorporate the latter earnings in a personal pension scheme. Any shortfall in benefits arising under an occupational pension scheme can be overcome by contemplating the payment of AVC's, either to trustees administering the scheme or under "free standing" contracts.

With the exception of retirement annuity arrangements commenced before July 1st, 1988, and which continue subsequently, personal pension schemes entirely replace those arrangements. This is achieved by precluding the introduction of any new retirement annuity arrangements on and after July 1st, 1988.

As the name implies, personal pension schemes are "personal" to the individual concerned. A scheme is retained when an individual changes jobs or becomes self-employed, although arrangements may be made to transfer from a personal pension scheme to an occupational pension scheme where an individual becomes a member of such a scheme.

Scheme requirements

Contracts for personal pension schemes are made between the individual and an approved institution including assurance companies, banks, building societies and friendly societies, among others. Each contract must be approved by the Inland Revenue and provide one or more of the following benefits:

a an annuity payable to the contributor and commencing on reaching an age between 50 and 75 years. A reduced age may apply by reason of early retirement on the grounds of ill-health, or perhaps engagement in an occupation where it is customary to retire before reaching 50;

b a lump sum not exceeding 25 per cent of the value of the annuity when it first becomes payable, with a correspondingly reduced future annuity;

c an annuity payable to the surviving spouse or dependants on the death of the contributor;

d a lump sum payable on the death of the contributor before reaching the age of 75;

e the return of contributions with interest and bonuses on the death of the contributor.

Allocation of contributions

Contributions paid under a qualifying personal pension scheme entitle the contributor to tax relief. It is possible for an individual to contemplate involvement in two or more schemes simultaneously, but a limit is placed on the aggregate relief which will be forthcoming for contributions paid.

Any contributions paid in a year of assessment ending on April 5th will be primarily allocated to that year. However, within a period of three months following the end of the year of assessment in which payment is made the taxpayer can elect for contributions to be treated as paid in the previous year, or perhaps earlier if there were no net relevant earnings in the previous year or earnings arose from Lloyd's underwriting activities.

14 *ALLOCATION OF CONTRIBUTIONS*

On September 29th, 1993 Harry paid a qualifying contribution of £6,000 (gross). In the absence of an election the contribution will be treated as paid in the actual year of payment, namely 1993–94.

However, not later than July 5th, 1994 Harry may elect to treat the contribution as having been paid in 1992–93 (or perhaps in 1991–92 if there were no net relevant earnings for 1992–93).

By re-allocating the contribution in this manner it may be possible to obtain relief for an earlier year which would otherwise be lost.

Limitations on relief

The maximum contributions paid, or deemed to be paid, in a year of assessment and which qualify for relief in that year are not to exceed 17.5 per cent of net relevant earnings. This percentage may be increased to the following levels for 1993–94 for those over the age of 35 on April 6th, 1993.

Age on April 6th, 1993	Percentage
36 to 45	20
46 to 50	25
51 to 55	30
56 to 60	35
61 and above	40

Where the personal pension scheme produces entitlement to a lump sum falling under **d** above the maximum contributions qualifying for relief and attributable to that scheme are not to exceed 5 per cent of net relevant earnings. This limitation of 5 per cent is not to increase the total relief above the 17.5 per cent (or higher amount for older taxpayers) level.

When applying the appropriate percentage to net relevant earnings for 1989–90, any excess of those earnings above £60,000 must be disregarded. This is in line with the earnings cap which applies to members of an occupational pension scheme, but the limit may be increased annually as the retail prices index increases.

Such increases occurred in earlier years but no increase was forthcoming for 1993–94. The earnings cap for each year is as follows:

Year of assessment	Maximum £
1989–90	60,000
1990–91	64,800
1991–92	71,400
1992–93	75,000
1993–94	75,000

Occasionally, both an employee and his or her employer may pay contributions under a personal pension scheme taken out by the employee. Any contributions discharged by the employer will be subtracted from the maximum amount on which the employee can otherwise obtain relief.

"Net relevant earnings" will comprise most items of income arising from an employment, office, trade or profession, after subtracting capital allowances and losses, among other items. There must be excluded earnings from an office or employment which entitles the employee to membership of an occupational pension scheme.

15 *CALCULATION OF RELIEF*

Sandra, a single woman aged 34, had profits of £37,000 assessable for 1993–94. On November 24th, 1993, she paid a contribution of £6,000 under an approved personal pension scheme which remained allocated to the year of payment.

	£
Total income	37,000
Less contribution	6,000
	31,000
Less Personal allowance	3,445
Tax chargeable on	£27,555

	£
Tax payable:	
Lower rate:	
On first £2,500 at 20 per cent	500.00
Basic rate:	
On next £21,200 at 25 per cent	5,300.00
Higher rate:	
On balance of £3,855 at 40 per cent	1,542.00
	£7,342.00

Unused relief

Contributions attributable to a year of assessment may fall below the maximum relief calculated by applying the 17.5 per cent, or some other, level. The unused relief may then be carried forward for a maximum period of 6 years and applied to relieve contributions paid in a future year which exceed the 17.5 per cent (or other) limit for that year. Relief is given for the year in which contributions are paid, or treated as paid, and not in the year during which unused relief arose.

Transitional relief

The method of providing relief for contributions paid under approved personal pension schemes is similar to that which applies to premiums paid under the "old" retirement annuity arrangements. This close relationship is recognised by transitional provisions which effectively preserve aggregate relief. For example, unused relief arising before July 1st, 1988, under the retirement annuity regime may be carried forward within the six-year period and absorbed by excess personal pension scheme contributions. In addition, personal pension scheme contributions paid after July 1st, 1988 could be carried back within the normal time limits and used against income for earlier years as if those payments were made under retirement annuity arrangements.

It is possible for an individual to pay both retirement annuity contributions and personal pension scheme contributions in the same year of assessment. Where relief is available for both, retirement annuity contributions are afforded priority. Before contemplating payments under both headings in the same year expert advice may well be required. This will recognise that whilst the earnings cap does not apply to retirement annuity arrangements, those arrangements may attract a reduced percentage of earnings qualifying for relief.

Deductions of tax

Personal pension scheme contributions will be discharged net, after deducting income tax at the basic rate of 25 per cent where the relevant earnings are assessable under Schedule E. Deduction and retention of tax in this manner provides the contributor with relief at the basic rate. This remains unaffected by the lower rate band of 20 per cent. Other contributions, namely those discharged by self-employed individuals, are paid gross and relieved when assessing relevant income. Relief at the higher rate will be given separately.

Contracting out

As an inducement to invest in a personal pension scheme employees are provided with a "contracting out" option. This is limited to those paying Class 1 national insurance contributions and can have no application to the self-employed. The purpose of contracting out is to remove the SERPS contribution element from Class 1 contributions. Unlike contracting out for members of an occupational pension scheme, the full Class 1 contributions are paid both by the employer and by the employee. The Department of Social Security will then contribute towards the employee's own personal pension scheme a sum representing:

16 *CARRYING FORWARD UNUSED RELIEF*

In the absence of sufficient premiums paid, Andrew had the following amounts of unused relief for earlier years:

	£
1987–88	740
1988–89	1,620
1989–90	5,800
1990–91	2,900
1991–92	3,250
1992–93	1,760

Andrew's net relevant earnings for 1993–94 were £40,000. He paid contributions of £17,000 on a qualifying personal pension scheme policy which were allocated to 1993–94. Assuming Andrew was 40 years of age on April 6th, 1993, and therefore qualified for the increased relief calculated at the rate of 20 per cent, these contributions will be absorbed as follows:

	£
Maximum relief for 1993–94	
20 per cent of £40,000	8,000
Unused relief brought forward (earlier year first)	
1987–88	740
1988–89	1,620
1989–90	5,800
1990–91	840
Total relief available for 1993–94	£17,000

Unused relief available for future years (subject to six-year time limit)

	£
1990–91 (balance)	2,060
1991–92	3,250
1992–93	1,760
1993–94	NIL

If Andrew is a married man with no other income, and entitled to the full married couple's allowance, the tax payable for 1993–94 becomes:

	£	£
Total income:		
Business profits		40,000
Deduct personal pension contributions		17,000
		23,000
Less		
Personal allowance	3,445	
Married couple's allowance	1,720	
		5,165
Tax chargeable on		£17,835
Tax payable:		
On first £2,500 at 20 per cent		500.00
On balance of £15,335 at 25 per cent		3,833.75
		£4,333.75

a the employer's contribution to the SERPS element, grossed up at 25 per cent; and

b the employee's contribution to the SERPS element not grossed up.

In addition, for a period of years ending on April 5th, 1993, the payment was increased by a bonus representing 2 per cent of the employee's earnings used to calculate the SERPS element, or £1 per week, whichever is the greater. A further bonus of 1 per cent applies from April 6th, 1993, for employees who have reached the age of 30.

Contracting out will only be permitted where the personal pension scheme provides a pension equal to that otherwise due under SERPS. Thus before electing to contract out individuals must recognise the loss of a future SERPS additional pension. Contracting out may also be possible for employees who contribute towards "free standing" AVC's which provide a sufficiently substantial alternative pension.

Husband and wife

Independent taxation requires that the relevant earnings of a husband and his wife are calculated separately and relief given to each individual without regard to the affairs of the other.

Interest paid

MANY INDIVIDUALS make payments of interest, particularly on mortgages or loans obtained to acquire their own homes. These individuals are entitled to income tax relief for interest paid if, but only if, a number of conditions are satisfied. When approaching this matter there are two quite separate problems to be resolved, namely the identity of the interest which qualifies for relief and also the manner in which that relief can be granted. For most payments of mortgage interest made after April 5th, 1993, relief is only available at the basic rate, with no relief at the higher rate of income tax. A further restriction confining relief to the lower rate of 20 per cent will apply from April 6th, 1994. Neither restriction extends, generally, to other qualifying interest payments.

No relief will be forthcoming for payments of interest on a bank overdraft or similar facility, unless those payments can be included in the calculation of business profits. Relief for other payments which do not comprise a business outlay will only be available if interest is payable on a debt incurred to finance expenditure falling under one of the headings discussed below. If the requirements of these headings are not satisfied the interest cannot qualify for relief when calculating the payer's liability to income tax.

PRIVATE RESIDENCES – MORTGAGE INTEREST

Occupation by borrower

Interest paid on a loan applied to acquire land or buildings in the United Kingdom or the Republic of Ireland will qualify for relief, if at the time the interest is paid the property is used as the borrower's only or main residence. Relief also extends to interest paid on a loan to purchase caravans and houseboats used for a similar purpose.

For interest paid within a period of twelve months, or perhaps longer at the discretion of the Inland Revenue, from the date of borrowing, relief will also be available should the property be used for a qualifying purpose at any time within the twelve-month period. In such cases it is immaterial whether the property was actually used at the time interest was paid.

The recent fall in property values has created many situations, known as "negative equity", where the value of a property is less than the outstanding mortgage. This may well prevent the owner of that property moving to acquire a new home. However, from March 16th, 1993, it may be possible to overcome this difficulty and retain an entitlement to interest relief. This will arise if:

a interest is being paid on a qualifying loan used to acquire the old property; and

b the lender agrees to substitute the new home for the old as security for the loan.

Although this arrangement will not result in a loan being obtained to acquire the new home, relief for interest paid will be forthcoming if the new home is a qualifying residence.

Occupation by dependent relatives and others

Relief may also be available for interest paid on a loan applied before April 6th, 1988, to purchase land, buildings, caravans and houseboats used as the only or main residence of:

a a dependent relative of the borrower; or

b a former or separated spouse of the borrower.

Occupation by a dependent relative will only be recognised if the property is provided rent-free and without other consideration. The expression "dependent relative" when applied to an individual means a relative of that individual, or his spouse, who is incapacitated by old age or infirmity from maintaining himself. It also includes the mother or mother-in-law of the individual if she is widowed, living apart from her husband or divorced.

This relief for property occupied by a dependent relative, a former spouse or a separated spouse is only available where the loan was applied before April 6th, 1988. No relief will be forthcoming for interest on loans applied on or after that date. It also remains a condition for obtaining relief that the individual occupying property before April 6th, 1988 continues to occupy the same property when future payments of interest are made on "old" loans. Should the "old" loan be replaced by a new loan, no relief can be allowed for interest on the replacement loan.

Improvement loans

The relief mentioned above was previously available for interest paid on a loan applied to improve property occupied by the borrower, a dependent relative or a former or separated spouse, as a qualifying residence. However, relief cannot apply to any home improvement loans granted after April 5th, 1988, unless the loan is used to finance the construction of a new building for occupation by the borrower and otherwise satisfying the remaining requirements governing relief. Interest on loans obtained before April 6th, 1988, continues to obtain relief. Should an older loan be replaced by a new loan on or after this date, no relief will be available for interest on the replacement loan.

Limitations of relief

A limitation is placed on the maximum amount of interest paid by an individual in the year ending on April 5th, 1994, which can qualify for relief. This limitation is imposed by restricting relief to interest on loans of £30,000. It is the amount of the qualifying loan, or loans, which establishes relief and not the amount of interest paid. £30,000 is an overriding maximum, incorporating all qualifying loans falling under this heading. Any loans applied after April 5th, 1988, which fail to qualify for relief may be disregarded when calculating the limit.

Notwithstanding independent taxation, a husband and wife "living together" cannot each obtain the benefit of the £30,000 limit. This limit applies to the aggregate amount of qualifying loans made to a husband and his wife. As will be seen later (page 47) there is considerable flexibility in selecting the spouse who can be treated as having paid interest qualifying for relief. Unfortunately, this flexibility has lost a great deal of its former attraction for interest payments made after April 5th, 1991. With very limited exceptions these payments will not qualify for relief at the higher rate (see page 40).

A problem may sometimes arise where a man and a woman were each obtaining relief for interest paid on loans of £30,000. If the couple subsequently marry, the limit of £30,000 will apply to the aggregate loans of both. This will result in a substantial reduction in the amount of future interest qualifying for relief.

Joint owners

The ceiling of £30,000 was previously applied to loans made to an individual, with an aggregate limitation of £30,000 for husband and wife "living together". This approach continues for loans applied for a qualifying purpose before August 1st, 1988. It was, however, considered unfair that two or more unmarried persons occupying a single property could each obtain relief for interest paid on maximum loans of £30,000, in contrast to a husband and wife who were limited to relief for interest on aggregate loans of £30,000 only. In the case of loans applied on and after August 1st, 1988, this anomaly is removed by restricting relief to £30,000 for all loans, or joint loans, affecting a single property. The maximum relief for interest on £30,000 will be shared equally between the several individuals involved. However, where there are unequal contributions, with the result that the interest paid by one individual is

17 *JOINT OWNERS*

On October 15th, 1989, three unmarried friends, Peter, Paul and Mary borrowed £90,000 to purchase a house which they subsequently occupied as their only residence. Peter borrowed £40,000, Paul £30,000 and Mary £20,000. Interest of £9,600 (gross) paid in 1993–94 was shared in these proportions.

Although each individual has borrowed a different amount, the limit of £30,000 must be shared equally, namely £10,000 each. Therefore the relief available to each joint owner will be calculated as follows:

Interest attributable to £30,000:

$$\frac{30{,}000}{90{,}000} \times £9{,}600 = \underline{\underline{£3{,}200}}$$

Each individual will obtain relief on:

$$⅓\text{rd} \times £3{,}200 = \underline{\underline{£1{,}067}}$$

less than his or her share of interest on £30,000, the balance may be transferred to other joint borrowers.

If the joint contributors include a husband and wife, each spouse counts as a separate share. These persons retain the ability to vary each other's shares, providing that the aggregate shares allocated to husband and wife are not altered (see page 47).

18 *JOINT OWNERS – RESTRICTION*

Adjusting the facts in Example 17, let it be assumed that Mary contributed a loan of £5,000, with Peter contributing £50,000 and Paul £35,000. Mary has been allocated interest relief on a loan of £10,000 but this must be limited to her actual contribution of £5,000. The balance of £5,000 will be re-allocated between Peter and Paul on the basis of their otherwise disallowed loans. This produces the following shares of the qualifying loan:

	£	£
Peter		
Basic allocation	10,000	
Add		
$\frac{40,000}{65,000} \times$ £5,000	3,077	13,077
Paul		
Basic allocation	10,000	
Add		
$\frac{25,000}{65,000} \times$ £5,000	1,923	11,923
Mary		5,000
		£30,000

Relief for aggregate interest of £3,200 will be allocated on this basis also.

Bridging loans

It has previously been pointed out that a property must be used for a qualifying purpose at the time interest is paid, or be so used within a period of twelve months following the acquisition date, before relief for interest will be forthcoming. This may give rise to difficulty where an individual moves from one property to another and delay is experienced in selling the old asset. To reduce hardship, interest paid on the old loan will usually continue to qualify for relief for a period of twelve months, and perhaps longer, following the cessation of use. In such cases the upper limit of £30,000 will apply separately to both the old and the new loan. This provides the exception to the general rule that relief will be limited to interest on qualifying loans not exceeding £30,000.

It was a condition of the extended relief that the individual obtained a fresh loan to acquire the new home. The relief was not available for individuals who moved into rented accommodation. This restriction no longer applies and from March 16th, 1993, the relief is available to all those moving from their homes, provided the property is placed on the market for sale.

Income tax relief at the higher rate is not generally available for payments of mortgage interest made after April 5th, 1991, but an exception arose in the case of bridging loans. Interest paid on the old, but not the new, loan continued to qualify for higher rate income tax relief if:

a the new loan was applied for the purchase of a property before April 6th, 1991; or

b a binding contract to acquire the new property was entered into before that date.

This was only a temporary measure which ceased to have any application shortly after April 6th, 1991.

Other matters

Subject to the exception which applies on leaving property, and the withdrawal or restriction of relief for new loans applied after April 5th or July 31st, 1988, relief can only be obtained for interest paid in relation to the only or main residence. Where an individual retains two or more residences, for example a town house used on weekdays and a country cottage occupied at weekends, it is not possible to choose the qualifying dwelling, as it only remains to determine which is the main residence.

This selection may prove troublesome where husband and wife are "living together" and each owns a separate property. The selection must be made, but where a husband uses, or intends to use, a property as his only or main residence and the wife uses, or intends to use, some other property for a similar purpose, the property first acquired must be taken as the qualifying residence.

Employees earning £8,500 or more and directors who receive loans either interest-free or at a rate of interest falling below a commercial rate may be assessed to income tax on the benefit arising (see page 84). However, where the notional interest creating the taxable benefit would produce relief by applying the above rules, if actually paid, a reduced liability to tax may arise.

JOB-RELATED ACCOMMODATION

Some employees may be required to reside in living accommodation provided by their employer for the purpose of carrying out the obligations of employment. This accommodation will normally comprise the employee's only or main residence and prevent relief being obtained for interest paid on a loan applied to acquire some other property. However, relief will be forthcoming for interest paid on a loan applied to purchase land, a building, a caravan or a houseboat which is also used as a residence by such an employee, or is intended to be used as the only or main residence on some future occasion, perhaps following retirement, where a number of conditions are satisfied. Included in these conditions is the requirement that living accommodation provided by the employer must be job-related. Living accommodation will only be job-related:

a where it is *necessary* for the proper performance of the duties of the employment that the employee should reside in that accommodation; or

b where the accommodation is provided for the *better performance* of the duties of the employment, and it is one of the kinds of employment in the case of which it is *customary* for employers to provide living accommodation for employees; or

c where, there being a special threat to the employee's *security*, special security arrangements are in force and the employee resides in the accommodation as part of those arrangements.

Most company directors are precluded from satisfying requirements **a** and **b**.

The availability of relief for interest paid by an employee occupying job-related accommodation is extended to certain self-employed individuals. These individuals must be carrying on a trade, profession or vocation and in this capacity be contractually bound to occupy living accommodation. This requirement will be satisfied if the taxpayer's spouse is similarly bound. Examples will include the proprietor of licensed premises required to reside in those premises under arrangements with brewers. The requirement cannot be satisfied where accommodation is supplied by certain persons closely associated with the self-employed individual.

In the case of both employed and self-employed individuals, relief remains governed by the ceiling of £30,000. In addition, payments made after April 5th, 1991, will not give rise to relief at the higher rate, and those taking place after April 5th, 1994, attract relief at the lower rate of 20 per cent only.

LOANS TO PURCHASE LIFE ANNUITY

Where at least 90 per cent of monies borrowed are applied to purchase an annuity ending on death, and the borrower is at least 65 years of age, interest on the borrowings may qualify for relief in full. It is a condition that the loan is secured on land in the United Kingdom or the Republic of Ireland, and that either the borrower or the annuitant uses the land as his or her only or main residence. This requirement is relaxed where the individual leaves the property after March 15th, 1993, as relief will remain available for interest paid in the succeeding 12 month period, and perhaps longer. Should the borrowing exceed £30,000, only interest calculated on this figure will be allowable. Here also higher rate income tax relief cannot be obtained for payments made after April 5th, 1991, but relief will continue to remain available at the basic rate of 25 per cent after April 5th, 1994.

PARTNERSHIPS

Interest paid to finance the purchase of an interest in a trading or professional partnership will qualify for relief without limitation. This relief will also extend to interest paid on monies borrowed which are applied as a contribution towards capital or loans and made to the partnership for use in the business. Relief is confined to persons who are members of the partnership at the time any interest is paid.

INDUSTRIAL CO-OPERATIVES

Interest on a loan obtained by an individual for the purpose of contributing capital to an industrial co-operative may be relieved.

EMPLOYEE CONTROLLED COMPANIES

Interest paid on a loan used to acquire ordinary shares in an employee controlled company will usually qualify for relief where paid by an employee of that company. The company's shares must not be quoted on a stock exchange, and several further conditions require satisfaction before relief will be forthcoming.

CLOSE COMPANIES

Interest paid to finance the purchase of ordinary shares issued by a company retaining "close company" status may often be relieved in full. This relief extends also to interest paid on monies which are reapplied in loaning funds to such a close company for use in its business. If the individual paying interest does not retain a significant shareholding, he or she must devote the greater part of their time to the company's affairs. Broadly, a company retains "close company" status if it is under the control of five or fewer shareholders, or is controlled by its directors. No relief can be obtained under this heading if shares issued by a company after March 13th, 1989, qualify for business expansion scheme relief.

PLANT AND MACHINERY FOR USE IN AN EMPLOYMENT

Interest paid by an employee on a loan obtained to finance the acquisition of plant or machinery for use in his or her employment will qualify for relief in full.

PERSONAL REPRESENTATIVES

Relief is available for interest paid on a loan used by personal representatives of a deceased person to satisfy inheritance tax becoming payable on death. This relief is limited to interest on money borrowed for the payment of tax before the grant of representation, or the delivery of an account, and applies only to tax on personal property. In addition, relief is restricted to interest paid in a period of one year from the making of the loan.

Where at the time of death a person could claim relief for interest paid on a loan applied to acquire land, buildings, a caravan or a houseboat used, or to be used, as an only or main residence, the obligation to satisfy future interest payments may be assumed by the personal representatives, or by trustees administering a settlement created by the deceased's will. These persons may continue to obtain relief for interest paid if the asset is used, or is intended to be used, by a surviving spouse of the deceased. Relief may also be available if the deceased died before April 6th, 1988, and a dependent relative was in occupation of the property at that time.

PROPERTY LET COMMERCIALLY

Interest paid on a loan to finance the purchase of land, a building, a caravan or houseboat which is not used as a qualifying residence as outlined on page 36 will only obtain relief if the property is let at a commercial rent. The property must be so let for at least 26 weeks in a 52-week period, and throughout the remainder of this time the property must either be available for letting or undergoing repair or improvement. The interest can only be set against rent received and not against income generally. Should the interest paid exceed the rent, any surplus may be carried forward and set against rental income for subsequent years.

BUILDING SOCIETY INTEREST

Mortgage interest paid to a building society will usually relate to a loan made for the acquisition of property. If the requirements outlined on the previous pages are satisfied, relief for the interest paid will be forthcoming, although after April 5th, 1991, this will usually be limited to relief at the basic rate only and further limited to the lower rate of 20 per cent after April 5th, 1994.

SHORT INTEREST

Where loans are granted for a period falling below 12 months in duration any interest paid will usually be termed "short interest". This will not qualify for the relief discussed above unless paid to a bank, discount house or a member of the Stock Exchange.

OVERSEAS INTEREST

Interest payable to a person residing overseas will not usually qualify for relief, unless it can be included in the calculation of business profits. Further, where land or buildings are situated outside the United Kingdom or the Republic of Ireland, for example, in the Channel Islands, the Isle of Man, Spain or Portugal, no relief for interest paid on a loan obtained to acquire those properties will be available.

HIRE-PURCHASE INTEREST

The so-called "interest" payable under the terms of a hire-purchase agreement is not really interest but a "hire charge". No relief can be obtained for such a payment, unless the payer may treat it as a business expense in computing profits.

BUSINESS EXPENSES

The requirements outlined above, which must be satisfied before payments of interest made by an individual can qualify for tax relief, have no application to "business" interest. An individual carrying on a trade, profession or vocation may include in the calculation of business profits or losses sums laid out "wholly and exclusively" for the purposes of the business. For example, interest paid by a sole trader on a loan applied to acquire assets used in the business, or to provide working capital, may usually be relieved in this manner without regard to the requirements outlined on the previous pages. However, relief for an interest payment cannot be obtained both as a deduction from business profits and also by reducing total income. In some situations it may be advisable to consider which form of relief is to be preferred.

COMPANIES

The above rules governing relief for interest paid have little application to companies, as special provisions apply for the purpose of determining liability to corporation tax.

How to obtain relief for interest paid

MORTGAGE INTEREST – RESTRICTIONS ON RELIEF

PAYMENTS OF INTEREST made on a loan applied to acquire an only or main residence may obtain relief where the requirements outlined earlier are satisfied. For payments made before April 6th, 1991, the payer could obtain relief at the basic rate and at the higher rate also where income was sufficiently substantial. Subject to rare exceptions which have long ceased to be available, no higher rate relief can be obtained for interest payments made on and after April 6th, 1991. Relief is now limited to tax at the basic rate only for qualifying interest paid on a loan to acquire an only or main residence. This extends to interest paid on a loan used to acquire an only or main residence of a dependent relative or other persons or to finance the improvement of property where the loan was obtained before April 6th, 1988. In addition, higher rate income tax relief can no longer be obtained on loans applied to acquire an annuity secured on land. A further restriction will be introduced on April 6th, 1994. From that date relief will be limited to the lower rate of 20 per cent only. Therefore, in a period of only three years, maximum relief will have fallen from 40 per cent to 25 per cent and then to 20 per cent.

The removal of relief at the higher rate and the forthcoming restriction to the lower rate does not extend to other payments of qualifying interest. These payments continue to support relief at the higher or basic rate, where of course the income of the payer is sufficiently substantial.

MORTGAGE INTEREST – THE MIRAS DEDUCTION SCHEME

Relief for payments of qualifying mortgage interest could be given either by adjusting the PAYE tax deductions made from earnings paid to employed persons or by deducting the interest from income on which tax is payable by direct assessment. This would give rise to considerable administrative difficulties, particularly in the case of PAYE, when frequent changes are made in the rate of mortgage interest payable.

To avoid these and other problems a mortgage interest relief at source scheme (MIRAS) is used. It must be emphasised that the purpose of the scheme is to provide a more efficient method of granting relief and it does not affect the net income tax liability of most individuals, although occasionally increased relief will be available to those having little or no liability to income tax. Not all payments of mortgage interest are brought within the scheme and any excluded qualifying interest will be relieved in the manner outlined later.

Basic rate relief – 1993–94

The substance of the MIRAS scheme is that when payments of interest are made to a qualifying lender during 1993–94 the payer will deduct and retain income tax at the basic rate of 25 per cent. There is a lengthy list of qualifying lenders, including building societies, banks, insurance companies, local authorities and others. The qualifying lender is obliged to allow the deduction of income tax and will recover the sums deducted from the Inland Revenue. The use of a 20 per cent lower rate band of income tax for 1993–94 will not affect the deduction of tax at the basic rate or the retention of that tax for this year.

The MIRAS deduction scheme applies to mortgage interest payable on a loan made to acquire an only or main residence in the United Kingdom which satisfies the requirements shown on page 36. It also extends to interest on a loan used to purchase other property by a person compelled

19 *RELIEF FOR INTEREST PAID – MIRAS*

In 1982 David obtained a mortgage loan of £35,000 from a building society to purchase his own home. The loan was repayable by monthly instalments, including interest. The interest element in monthly instalments paid during 1993–94 aggregated £2,860, before deducting income tax at the basic rate of 25 per cent.

The total amount of interest actually paid in the year will be:

	£
Gross interest	2,860
Less income tax deducted at 25 per cent	715
Payments actually made	£2,145

The only income of David for 1993–94 comprised a salary of £24,000. The income tax payable on this salary, assuming the taxpayer is a married man entitled to the full basic married couple's allowance, will be:

	£	£
Total income		24,000
Less		
Personal allowance	3,445	
Married couple's allowance	1,720	5,165
Tax chargeable on		£18,835

Tax payable:	
On first £2,500 at 20 per cent	500.00
On balance of £16,335 at 25 per cent	4,083.75
	£4,583.75

The net income tax burden is:

	£
Tax payable	4,583.75
Less tax retained by deduction	715.00
Net tax suffered	£3,868.75

to reside in job-related accommodation, and to the purchase of an annuity secured on land as discussed on page 41. Where the amount of any loan exceeds the £30,000 limit governing relief for interest paid, qualifying lenders will operate MIRAS on that part of the loan which does not exceed £30,000.

It is important that borrowers fully advise lenders of any other qualifying loans existing at the time of new borrowings as these other loans may affect the availability of relief under the MIRAS scheme. Notification must also be made where interest on a loan ceases to qualify for relief. This is a most significant matter as the Inland Revenue have often expressed concern that the MIRAS deduction scheme is being heavily abused. Responsibility for its operation rests primarily between the lender and the borrower. Once errors or maladministration have been detected, serious financial consequences will arise.

The MIRAS deduction scheme is limited to income tax at the basic rate of 25 per cent. The gross amount of interest paid will be deducted in calculating total income used to establish whether the increased personal allowance or the increased married couple's allowance can be obtained by elderly taxpayers. However, as the amount of tax deducted can be retained, it is not also possible to subtract interest when calculating income chargeable to income tax. If the taxpayer has insufficient income to produce tax liability, for example where income is exceeded by allowances, or is only liable at the lower rate of 20 per cent, the basic rate income tax deducted can still be retained.

20 *RELIEF FOR INTEREST PAID GROSS*

Mark obtained a loan from a person who was not a qualifying lender within the MIRAS scheme. The loan was applied to acquire Mark's home. Interest amounting to £2,860 was paid gross in 1993–94 and qualified for relief. The only income of Mark, a married man, was a salary of £24,000. No election had been made to apportion the married couple's allowance.

Income tax payable for 1993–94 becomes:

	£	£
Total income		24,000
Less		
Personal allowance	3,445	
Married couple's allowance	1,720	
Interest	2,860	8,025
Tax chargeable on		£15,975

Tax payable:	
On first £2,500 at 20 per cent	500.00
On balance of £13,475 at 25 per cent	3,368.75
	£3,868.75

It will be seen that the tax payable of £3,868.75 is identical to the net tax suffered by David in Example 19 on page 45, who paid interest falling within MIRAS. This illustrates that the purpose of MIRAS is to provide income tax relief at source, rather than when calculating the liability of the payer.

Lower rate relief – 1994–95

The MIRAS arrangements will continue in 1994–95, but with one significant amendment. Tax will only be deducted and retained at the lower rate of 20 per cent. No other relief will be available to payers and it will not be possible to contemplate relief at some additional rate also.

MORTGAGE INTEREST – RELIEF OUTSIDE THE MIRAS SCHEME

Not all payments of mortgage interest are brought within the MIRAS scheme; for example, where interest is paid to a person whose name does not appear on the list of qualifying lenders. In these circumstances interest will be paid gross, leaving the taxpayer to obtain relief either in the PAYE notice of coding or by deduction from direct assessment.

One disadvantage of this approach is that where there is no taxable income, the taxpayer will obtain no effective relief for interest paid. If there is sufficient income to produce liability at the lower rate of 20 per cent only for 1993–94, it is at this rate that the relief will be effectively given.

MORTGAGE INTEREST – HUSBAND AND WIFE

Where a husband and wife are "living together" there can be only one qualifying residence between the parties. Interest paid on a loan applied to acquire that residence will qualify for tax relief in the normal manner. This requires that where a husband and his wife jointly acquire a

21 *RELIEF FOR INTEREST PAID – HIGHER RATE*

In 1984 Michael borrowed a substantial sum of money which he applied to acquire shares in a close company. Interest of £4,500 was paid gross on the borrowings in 1993–94 and qualified for relief. Michael was a married man entitled to the full basic married couple's allowance. His only income for the year comprised a salary of £42,000 from the company. Income tax payable will be:

	£	£
Total income		42,000
Less		
Personal allowance	3,445	
Married couple's allowance	1,720	
Gross interest	4,500	9,665
Tax chargeable on		£32,335

Tax payable:	
Lower rate:	£
On first £2,500 at 20 per cent	500.00
Basic rate:	
On next £21,200 at 25 per cent	5,300.00
Higher rate:	
On balance of £8,635 at 40 per cent	3,454.00
	£9,254.00

The gross interest of £4,500 has reduced taxable income by the same amount and therefore obtained relief at the full higher rate of 40 per cent.

property the maximum ceiling of £30,000 will be divided equally, with each able to obtain relief for interest on £15,000. If the loan is made to one spouse only that individual will obtain relief for interest paid on a loan up to the maximum of £30,000.

However, it is possible to submit an "allocation of interest" election. Where the election applies the interest paid by either, or both, parties to the marriage can be allocated between them in whatever proportions they consider appropriate. The election may also allocate the collective interests held by husband and wife between the parties where there are two, or perhaps more, individuals retaining interests in a single property and the £30,000 limit must be apportioned.

The election must be made jointly by husband and wife before a period of 12 months has elapsed following the end of the year of assessment to which the election relates. The election will then apply not only for the year of assessment concerned but for all following years. However, either husband or wife may withdraw the election. Notice of withdrawal must be given within a period of 12 months following the end of the year of assessment to which the withdrawal relates. Once a valid withdrawal has been submitted the normal rules will apply, unless of course the parties submit a revised election.

For 1990–91 the election was widely used where one spouse incurred liability to income tax at the higher rate but the other spouse did not. There would usually be an advantage in all interest being treated as paid by the spouse with the higher income. With the removal of higher rate relief for most items of mortgage interest paid after April 5th, 1991, the "allocation of interest" election has lost much of its former attraction. In limited situations it may still be beneficial; for example, where:

22 RELIEF FOR INTEREST PAID – LET PROPERTY

A single man obtained a loan in 1980 for the purpose of acquiring an investment property. Interest amounting to £5,800 was paid on this loan in 1993–94 and rental income of £4,700 arose in the same year. The only other income was £18,000 from an employment.

The interest paid must be set against rental income received, thereby reducing that income to nil. The surplus interest of £1,100 (£5,800 less £4,700) can only be carried forward and set against rental income for 1994–95 and future years.

Tax payable for 1993–94 becomes:

	£	
Total income	18,000	
Less Personal allowance	3,445	
Tax chargeable on	£14,555	
Tax payable:		
On first £2,500 at 20 per cent		500.00
On balance of £12,055 at 25 per cent		3,013.75
		£3,513.75

a interest is paid outside the MIRAS scheme and there is insufficient taxable income of one spouse to absorb the relief; or,

b increased personal allowances and married couple's allowances are available to individuals over the age of 64.

OTHER INTEREST

Although most items of interest qualifying for relief and paid by an individual will comprise mortgage interest falling to be relieved in the manner outlined above there are other classes of interest which may also obtain relief for income tax purposes. This other interest will be paid gross without deduction of income tax unless, exceptionally, it is paid to a lender residing overseas. The payment will qualify for relief at the lower rate, the basic rate and the higher rate of tax where these rates are suffered by the payer.

LET PROPERTY

An exception arises in the case of interest paid on a loan applied to acquire let property. This interest can only be offset against letting income. Should the income be insufficient to absorb interest paid in a year of assessment the unrelieved interest may be carried forward and relieved against similar income in succeeding years.

Other reliefs

National insurance contributions

NATIONAL INSURANCE contributions are payable by many employed and self-employed individuals. There are numerous exceptions and the level of contributions due will frequently be governed both by the amount of earnings and also by upper and lower thresholds. In summary form, the scope of the four contribution Classes is as follows:

Class 1 An employee pays primary contributions based on a percentage of earnings. A secondary contribution, also based on a percentage of employee's earnings, is payable by the employer.

Class 2 Self-employed individuals pay a flat rate contribution.

Class 3 Some individuals may pay voluntary flat rate contributions for the purpose of securing social security benefits.

23 *NATIONAL INSURANCE CONTRIBUTIONS*

John is a married man deriving his sole livelihood from a business. Profits of the business assessable for 1993–94 amounted to £29,100 and John paid maximum Class 4 national insurance contributions of £976 for the year. No election had been made to apportion the married couple's allowance.

Income tax payable for 1993–94 becomes:

	£	£
Total income		29,100
Less		
Personal allowance	3,445	
Married couple's allowance	1,720	
Class 4 contributions ½ × £976	488	5,653
Tax chargeable on		£23,447
Tax payable:		
On first £2,500 at 20 per cent		500.00
On balance of £20,947 at 25 per cent		5,236.75
		£5,736.75

Class 4 In addition to Class 2 flat rate contributions, self-employed individuals suffer a percentage rate Class 4 contribution based on taxable profits.

Secondary Class 1 contributions paid by an employer may usually be deducted when calculating taxable profits of the employer's business, if the contributions are satisfied for an employee engaged in such a business. Subject to this, no relief is generally available in respect of national insurance contributions paid when calculating the contributor's liability to income tax.

An exception applies to Class 4 contributions paid by a self-employed individual. One-half of these contributions attributable to a year of assessment may be deducted from total income when arriving at liability to income tax for that year. No similar deduction is available for Class 2 flat rate contributions. It must be emphasised that the one-half deduction is not made when calculating the *amount* of profits assessable to income tax, as relief is given in *charging* liability to that tax.

Business expansion scheme

THE AMOUNT of income tax payable by an individual may be reduced by subtracting allowances and a range of outgoings when calculating income chargeable to tax. Comments on the previous pages have examined such matters as personal and other allowances, together with deductions made for pension contributions, interest and Class 4 national insurance contributions. A further doduction which will be of considerable interest to some taxpayers involves relief for expenditure incurred under the business expansion scheme. This scheme was introduced to generate funds for businesses by providing income tax relief to individuals contributing those funds and will end on December 31st, 1993. Relief is confined to the cost of subscribing for eligible shares issued by a company. Most shares are eligible unless they carry unusual or preferential rights.

A large number of requirements must be satisfied, both by the individual subscriber and by the share issuing company, before relief will be available. The more significant requirements are reviewed below.

INDIVIDUALS WHO QUALIFY

At the time of the issue, the individual subscriber must be resident and ordinarily resident in the United Kingdom. Throughout a period commencing two years before the issue date and ending five years after that date, the individual must not:

a be an employee of the company;

b be a director of the company unless he or she acts in an unpaid capacity;

c have an associate, namely a spouse, parent, grandparent, child or grandchild, who is an employee or paid director of the company; or

d either on his own or with associates retain more than 30 per cent of the issued ordinary share capital, loan capital or voting power.

Where shares are issued after March 15th, 1993, the holder of those shares will be disqualified from obtaining relief if a loan is made linked with the shares during the above period of seven years.

QUALIFYING COMPANIES

The company issuing shares must be incorporated in the United Kingdom. Throughout a period of three years following the issue of shares, or the commencement of trading if later, the company must:

a not have a share quotation on the Stock Exchange or be dealt in on the Unlisted Securities Market;

b remain resident in the United Kingdom;

c exist wholly or mainly for the purpose of carrying on a qualifying trade, or be a holding company with subsidiaries carrying on qualifying trades;

d have no unpaid share capital;

e not be under the control of a second company.

Most trades carried on by a company will comprise 'qualifying trades', with the exception of dealing, banking, insurance and leasing, among others. Companies whose activities are confined to the retention of wines, antiques and other assets for a lengthy period are not treated as carrying on a qualifying trade. In addition, companies retaining substantial holdings of land and buildings are excluded.

A relaxation in these requirements applies to certain companies issuing shares after the end of July 1988. During this period, qualification is extended to include a company acquiring or constructing buildings to be let on assured tenancies. A limitation is placed on the cost of individual properties but a company will not be excluded from qualifying status only on the grounds that a substantial part of its assets are invested in land and property.

The maximum amount of capital carrying business expansion scheme relief which a company may raise in any 12-month period is now limited to £750,000. This is increased to £5 million for companies engaged in ship chartering or assured tenancy investment.

RELIEF FOR INVESTMENT

Subject to these and other requirements, it is immaterial whether the company issuing shares commences a new business or has been in existence for many years. Where the requirements are satisfied the individual subscribing for shares may expect to obtain tax relief for his or her outlay.

The maximum relief for each individual is limited to £40,000 for share subscriptions made in a year of assessment ending on April 5th. If any part of this maximum amount is not utilised, it cannot be carried forward and used in a succeeding year. An investor may subscribe for shares issued by a single company or by any number of companies, but a subscription will only qualify for relief if at least £500 is invested in acquiring shares issued by a particular company during a single year.

The calculation of relief for a year of assessment will be primarily governed by subscriptions actually made in that year. However, where a qualifying investment is made not later than October 5th, one-half of the subscription may, at the taxpayer's option, be treated as taking place in the previous year of assessment ending on April 5th. The maximum subscription which can be related back to an earlier year is not to exceed £5,000. There is the additional requirement that the amount related back cannot increase relief for the earlier year above the maximum limit of £40,000.

Many individuals place their monies with the managers of approved funds who apply those monies for the subscription of shares issued by qualifying companies. Investments made in this manner are not subject to the minimum £500 requirement. A further distinction is that relief will be given by reference to the closing date for investment in the fund and not the date on which the share subscription is made.

Relief once granted may be withdrawn retrospectively if the individual, or the company, ceases to satisfy the several requirements at any time in the appropriate period. There may also be the complete or partial withdrawal of relief should the individual dispose of his or her shareholding within a period of time, usually five years from the issue date.

Claims for relief in respect of business expansion scheme investments can be submitted immediately the issue takes place and other necessary formalities are observed. Subscribers need not await the submission of annual income tax returns.

No liability to capital gains tax will arise on the subsequent disposal of

24 *BUSINESS EXPANSION SCHEME – ALLOCATION*

During the year ended April 5th, 1993, Ann subscribed £37,000 for shares issued under the business expansion scheme. She made the following share subscriptions in the year to April 5th, 1994:

	£
August 1993	12,000
December 1993	20,000

Ann can claim to treat one-half of the subscriptions made in the six months ending on October 5th, 1993, as taking place in 1992–93. However, as ½ × £12,000 exceeds £5,000, the amount carried back must be restricted to £5,000. Relief has already been granted on £37,000 in 1992–93, leaving a balance of only £3,000 required to achieve the maximum investment of £40,000. The amount carried back must therefore be further restricted to £3,000, leaving a balance of £9,000 (£12,000 less £3,000) treated as paid in 1993–94. This will be added to the further investment of £20,000 made in December 1993.

25 *BUSINESS EXPANSION SCHEME – RELIEF*

A married man received a salary of £95,000 in 1993–94. During the year, but before December 31st, 1993, he subscribed £40,000 for shares issued by a company. It was agreed this investment qualified for business expansion scheme relief which should be given in 1993–94 only. No election had been made to apportion the married couple's allowance.

		£
Total income		95,000
Less	£	
Personal allowance	3,445	
Married couple's allowance	1,720	
Business expansion scheme relief	40,000	45,165
Tax chargeable on		£49,835

Tax payable:	£
Lower rate:	
On first £2,500 at 20 per cent	500.00
Basic rate:	
On next £21,200 at 25 per cent	5,300.00
Higher rate:	
On balance of £26,135 at 40 per cent	10,454.00
	£16,254.00

shares issued after March 18th, 1986, if business expansion scheme relief has been obtained and not withdrawn.

On earlier occasions it was possible to obtain income tax relief for interest paid on monies borrowed to finance the acquisition of shares qualifying for business expansion scheme relief, if the company involved retained close company status. No relief is now available for such payments of interest, where the share subscription occurred after March 13th, 1989.

HUSBAND AND WIFE

For 1989–90 and earlier years the maximum of £40,000 governed the aggregate share subscriptions capable of being made by a husband and wife "living together". With the introduction of independent taxation, this limitation was abandoned and each spouse is independently subject to the £40,000 restriction and other limits. Notwithstanding this, where one spouse acquires eligible shares and subsequently transfers those shares to the other, this will not represent a disposal withdrawing relief.

TERMINATION OF SCHEME

The business expansion scheme will terminate on December 31st, 1993. Investments made after this date will not obtain relief.

Life assurance premiums

TAX RELIEF may be available where premiums are paid on older qualifying life assurance and other policies. This relief applies only to premiums on policies made before March 15th, 1984, and cannot be obtained for new policies entered into on or after that date. Changes to a pre-1984 policy which secure increased benefits may result in relief being withdrawn from the date of the change. Where relief is available this has no effect whatsoever on the policyholder's liability to income tax but merely reduces the amount of the premium.

When paying premiums on an approved pre-1984 policy the policyholder will deduct and retain income tax at the rate of 12.5 per cent. It is immaterial whether the individual is liable to income tax, or exempt on the grounds that his or her income is insufficient to justify liability. In all cases the deduction can be made. A restriction arises, however, where the premiums paid in any one year exceed £1,500, as relief will be limited to deductions of £1,500 or one-sixth of the individual's total income, whichever is the greater. If the amount deducted at the rate of 12.5 per cent exceeds these limits the policyholder will be required to refund the excess.

Separate calculations of total income must be prepared to establish whether premiums paid by a husband or his wife exceed the one-sixth limit.

Medical insurance premiums

TAX RELIEF may be available for premiums paid under a private medical insurance contract. This relief is limited to premiums paid on a policy for the benefit of an individual aged 60 years or over. In the case of husband and wife, only one spouse need have achieved this age. The policy must be in a form approved by the Inland Revenue, be limited to a period not exceeding twelve months and provide medical cover. The provision of cash benefits must usually be excluded. Subject to this the contract may cover charges for medical and surgical procedures, including diagnosis, the purpose of which is the relief of illness or injury. It is a general requirement that the procedures must be given or controlled by a registered medical or dental practitioner in the United Kingdom, but physiotherapy, following consultation with a general practitioner, is also included.

Relief will not be confined to premiums paid by the person insured but may extend to premiums paid by some other person, perhaps a son or daughter, providing the insured has reached the required age.

26 *MEDICAL INSURANCE PREMIUMS*

William is a single man aged 48 earning £24,500. He pays a premium of £700 on an approved medical insurance policy providing cover for his elderly mother. The actual premium paid will be:

	£
Gross payment	700.00
Less tax at 25 per cent	175.00
Actual payment	£525.00

	£
Total income	24,500
Less Personal allowance	3,445
Tax chargeable on	£21,055

Tax payable:	
On first £2,500 at 20 per cent	500.00
On balance of £18,555 at 25 per cent	4,638.75
	£5,138.75

The tax of £175 deducted on payment of the premium can be retained, which effectively reduces the tax suffered from £5,138.75 to £4,963.75.

Qualifying premiums will be paid after deduction of income tax at the basic rate under a scheme similar to MIRAS, which applies to payments of mortgage interest (see page 44). In common with the MIRAS scheme, tax deducted at the basic rate may be retained whether or not the payer is liable to income tax at that rate. Unlike MIRAS, however, contributors liable to tax at the higher rate may obtain relief on the excess over the basic rate, either through the PAYE notice of coding or against direct assessment. The restriction of relief under MIRAS to the lower rate of 20 per cent for 1994–95 does not apply to medical insurance premiums.

In the case of a married couple it may be worth considering whether the contract should be entered into and premiums paid by a husband or his wife. If only one spouse is liable to income tax at the higher rate of 40 per cent, that spouse should be selected, where possible. In the case of joint policies relief is given to the spouse actually paying premiums.

Vocational training

A tax relief designed to encourage vocational training came into operation on April 6th, 1992. This relief is available for study and examination fees paid by an individual resident in the United Kingdom who undertakes qualifying training. Detailed arrangements have to be observed but to qualify for relief the training must lead to National Vocational Qualifications or Scottish Vocational Qualifications at levels 1 to 4. These are qualifications accredited by the National Council for Vocational Qualifications which covers England, Wales and Northern

Ireland, or by the Scottish Vocational Education Council. Levels 1 to 4 incorporate training up to middle management and supervisory skills. Level 5, which is not included, extends to senior managerial and professional skills including degree level qualifications.

Tax relief will be given on a basis similar to that which applies to interest payments under the MIRAS scheme outlined on page 44. When making qualifying payments of study and examination fees the payer will deduct income tax at the basic rate. The tax deducted may be retained whether or not the payer is liable to income tax at that rate. Unlike MIRAS, however, payers who are liable to income tax at the higher rate may deduct their outgoing when calculating liability at this rate. Relief for payments made after April 5th, 1994, will not be restricted to the lower rate of 20 per cent which applies to MIRAS from that date.

Persons providing training and who receive fees after deduction of income tax at the basic rate can obtain repayment of the tax deducted from the Inland Revenue.

Employments

Pay As You Earn

PAYE is *not* a separate tax but a scheme whereby income tax on wages, salaries and other earnings is collected by deduction as and when the wages and salaries are paid. A "receipts basis" governs the year of assessment into which earnings fall. The rules which determine the time of "receipt" are discussed on page 65. Identical rules apply to establish the date of "payment" for the purposes of PAYE.

Although all wages and salaries are subject to assessment under Schedule E, circumstances occur where it is impractical to operate a PAYE scheme of tax deduction. For example, an individual employed abroad by a foreign employer may be liable to tax on his earnings but the employer could not operate PAYE, and in such a case the employee will be assessed direct. PAYE extends to all income tax payable on earnings to which the scheme relates, including tax at the lower rate, the basic rate and the higher rate.

In most situations it will be apparent whether an individual rendering services holds an office or employment to which the PAYE deduction scheme applies. There are, however, inevitably borderline cases where the distinction between employment and self-employment is not easy to resolve. Some employers choose to disregard this distinction and discharge earnings without deducting PAYE. This is a most dangerous practice, as subsequent detection by the Inland Revenue may have serious financial and other consequences.

Many individuals whose services are supplied through agencies and who do not technically become employees of the person to whom services are supplied are regarded as "employees" for income tax purposes. PAYE will be applied to any remuneration paid by the employer of such persons. However, certain individuals engaged in diving operations who could be correctly treated as employees may be regarded as self-employed and outside the PAYE scheme.

The collection of tax on most unemployment benefits paid to the unemployed is brought within the PAYE deduction scheme. The scheme also applies to the collection of tax on social security maternity pay, payments of statutory sick pay made by an employer and to many pensions paid under occupational schemes.

CODE NUMBERS

Each employee should have a code number and this is arrived at by the tax office from the income tax return or other information disclosing details of allowances claimed. All the allowances are added together and if the employee has no other income the total of his allowances, less the last figure, will fix his code number.

If the taxpayer has other income, e.g. a retirement pension, untaxed interest or income from property, the estimated amount of this income may be deducted from the total allowances to calculate the code number. Whilst this will increase the amount of tax deducted under PAYE, it will avoid the need to raise assessments directly on the taxpayer to recover tax on the other income. Tax on car and car fuel benefits enjoyed by directors and higher paid employees is also collected through the PAYE system. This was previously achieved by deducting the estimated benefits from total allowances when fixing the code number. However, on April 6th, 1993, a new "K" code procedure was introduced to replace the previous practice (see page 61).

No adjustment is usually made on the coding notice for contributions to an occupational pension scheme or superannuation fund as these will be deducted from earnings in arriving at the net earnings chargeable to tax. A number of special adjustments will be required to the code number where tax has been underpaid for earlier years, tax is being deducted from annual payments made, or liability arises at the higher rate. Code 0 will frequently apply where an individual has two or more employments. The full allowances will be used in calculating the code number for the main employment, leaving no allowances available for the subsidiary employment.

The letters "L", "H" or "T" will often appear at the end of the code number, e.g. Code Number 516H. The letter "L" indicates that the individual concerned is entitled to the basic personal allowance and the letter "H" that the married couple's allowance, or the additional personal allowance available for single parent families, is available. The use of these letters enables the code to be adjusted quickly where there is any future change in the rate of allowances.

The letters "L" and "H" do not indicate the remaining allowances or reliefs to which an employee may be entitled, but if the employee does not wish his employer to know which allowance is available he may request the Tax Office to replace the letter "L" or "H" with the letter "T". The letter "T" will also be used where no personal allowance is available, e.g. where an individual has two employments and the personal allowance and any other allowances have been applied in calculating the code number for the main employment only. Code numbers issued to elderly taxpayers entitled to claim the increased personal allowance or increased married couple's allowance have the letter "P" to denote a single person and "V" for a married man.

Although these are the main letters used, others apply in special circumstances. For example, BR indicates that tax is to be deducted at the basic rate and NT shows that no tax is to be deducted. D implies that tax will be deducted at the higher rate and F requires that tax due on a social security pension or benefit is being collected from earnings or a pension from a previous employment. Social security retirement pensions and widows' benefits are paid gross, without deduction of income tax. This requires that where tax is due, recovery of that tax must be made by adjusting the PAYE code number of an employment or by direct assessment.

CHANGES IN THE CODE NUMBER

Should any change in the available allowances occur during the year the Tax Office must be notified immediately as this will enable the code number to be quickly altered. The need for an alteration may arise, for example, where a taxpayer marries and qualifies for the married couple's allowance, becomes entitled to the additional personal allowance for children or qualifies for the widow's bereavement allowance.

DEDUCTIONS WORKING SHEETS

Tax tables are supplied to all employers so that the actual tax deductions can be calculated. The amount of the deduction in any particular case depends upon the code number, and the employer is advised of this number so that the correct amount of tax to be deducted can be ascertained by him from the tax tables. Employers are provided with official Deductions Working Sheets for each employee, unless the employer chooses to use a similar record of his own design. Details of payments made to employees are entered on these sheets together with information extracted from the tax tables. This enables the employer to calculate the amount of PAYE deductions which should be made. At the end of the income tax year the employer completes End of Year Returns, or similar documents, and forwards these to the Tax Office.

The Inland Revenue then knows the total earnings for the year and the total amount of tax suffered by deduction by each employee. The exact amount of tax which should be paid on the total earnings of the year can then be calculated. If any tax has been under- or over-paid, this adjustment will usually be carried forward to the following year; but the taxpayer has the right to require any tax overpaid to be refunded instead of having it carried forward. Should the amount under-deducted be substantial, the employee may be required to pay this amount to the Inland Revenue by direct assessment.

Class 1 national insurance contributions are also entered on the Deductions Working Sheets. However, these contributions do not represent the payment of income tax and are only dealt with under the PAYE scheme for administrative reasons.

Failure on the part of an employer to submit in good time End of Year Returns and other documents for 1993–94 may result in a demand for penalties.

REPAYMENT OF TAX

If current earnings are smaller than those for earlier weeks or months falling in the same tax year, it is possible that some tax will be repaid to the employee. This may happen if the tax paid for previous weeks or months is greater than the tax due up to the end of the week or month in respect of which the earnings are small. It may also occur where entitlement to some further allowance or relief arises. In these circumstances the employer will refund to the employee part of the tax deducted on earlier occasions.

UNEMPLOYMENT

Most unemployment benefits are now taxable. However, no deduction of tax will be made until the period of unemployment has ended.

On becoming unemployed an individual will be handed a leaving certificate, Form P45. If he or she claims unemployment benefit the form must be handed to the benefit office. On subsequently finding a new employment the individual will deliver a completed card UB40 to the benefit office. This office then issues the individual with an updated Form P45, including the amount of taxable benefit, and will make any repayment of PAYE deductions which may be due. The new employer uses the information shown on the P45 to make future deductions from earnings. If the period of unemployment extends to the following April 5th, the benefit office will make any repayment of PAYE which may be due.

It follows that where an individual becomes unemployed, no repayment of PAYE deductions can be obtained until the end of the tax year, or the end of the period of unemployment, whichever occurs first. Persons becoming unemployed by reason of strike action cannot obtain repayment of PAYE until the strike ends.

The purpose of withholding refunds during a period of unemployment, and refraining from deducting PAYE on benefits paid, is one of administrative convenience. In many cases the amount due to be refunded will be similar to the tax due on taxable social security benefits.

THE NEW "K" CODE

The PAYE scheme is used to collect income tax by deduction when earnings are paid. Not all rewards chargeable to income tax are received in the form of cash payments. Examples include a large number of benefits in kind enjoyed by directors and employees (see page 76). It was previously the practice to collect tax indirectly on these non-cash sums by subtracting the estimated taxable benefits from allowances when arriving at the code number used to operate PAYE. However, this approach was not fully effective where the total non-cash items exceeded the amount of the allowances, as it was not possible to use a negative code number. Where excessive benefits arose, the Inland Revenue were required to raise an assessment on the taxpayer with the inevitable delay in collecting tax due.

To resolve this problem a new "K" code procedure was introduced on April 6th, 1993. This procedure does not require any amendment to code numbers. Instead, additions are made to the amount of taxable pay from which PAYE deductions must be subtracted. The additions, to be made at agreed rates, reflect the value of taxable benefits and enable income tax to be collected on those benefits through the PAYE system.

The new "K" codes also replace the special "F" codes given to pensioners whose social security retirement pensions exceed their personal tax allowances.

It may be found that by adding notional earnings, reflecting taxable benefits, to actual earnings the amount of PAYE to be deducted from payments made is excessively high, or may even exceed the amount of the actual payment. To avoid distortions of this nature a restriction is placed on the maximum deduction, which will not usually exceed 50 per cent of the actual pay. Subject to this modification, the existing PAYE procedure will apply generally to those taxpayers allocated "K" codes for 1993–94 and future years.

CHANGING JOBS AND NEW EMPLOYMENTS

If an individual changes his job he will receive from his old employer a leaving certificate (Form P45) which sets out the code number, the total pay to date and the total tax that has been deducted in the tax year. This certificate should be handed to the new employer, if any, who will then continue the deductions from the later earnings of the same tax year. It is often found that delay occurs in obtaining a Form P45, and some individuals may fail to take proper care of the form handed to them. This causes considerable work, both for the new employer and also the Inland Revenue, as laborious steps must be taken to trace details relating to the tax affairs of the employee. Individuals should take great care of a Form P45 and hand it to the new employer at the earliest opportunity. If they do not, excessive PAYE deductions may be made by the new employer until a revised notice of coding is issued. To avoid problems of this nature a special procedure is used. This procedure, which applies where a Form P45 is not handed to the new employer promptly, requires the issue of a short questionnaire. The questionnaire urges the new employee to contact his old employer for the speedy production of Form P45 and also requires the provision of sufficient information for the Tax Office to compute a provisional code if there is further delay.

School leavers and others commencing employment for the first time should be placed on an emergency code until they have completed an income tax return which enables an accurate code to be issued. However, such persons will, after signing a simple declaration, be given a code number for a single person and no income tax return will be issued, unless requested by the taxpayer.

Taxpayers starting an additional job are placed on an emergency code, if their earnings are sufficiently substantial, or may have no tax deducted until the Tax Office issues a code number. Tax deductions made from earnings arising from the additional job are imposed at the basic rate of 25 per cent.

Where the "K" code procedure outlined above applied to the old employment, this will be reviewed by the Inland Revenue to establish whether it should be continued by the new employer, if any.

ACCOUNTING FOR DEDUCTIONS

Most employers are required to pay over to the Collector of Taxes, not later than fourteen days after the end of each tax month, deductions made in the previous month. A tax month ends on the fifth day with the result that the employer's liability to account for deductions arises on the nineteenth of each month. A similar procedure applies to the discharge of Class 1 national insurance contributions.

However, a change in the accounting procedure is available for small employers. If the average aggregate monthly payments of PAYE deductions and national insurance contributions fall below £450 the employer may adopt a quarterly, rather than a monthly, accounting basis. Payments will then fall due fourteen days after the end of each quarter terminating on July 5th, October 5th, January 5th and April 5th.

Contractors in the construction industry may also adopt a quarterly basis when accounting for deductions from payments to sub-contractors (see page 101) where the average aggregate monthly payments of PAYE, national insurance contributions and sub-contractors' deductions fall below £450.

OMISSION TO DEDUCT TAX

The purpose of the PAYE deduction scheme is to collect tax on earnings when emoluments are paid to an employee. However, the employer's obligation is not limited to the satisfaction of sums actually deducted but extends to the amount of deductions which ought to have been made, less repayments properly due to employees. Failure on the part of the employer to make the full deductions may therefore have serious consequences, as the Inland Revenue may demand payment of the full sums due. This situation often arises following an investigation of an employer's affairs and the allegation that the deduction procedure has not been properly applied.

In two situations the employer may be relieved of his or her obligation to account for deductions which have not been made. First, where the Collector of Taxes can be satisfied that the employer took reasonable care to comply with the PAYE regulations, and the under-deduction was due to an error made in good faith, he may direct that the outstanding sum should be recovered from the employee or employees concerned. The effect of such a direction is to absolve the employer from further liability.

The second exception arises where the Commissioners of Inland Revenue (and not the Collector of Taxes) are of the opinion that an employee has received his emoluments knowing that the employer has wilfully failed to make the deductions required by the PAYE regulations. In these circumstances also the Commissioners may absolve the employer from liability to account for under-deductions and recover the proper amount of tax from the employee or employees.

The application of either approach is very much a matter for the discretion of the Inland Revenue, and no employer should anticipate that an appropriate direction will be issued. This merely serves to emphasise the obligation placed on employers to ensure that the proper PAYE deductions are made when paying emoluments to employees.

There are similar provisions which enable underpayments of national insurance contributions to be recovered.

RECOVERY OF TAX AND INTEREST

Some employers fail to account for PAYE deductions made, or indeed to operate properly the statutory requirements. HM Inspector of Taxes may then determine the amount thought to be due and raise an assessment. If the amount of such an assessment, known as a Regulation 29 determination, is to be disputed the employer must provide notice of appeal within a period of thirty days from the issue date. Failure to provide the required notice of appeal will result in the tax shown by the assessment falling due for payment. Frequently the amount of tax shown by a disputed assessment which is under appeal will be settled by agreement between the parties, but where it is not, the appeal will be heard by a body of Commissioners. A liability to satisfy interest will usually arise where action is taken under Regulation 29 and an amount of tax falls due.

In many situations the Inland Revenue have been unable to impose an interest charge where there has been delay in accounting for PAYE deductions. However, this obstacle has now been removed and where PAYE deductions have not been paid over to the Collector of Taxes within 14 days after the end of a year of assessment (namely, by April 19th) a general interest charge may be imposed. This first applies to deductions made in 1992–93 where the amount deducted was not paid over by the employer by April 19th, 1993. The rate of interest charged will vary in line with changes in the money market generally but is imposed at rates identical to those which apply for late payments of tax (see page 165). It will not be overlooked that any interest commitment discharged in this manner cannot form an ingredient in the calculation of profits chargeable to tax.

The interest charge is limited to sums remaining outstanding 14 days following the end of the year of assessment. It does not apply to late monthly or quarterly payments made during the year.

Similar interest procedures also apply to deductions made under the sub-contractors' scheme (see page 101) and to late payments of Class 1 national insurance contributions.

ASSESSMENTS

After April 5th, 1994, when the Tax Office receives all 1993–94 returns from employers, the tax deducted is checked. If the amount deducted correctly represents the tax payable for 1993–94 and the code number does not require adjustment due to any alteration in the taxpayer's allowances, no formal notice of assessment will be sent to the taxpayer. But the latter has the right to give written notice to the Tax Office within five years from April 5th, 1994, requiring an assessment to be made upon him showing the manner in which the tax paid is to be calculated.

ASSESSING TOLERANCE

It is apparent that the administrative cost of raising assessments to collect small amounts of tax may substantially exceed the tax eventually collected. This is recognised by the Inland Revenue who apply an "assessing tolerance" of £30 below which the tax is not assessed or collected. However, if an assessment is raised, particularly where the taxpayer has requested such an assessment, steps will be taken to collect the tax, notwithstanding that the amount involved is small. Where the tax payable exceeds the assessing tolerance by a small amount, all tax will be collected and not only the excess.

Widows and single women pensioners under the age of 65 may receive social security pensions on which any tax due must be recovered by direct assessment. No assessments will be raised on such persons to recover small amounts falling within the assessing tolerance.

BASIS OF ASSESSMENT AND BACK PAY

The assessment of earnings is based on the amount of those earnings "for" the year of assessment ending on April 5th. In earlier years it was necessary to allocate earnings to a year of assessment, particularly where earnings were paid late or in arrears. There were two main problem areas and the first arose where bonuses, fees or commissions were paid for a period overlapping April 5th, or perhaps after the end of the year of assessment to which they referred. For example, a bonus for the year ending September 30th, 1988, may have been paid in, say, December of the same year. It was then necessary to allocate the bonus as to one-half for 1987–88 and one-half for 1988–89. As a result there would be an under-deduction of PAYE for the earlier year to be recouped in the following year. This process could continue annually where a bonus or some other payment fell due in successive years.

The second situation recognised that some employees, particularly directors, would receive a bonus or other sum based on the results shown by a company's financial accounts. Few accounting periods conveniently terminated on April 5th and strictly the bonus had to be allocated between two different years of assessment. In practice, this approach was often relaxed by adopting an "accounts basis", whereby a bonus and other items of remuneration were treated as income for the year of assessment in which the employer's accounting year ended. This practice could only be adopted with the taxpayer's consent and did not apply in the opening and closing years of an employment.

These two alternatives ceased to apply after April 5th, 1989. From this date earnings must be allocated to, and assessed for, the year of assessment in which they are received. There is no longer any need to apportion earnings between one year of assessment and another, to make an adjustment where earnings are received late or to apply the "accounts basis". In all cases the date of receipt will determine the year of assessment into which earnings fall.

DATE EARNINGS RECEIVED

For most employees, earnings will be treated as "received":

a on the date emoluments are paid; or

b on the date an employee becomes entitled to those emoluments,

whichever event first occurs.

These rules apply also to company directors but for such individuals there are three further possible dates, namely:

c the date emoluments are *credited* in the accounts or records of the company;

d if emoluments for a period are *determined* before the end of that period – the last day of the period; or

e if emoluments for a period are *determined* after the end of that period – the date of determination.

In all cases it is the earliest of the possible dates which establishes the time of receipt. Particular caution must be exercised when dealing with remuneration payable to directors of family companies for the purpose of ensuring that the date of "receipt" is not unduly advanced.

The "receipt" date will also establish that on which earnings are treated as "paid" for PAYE purposes.

OVERSEAS EMPLOYMENTS

Earnings from an office or employment are only capable of being assessed to income tax under Schedule E and cannot be dealt with under any other Schedule. For this purpose it is immaterial whether duties are performed in the United Kingdom or in some territory overseas. However, the liability to United Kingdom taxation in respect of earnings from employments undertaken wholly or partly outside the United Kingdom will largely depend on whether the employee is resident here or abroad and also the place where duties are actually carried out.

Employees resident and ordinarily resident

If an employee is both resident and ordinarily resident in the United Kingdom, all earnings, whether from duties carried out at home or overseas, are initially liable to tax. It may be possible to reduce the amount of taxable earnings by applying a "foreign earnings deduction" where duties are performed overseas, but the application of this deduction is severely limited.

Where an employee works full-time overseas for a qualifying period of 365 days or more, he may deduct 100 per cent of his overseas earnings when calculating liability to United Kingdom taxation, and therefore avoid any liability in respect of those earnings. A period is treated as a "qualifying period" for this purpose unless during that period the employee was present in the United Kingdom:

a on more than 62 consecutive days; or

b for more than one-sixth of the total number of days in that period.

The "foreign earnings deduction" is limited to earnings for duties carried out overseas and cannot extend to duties performed in the United Kingdom, unless those duties are merely incidental to the overseas activities.

For seafarers the number of days in **a** is increased to 183 days and the factor in **b** to one-half.

The Gulf war

The crisis in the Gulf compelled many employees to return unexpectedly early to the United Kingdom. This may well have prevented those individuals establishing the required 365-day qualifying period. However, special relief is available for employees who were working in Kuwait or Iraq on August 2nd, 1990, or at any time in the previous 62 days, under a contract of employment requiring the whole or a substantial part of the duties to be performed in Kuwait or Iraq. The relief will enable the 100 per cent deduction to be obtained for earnings up to the date of return to the United Kingdom if, disregarding the Gulf crisis, the 365-day continuing period would otherwise have been achieved.

Some relaxation is also available in the rules which apply to determine whether an individual is "resident" in the United Kingdom (see page 161).

Other employees

An individual who is either not resident or not ordinarily resident in the United Kingdom will be charged to tax on his earnings for work undertaken in the United Kingdom. This charge does not extend to earnings for work performed overseas.

Special rules apply to employees domiciled outside the United Kingdom and employed by non-resident employers. If these individuals perform the whole of their duties overseas only sums remitted to the United Kingdom will be chargeable to tax.

PROFIT-RELATED PAY

The calculation of earnings received by employees will sometimes be influenced by the level of profits achieved by the employer. Earnings of this nature are fully chargeable to income tax unless they comprise profit-related pay.

To achieve relief from taxation, profit-related pay must arise under a scheme approved by the Inland Revenue. The scheme enables employees to receive profit-related pay based on the employer's profits for a profit period, in addition to the employees' normal earnings. A profit-related pay scheme is applied to an "employment unit" and need not necessarily extend to all business activities of the employer. At least 80 per cent of employees working in that employment unit must be members of the scheme, although part-time staff working less than 20 hours weekly and new employees having less than three years of service may be excluded. Controlling directors must not be permitted to participate and the scheme is limited to employees in the private sector. A profit-related pay scheme can be introduced for a single accounting period of twelve months in duration or extend throughout a longer period.

A participating employee will receive both normal earnings and profit-related pay. However, the profit-related pay may be wholly or partly exempt from income tax. The level of exemption has changed from time to time but, for profit periods commencing after March 31st, 1991 the exemption will comprise the lower of:

a the actual profit-related pay;

b one-fifth of normal pay plus profit-related pay; and

c £4,000.

When applying the PAYE deduction scheme the employer will disregard the exempt profit-related pay and confine deductions to net earnings remaining. The exclusion of pay in this manner has no application to the calculation of national insurance contributions, which extends to the full earnings.

Applications to register a profit-related pay scheme may be submitted at any time, but the scheme must be registered before the commencement of the employer's first profit period used to measure profit-related pay if the tax exemption is to be obtained.

27 *PROFIT-RELATED PAY*

Mr R was a member of an approved profit-related pay scheme throughout the twelve-month profit period to September 30th, 1993. On January 15th, 1994, he received profit-related pay of £3,500 for that period. Normal pay received by Mr R in the year ended September 30th, 1993, was £12,000.

The profit-related pay of £3,500 comprises income for 1993–94. However, the exempt amount will be the smaller of:

		£
a	Profit-related pay	3,500
b	$\frac{1}{5}$ × (£3,500 + £12,000)	3,100
c	maximum	4,000

Calculation **b** produces the smaller figure and the taxable part of profit-related pay becomes £400 (£3,500 less £3,100).

PENSIONS

Any pension from an office or employment in the United Kingdom is assessable to income tax under Schedule E. In most cases the pension will be subject to deduction of tax under the PAYE scheme outlined above. By concession, any additional pension awarded due to injury, work related illness or war wounds is not charged to tax.

An exception arises where the pension is paid by an overseas employer to a former employee resident in the United Kingdom, as in such a case PAYE will not usually apply. Overseas pensions are chargeable to tax under Schedule D but assessment is limited to 90 per cent of the pension, whether it is remitted to the United Kingdom or not. The remaining 10 per cent will escape liability.

EXPENSES

Any expenses which the holder of an office or employment is *necessarily obliged* to expend *wholly, exclusively and necessarily* in the *performance of the duties of the office*, including expenses of travelling, may be deducted from the earnings to be assessed. Before an expenses claim is admitted by the Inland Revenue the items of expenditure are closely scrutinised to establish whether the requirements have been satisfied. For example, the cost of travelling from home to the place of employment cannot be allowed, as travelling is not undertaken whilst performing the duties of the office but to place the individual in a position from which to carry out those duties. On the other hand, once the place of employment has been reached the cost of any further business journeys will usually qualify for relief. When determining those expenses which may obtain relief, a distinction must be drawn between expenses which are personal to an employee and those which would be incurred by any holder of the office. For example, an incapacitated employee may have to incur expenses by reason of his incapacity, e.g. the maintenance of a guide dog by a blind person, but this expense would not be incurred by *any* holder of the office and it must be disallowed.

An expenses claim should show, where possible, each individual item making up the total sum claimed. Vouchers and receipts must always be obtained when making payments and subsequently submitted in support of the claim. Unless these details are tendered they will usually be asked for and in the absence of sufficient information the claim may well be rejected. Many trade unions have negotiated round sum allowances on behalf of their members. These allowances should be granted without further enquiry, although individual employees may attempt to establish increased relief if supporting evidence can be supplied.

Employees performing services wholly outside the United Kingdom under the terms of a separate contract may usually deduct the cost of travelling from, and returning to, the United Kingdom.

Fees and subscriptions paid to a large number of professional bodies and learned societies may be deducted from earnings. The Inland Revenue retains a list of approved bodies and only subscriptions paid to a body or society whose name appears on the list can be deducted.

Examples of expenditure which can be included in an expenses claim:

a **Hotel Expenses** for sales representatives and others who have to go from place to place in the performance of their duties. No restriction will normally be necessary for any "home saving" effected by the employee while away on business trips.

b **Office Accommodation**, clerical assistance, stationery, and similar expenses where necessary to the employment.

c **Overalls, Clothing and Tools** where the employee must supply these items specially for his employment. Many trade unions have negotiated round sum allowances for these items on behalf of their members.

d **Travelling Expenses** actually incurred in performing the duties.

e **Professional Fees and Subscriptions** paid to Societies with activities related to an employee's work.

f **Rent** and other outgoings incurred by clergymen and ministers of religion.

Examples of expenditure which cannot be included in an expenses claim:

a **Travelling Expenses** in travelling to and from the taxpayer's place of employment, unless the employment is carried out overseas.

b **Instruction Fees and Cost of Books** where incurred by the employee to enable him to qualify in his appointment or to put him in a position to carry out his employment. There may be some relief for expenditure incurred on approved vocational training (see page 56).

MOTOR MILEAGE ALLOWANCES

Where an employee uses his or her own motor car for business purposes the employer will usually pay a motor mileage allowance. This allowance may be generous or austere, but any sum paid is strictly income chargeable to income tax with PAYE deductions being imposed. It then remains for the employee to submit an expenses claim in an endeavour to obtain relief from income tax suffered.

This is a cumbersome and time-consuming exercise and considerable administrative savings may be achieved by adopting the "Fixed Profit Car Scheme", with the approval of the Inland Revenue. The broad effect of this scheme is that the Inland Revenue announce the maximum amount of mileage allowances which will not result in the employee becoming chargeable to income tax. Motor cars are graded into a number of bands for this purpose.

To the extent that mileage allowances exceed the approved levels, the excess will be treated as income chargeable to income tax without the benefit of any expenses claim.

The Fixed Profit Car Scheme is limited to mileage allowances paid for business motoring and has no application to other matters. Employees are not obliged to adopt the scheme and may choose to apply the statutory basis. Whilst consideration must be applied to individual circumstances, it is unlikely that the statutory basis will result in any increased exemption from taxation.

The mileage rates used for the Fixed Profit Car Scheme take account of depreciation, insurance, road tax, fuel, services and repairs attributable to the business miles travelled. They do not include interest. It follows that any interest paid on a loan applied to acquire a motor car may well enable the employee to obtain relief for the business proportion of that interest.

The rates used for the purposes of the Fixed Profit Car Scheme for both 1992–93 and 1993–94 are shown below.

FIXED PROFIT CAR SCHEME

TAX-FREE LIMITS 1992–93

Cylinder capacity	Up to 4,000 miles per mile (p)	Over 4,000 miles per mile (p)
Up to 1,000	25	14
1,001–1,500	30	17
1,501–2,000	38	21
2,001 and above	51	27

TAX-FREE LIMITS 1993–94

Cylinder capacity	Up to 4,000 miles per mile (p)	Over 4,000 miles per mile (p)
Up to 1,000	26	15
1,001–1,500	32	18
1,501–2,000	40	22
2,001 and above	54	30

28 FIXED PROFIT CAR SCHEME

Throughout the year of assessment 1993–94 Mr S used his own motor car when travelling on his employer's business. The vehicle was of 1,600 cylinder capacity and 6,200 miles of business motoring were involved in the year. The employer paid a mileage allowance at the rate of 42p per mile and the Fixed Profit Car Scheme applied. The tax-free mileage allowance for 1993–94 will be calculated as follows:

	£
First 4,000 miles at 40p	1,600.00
Next 2,200 miles at 22p	484.00
	£2,084.00
Total mileage allowances paid	
6,200 at 42p	£2,604.00

Mr S will suffer income tax on £520 (£2,604 less £2,084). This tax should be imposed through the PAYE system. There can be no expenses claim, or claim for capital allowances on the cost of the motor car.

Benefits in kind

ALL EMPLOYEES

ASSESSMENT UNDER Schedule E extends to "emoluments" arising from an office or employment. The expression "emoluments" is defined to include all salaries, fees, wages, perquisites and profits whatsoever. This definition will embrace most "rewards" received by an employee but some advantages may be enjoyed which are not necessarily subject to tax, including earnings arising under a profit-related pay scheme. As a general rule, any advantages which can be turned into money will be taxed but those which cannot may escape liability. For example, an employee may enjoy the use of a company car but as such an advantage cannot be converted into money no liability will arise. This remains subject to the special rules, discussed on page 78, which apply to directors and many employees.

In those cases where an employee receives "money's worth" which is chargeable to tax, liability will arise on the market value of the benefit and not necessarily on the cost to the employer of providing that benefit, but there are many exceptions. An employee who is provided with a voucher, by reason of his office or employment, will be taxed on the cost to the employer in providing the voucher and not on the value of goods for which that voucher can be exchanged. Advantages which arise from the provision of season tickets financed by an employer, or the use of an employer's credit card, incur liability to income tax. Payments made to an employee during a period of sickness or disability are taxable, except to the extent that the payments are funded from contributions made by the employee. This is in addition to the tax imposed on statutory short term sickness benefit paid by an employer. The provision of luncheon vouchers remains exempt unless, or to the extent that, they exceed 15p in value. Travel vouchers, warrants and allowances made available to members of the armed forces when going on, or returning from, leave are not chargeable to tax.

Where an employer satisfies a personal obligation of an employee the amount involved will be assessable. An illustration may involve the employer who satisfies the council tax payable by an employee, unless the tax is attributable to property occupied by the employee as part of his or her employment.

In practice, the Inland Revenue do not seek to charge tax in respect of awards made to directors and employees as testimonials to mark long service where the period of service is not less than twenty years and no similar award has been made to the recipient within the previous ten years. This concession is broadly limited to tangible articles, for example a watch or television set, having a cost or value not exceeding £20 for each year of service but may also include the provision of shares in the employing company. Also by concession, rewards paid under a genuine suggestion scheme, the reimbursement of expenses where an employee has been required to make alternative travelling or accommodation arrangements due to industrial disputes, the cost of late night journeys where an employee is occasionally required to work late and the provision of financial assistance to severely disabled employees when travelling from home to work do not create a liability to income tax. Nor will liability arise where an employee is reimbursed the cost of car parking at or near the place of work.

Some employees receive gifts from third parties. The value of these gifts will not be taxed if they are unsolicited. It is a requirement that gifts received from the same source do not exceed £100 in any year and the exemption does not extend to cash gifts or tips. However, a payment made to an individual as an inducement to take up employment, sometimes referred to as a "Golden Hello", is likely to be fully taxable.

Where an employee is working wholly abroad the reimbursement of travelling and hotel expenses by the employer will not create an emolument assessable to income tax. A similar exemption applies where the employer bears the cost of travel incurred by an employee's spouse and children. It is a necessary requirement that the family travel to and from the country where the employee is working and the United Kingdom. Expenses incurred by, or reimbursed to, a non-domiciled individual when travelling to the United Kingdom for employment purposes are also exempt, but this extends only to travelling within a period of five years from the initial date of arrival in this territory.

The ability of an employee to acquire shares or securities on advantageous terms will often create liability to income tax. However, exemption may be available where shares or securities are acquired under an approved profit sharing scheme, a savings-related share option scheme or an approved share option scheme.

PROVISION OF LIVING ACCOMMODATION

An additional liability to income tax may arise where an employee is provided with living accommodation by reason of his or her employment. This liability also applies where such accommodation is provided for use by the employee's wife or husband, son or daughter, son-in-law, daughter-in-law, parent, servant, dependant or guest. There are, however, exceptions and no liability will accrue where the employer is an individual and the accommodation is made available in the normal course of a domestic, family or personal relationship. Nor will it apply to most accommodation used by employees of a local authority. In addition, no liability will arise on the provision of living accommodation for an employee:

a where it is necessary for the proper performance of the employee's duties that he or she should reside in the accommodation, or

b where the accommodation is provided for the better performance of the duties of employment, and this is one of the kinds of employment in the case of which it is customary for employers to provide living accommodation for employees, or

c where, there being a threat to the employee's security, special security arrangements are in force and the employee resides in the accommodation as part of those arrangements.

The exclusions under **a** and **b** have little application to most company directors.

Where liability does arise, the employee is treated as receiving an additional emolument taxable under Schedule E. This emolument will comprise an amount equal to:

a the value of the accommodation for the period of availability in each year of assessment; less

b contributions made by the employee.

It will be clear that no additional emolument will arise where a rent is paid by the employee which equals or exceeds the value under **a**.

For properties in the United Kingdom, the value of the accommodation will comprise the gross rateable value used for rating purposes or, if it is greater, any rent paid by the person providing accommodation. To eliminate distortions in Scotland where properties have been uprated, the former rateable value continues to be used. Although general rates were replaced in Great Britain by the community charge, which in turn was replaced by yet another system, the council tax, rateable values continue to be used as a "measure" for income tax purposes. In the case of new properties it will be necessary to estimate a comparable rateable value.

29 *PROVISION OF ACCOMMODATION*

In 1983 Company A purchased a residential property in Surrey having a gross rateable value of £2,500. Mr B is an employee of the company and throughout the year ending on April 5th, 1994, occupied the property as his private home. No rent was paid in return for the provision of living accommodation.

The emolument on which Mr B will suffer income tax for 1993–94 must be calculated as follows:

	£
Value of accommodation – gross rateable value	2,500
Less contribution	NIL
Emolument 1993–94	£2,500

Expensive accommodation

A further liability to income tax may arise where an employer provides an employee with more expensive living accommodation. This is in addition to the liability mentioned above and remains subject to the exclusions and exemptions referred to earlier.

The further liability is confined to living accommodation obtained at a cost exceeding £75,000, and can have no application where cost falls below this figure. "Cost" includes not only expenditure laid out to acquire accommodation but includes any further outgoings on carrying out improvements, where those outgoings have been incurred before the commencement of the year of assessment concerned. In some situations, where property has been retained for more than six years before the employee enters into occupation, "cost" may be replaced by "market value".

Where the cost, or market value if appropriate, of providing living accommodation does exceed £75,000, the excess over this figure must be established. The further emolument then represents "the additional value of the accommodation", which is calculated by applying the official rate of interest at the beginning of the tax year to the excess. This rate is altered from time to time, but on April 6th, 1993, was 7.75 per cent per annum.

If the employee provides rent, or makes some other contribution for the use of living accommodation, this may be subtracted from the additional emolument, but only to the extent that it exceeds the gross rateable value of the property, or rent paid by the employer, whichever is the higher.

Therefore, for 1993–94 two different emoluments may arise where expensive living accommodation is made available. This combined liability affects all employees and is not confined to directors and the higher-paid.

30 *PROVISION OF EXPENSIVE ACCOMMODATION*

Using the facts of Example 29, let it be assumed that Company A paid £150,000 to acquire the residential property in 1983. Further expenditure of £40,000 was incurred before April 6th, 1993, in carrying out improvements to the property. As the official rate of interest on April 6th, 1993, was 7.75 per cent per annum, the emoluments arising to Mr B for 1993–94 become:

		£	£
a	Emolument as calculated in Example 29		2,500
b	Additional emolument:		
	Cost of providing accommodation:	£	
	Cost of acquisition	150,000	
	Improvements	40,000	
	Aggregate cost	190,000	
	Less to be excluded	75,000	
	Excess	£115,000	
	Emolument:		
	£115,000 × 7.75 per cent		8,912
	Total emoluments from living accommodation		£11,412

EMPLOYEES EARNING £8,500 OR MORE AND DIRECTORS

The assessment of fringe benefits is broadened considerably for most company directors and many employees. The persons affected are employees earning £8,500 or more and directors, an approach which incorporates:

a all directors, except certain directors earning less than £8,500 per annum and who do not, either individually or with certain members of their family, retain a substantial shareholding interest in the company. This exception is limited to full-time working directors and directors of non-profit making companies or charitable bodies; and

b all employees earning £8,500 or more per annum.

For the purpose of establishing whether a director or employee earns £8,500 or more per annum and is therefore subject to the additional liabilities discussed below, his or her actual earnings must be increased by:

a adding the value of any benefits mentioned on the previous pages;

b adding the value of any benefits referred to below;

c ignoring any expenses which may be deducted from earnings.

This implies that many employees earning less than £8,500 per annum may become assessable on "fringe benefits", once the adjustments have been made to the calculation of their notional income.

Assessment of benefits

The assessment of benefits is not limited to facilities and advantages made available to a director or employee personally but extends also to benefits provided for that person's spouse, his sons and daughters and their spouses, his parents, servants, dependants and guests.

Where an employer pays a sum representing "expenses" to a director or employee this sum will comprise an additional emolument and it remains for the director or employee to submit an acceptable expenses claim if additional liability to income tax is not to arise. In many cases this formality can be avoided by obtaining a dispensation from HM Inspector of Taxes. In those cases where a director or employee provides his or her own motor car for business travel and receives a mileage allowance, the Fixed Profit Car Scheme outlined on page 70 may also be used to avoid the formality of a claim for expenses.

Should an employer incur expense in providing some facility or advantage for the benefit of a director or employee the cost incurred by the employer, referred to as the "cash equivalent', is treated as additional remuneration unless, or to the extent that, the cost is made good by the recipient. For example, should an employer purchase a television set for, say, £300 and immediately transfer the ownership of that set to a qualifying director or employee for no consideration, a benefit of £300 will be assessable to income tax.

The calculation of the cash equivalent previously gave rise to uncertainty where an employee made facilities available to employees on advantageous terms. This could affect employees at private schools whose children were educated at a reduced fee and employees of transport undertakings able to travel at a price lower than that charged to full fare paying customers. The Inland Revenue now accept it is only the additional cost incurred by the employer in making these facilities available which represents the "cash equivalent".

Liability will not extend to the cost of providing meals in a canteen where those meals are available to all employees, to certain accommodation provided for an employee who is required as a condition of his employment to use the accommodation, or to the cost of providing future pensions. An employer will often incur expenses in providing a Christmas party, annual dinner dance or similar function for the benefit of employees. In practice, no taxable benefit will arise on those attending when the cost does not exceed £50 per head. Nor will liability accrue from the provision of in-house sports facilities provided by the employer after April 5th, 1993.

A taxable benefit may be provided by some person other than the recipient's employer. However, where entertainment is made available for a director or employee by a third party no benefit will arise unless the advantage arose under an arrangement with the employee's own employer or was given in return for some service or anticipated service. "Entertainment" may also include the provision of seats at a sporting or cultural event.

Scholarship awards

The employer of a director or employee may sometimes finance the cost of scholarships awarded to a child of that individual. This is frequently achieved by a company contributing funds to the trustees of an educational trust who provide the award to selected children. Arrangements of this nature will result in the parent being assessed on the cost involved.

Workplace nurseries

Benefits arising from a limited range of child care facilities are not assessable on those earning £8,500 or more. Exemption extends to nurseries run at the workplace or elsewhere by the employer. It will also extend to nurseries run by employers jointly with other employers, voluntary bodies or local authorities, and include facilities made available for older children after school or during school holidays. A condition for obtaining exemption requires that the child care facilities must comply with any local requirement for registration by the appropriate local authority. No exemption will be forthcoming if the child care facilities are made available in domestic premises.

The exemption will not extend to the provision of cash allowances for child care or the payment by an employer of an employee's bills. Nor will it be available where the employer provides vouchers which can be used by the employee to discharge child care expenses.

Use of assets

Many items of expenditure incurred, or deemed to have been incurred, by an employer will not result in the transfer of any asset to the director or employee. Detailed rules must then be applied to calculate the benefit assessable to income tax and for this purpose a distinction is drawn between the provision of motor cars, fuel for private motoring, mobile telephones, motor vans, loan facilities, and other assets or advantages. The application of these special rules is discussed below.

Motor cars

In those cases where a motor car is made available for private use by a director or employee the size of the taxable benefit will be governed, in part, by the amount of business mileage. Subject to the amount of this mileage, it must be emphasised that it is the *availability* of a motor car for private motoring which produces a benefit and not the actual use to which the vehicle is applied.

For 1993–94 and earlier years, standard scale charges have been used to calculate the taxable benefit arising from the availability of a motor car for private motoring. The scale charges were broadly increased by 8 per cent for 1993–94 when compared with the previous year. To assist comparison the scale charges for both 1992–93 and 1993–94 are shown on the following page.

An entirely new system for calculating taxable benefits attributable to the availability of motor cars for private motoring is being introduced on April 6th, 1994. This system abandons the use of standard car charges and is briefly explained on page 80.

The collection of tax on car benefits was previously achieved by adjusting the code number of a director or employee. As that number was reduced the amount of tax subtracted under the PAYE scheme was correspondingly increased. This approach has largely been abandoned from April 6th, 1993, and replaced by the new "K" codes. The function of these codes is reviewed on page 61.

Substantial business use – 1993–94

If the annual business use of a motor car is "substantial" the assessable benefit for 1993–94 will be calculated by reference to the second table on the following page. Business use is regarded as "substantial" for this year if, but only if, there is more than 2,500 miles of business motoring. Where two or more vehicles are supplied for a director or employee, only one can qualify as involving "substantial" business use. This will be identified as the vehicle, if any, used to the greatest extent for business travel.

No additional benefit will arise from the availability of a motor car unless the employer provides a chauffeur. Where a chauffeur is provided his wages and any other expenses will represent an additional benefit derived by the director or employee. The provision of a car parking space at or near the place of work will not be treated as producing a taxable benefit. The use of a car telephone did not previously produce any benefit but further liability may arise from April 6th, 1991 (see page 83).

The annual benefit will be reduced by one-half if the employee is required to use the motor car mainly for business travel which amounts to at least 18,000 miles in the year ended on April 5th, 1994.

No benefit will usually arise from the use of a motor car forming part of a "pool" provided that:

Car scale benefits 1992–93

	Age of car: Under 4 years	Age of car: 4 years or more
Cars having a market value up to £19,250 when first registered	annual benefit £	annual benefit £
Cars having a cylinder capacity:		
1,400 or under	2,140	1,460
1,401 to 2,000	2,770	1,880
2,001 or more	4,440	2,980
Non-cylinder capacity cars:		
Original market value		
Under £6,000	2,140	1,460
£6,000 to £8,499	2,770	1,880
£8,500 to £19,250	4,440	2,980
Cars having a market value of more than £19,250 when first registered		
Original market value		
£19,251 to £29,000	5,750	3,870
£29,001 or more	9,300	6,170

Car scale benefits 1993–94

	Age of car: Under 4 years	Age of car: 4 years or more
Cars having a market value up to £19,250 when first registered	annual benefit £	annual benefit £
Cars having a cylinder capacity:		
1,400 or under	2,310	1,580
1,401 to 2,000	2,990	2,030
2,001 or more	4,800	3,220
Non-cylinder capacity cars:		
Original market value		
Under £6,000	2,310	1,580
£6,000 to £8,499	2,990	2,030
£8,500 to £19,250	4,800	3,220
Cars having a market value of more than £19,250 when first registered		
Original market value		
£19,251 to £29,000	6,210	4,180
£29,001 or more	10,040	6,660

a the vehicle is actually used by two or more employees;

b any private use by the employee is merely incidental; and

c the vehicle is not normally kept overnight in or near the vicinity of the employee's home.

Adjustments to the scale benefits shown on the previous page may be necessary if the director or employee is required to contribute towards the cost of providing a motor car or the vehicle is available for use during part only of the year of assessment.

31 MOTOR CARS – SUBSTANTIAL USE

An employer purchased a new car at a cost of £18,750 in December 1991. The vehicle had a cc of 2,200 and was available for use by a director, X, throughout the year 1993–94. The total annual business mileage of 10,000 miles was "substantial".

The vehicle is less than four years old and X will derive a taxable benefit of £4,800 for 1993–94. The corresponding taxable benefit for 1992–93, assuming the vehicle was available throughout the year, would have been £4,440.

Insubstantial use – 1993–94

A different basis will be used to measure the taxable benefit for 1993–94 where the business use fails to exceed 2,500 miles annually. This basis applies also where two or more vehicles are available to a director or employee, as only one vehicle can be the subject of "substantial" business use. In such cases, the benefit will comprise one and a half times the scale charge shown by the second table on the previous page, with an addition for a chauffeur's wages and expenses, if any. Here also an adjustment to the taxable benefit will be necessary if the director or employee is required to contribute towards the cost of providing the vehicle, or the car is available for only part of the year.

32 MOTOR CARS – INSUBSTANTIAL USE

Using the facts in Example 31, let it be assumed that the vehicle was not used for any business mileage. The taxable benefit for 1993–94 then becomes:

Scale charge £4,800 + 50 per cent	£7,200

Future changes – 1994–95

A new system for measuring the taxable benefit arising from the availability of a car for private motoring will come into operation on April 6th, 1994, and affect 1994–95 and future years. Under this system the basic taxable benefit will comprise 35 per cent of the price of the car. "Price" will represent the aggregate (inclusive of tax) of:

a the list price of the vehicle when it was first registered; plus

b the price of "extras" provided with the car.

Where business travel exceeds 2,500 miles in a year of assessment, the basic taxable benefit will be reduced by one-third. A reduction of two-thirds is available where business travel amounts to at least 18,000 miles during the year.

The taxable benefit will be reduced by a further one-third for vehicles which are four or more years of age at the end of the tax year.

Vehicles which are more than fifteen years of age and have a market value of more than £15,000 will be included in the scheme at their open market value in substitution for "price".

The existing rules which apply to "second cars" and vehicles forming part of a "pool" will be preserved.

The effect of these changes on the taxable benefit assessable to income tax will be governed by price. Many inexpensive vehicles will attract a reduced charge and this may apply also to those in the expensive range. It is likely, however, that the availability of vehicles in the middle range will give rise to a considerably increased taxation commitment.

Petrol and other fuel supplied for private motoring

The scale charges which apply to create a taxable benefit where a motor car is provided for private motoring during 1993–94 will not necessarily exhaust all liability for the same year. There may be additional fuel benefit charges. These potential fuel benefits arise whenever a motor car is made available to a director or employee (including members of those individuals' families and households). Therefore, where a car benefit arises from the availability of a motor car (as discussed on page 78), a car fuel benefit will also potentially arise.

Car fuel benefits are measured by reference to scale charges, which are simpler to apply than those attributable to the availability of motor cars. The scale charges for 1993–94 are shown by the table on the following page. This discloses an increase of some 20 per cent above the figures for the previous year.

When applying the scale charges no distinction is drawn between substantial and insubstantial use, nor is the age of the car significant. Where 18,000 miles or more of business travel took place in 1992–93, the scale charge for that year was reduced by one-half. No similar reduction is available for 1993–94.

Should a vehicle be available for part only of the year, or a vehicle falling within one scale charge be replaced by a vehicle falling within a different scale, the benefit must be suitably adjusted.

There will be no scale charge if the employer only provides petrol or other fuel for business travel. Contributions towards the cost of fuel supplied for private motoring will only be recognised to eliminate the scale charge if both:

a the director or employee is *required* to make good the whole of the expense incurred when providing fuel for private motoring; and

b the *whole* cost is actually satisfied.

Arrangements for collecting income tax on car fuel benefits through the PAYE system are similar to those mentioned on page 78.

The restructuring of taxable benefits, which applies to the availability of a car for private motoring on April 6th, 1994, has no application to the car fuel benefits. These benefits will continue to be based on scale figures.

Car fuel scale benefits 1993–94

PETROL FUEL

Cars having a recognised cylinder capacity	**Annual benefit**
Cylinder capacity:	£
1,400 or under	600
1,401 to 2,000	760
2,001 or more	1,130
Other cars	
Original market value:	£
under £6,000	600
£6,000 to £8,499	760
£8,500 or more	1,130

DIESEL FUEL

Cars having a recognised cylinder capacity	**Annual benefit**
Cylinder capacity:	£
2,000 or under	550
2,001 or more	710
Other cars	
Original market value:	£
under £8,500	550
£8,500 or more	710

33 *MOTOR CAR AND FUEL BENEFITS*

A company purchased a new 1600 cc motor car using petrol at a cost of £14,000 in August 1992. The vehicle was used by a director for business and private travel throughout 1993–94 and 8,000 miles of business mileage was involved. All petrol used for both business travel and private motoring was supplied by the company. No contribution was made by the director.

The taxable benefits for 1993–94 will comprise:	£
Availability of motor car – scale charge	2,990
Provision of fuel for private motoring – scale charge	760
Total taxable benefits	£3,750

National insurance contributions

Before April 6th, 1991, the availability of a motor car for private motoring did not create earnings for the purpose of calculating liability to Class 1 national insurance contributions. Liability arose from some arrangements involving the supply of fuel for private motoring but there were several exceptions. From April 6th, 1991, however, the position changed significantly. In those cases where a director or higher-paid employee has the use of a motor car for private motoring the income tax scale benefit charges are now used to establish earnings for Class 1 purposes. A similar approach is applied to the supply of fuel for private motoring, with the income tax scale charges being used. This approach does not require the satisfaction of primary Class 1 contributions by the employee. However, the employer must discharge secondary contributions at the rate of 10.4 per cent. The amount of contributions arising under this heading is calculated after the end of each year of assessment and accounted for in the following June.

Mobile telephones

Also before April 6th, 1991, no taxable benefit arose from the private use of a telephone fitted in a motor car, although benefits did arise from the private use of other mobile telephones. From April 6th, 1991, a standard taxable benefit is created from the private use of a mobile telephone whether fitted in a motor car or not. The standard annual charge comprises £200 for each mobile telephone. The taxable benefit will only be avoided if there is either no private use whatsoever or, where private use does arise, the employee is required to make good the whole cost, including an appropriate proportion of subscriber charges and other standing costs.

Vans

No special provisions were previously in place for calculating the taxable benefit arising from the availability of a van, as opposed to the availability of a motor car. Where vans were used for non-business purposes the general approach mentioned on page 76 was applied to calculate the benefit. This general approach no longer applies and special provisions have been introduced to calculate the value of a taxable benefit from April 6th, 1993.

These provisions apply a standard charge for the use of all vans. The word "vans" identifies vehicles built primarily to carry goods or other loads with a gross vehicle weight not exceeding 3,500 kilograms. Where a van is made available for non-business travel, particularly involving travel from home to work, a standard benefit of £500 arises for 1993–94. This is reduced to £350 for vehicles more than four years old at the end of the tax year. In those cases where the use of a van is shared between two or more employees the standard charge of £500, or £350, must be suitably apportioned.

The standard charge will be reduced pro rata for vans which become, or cease to be, available or are incapable of being used for thirty or more consecutive days during the year. In the rather unusual situation where an employee has more than two vans available simultaneously, a standard charge will arise in respect of each vehicle. No taxable benefit will arise in the case of pooled vans unless the vehicle is normally kept at or near the homes of the employees who share the van. There will be no additional charge for the use of petrol or diesel fuel.

The standard charge has no application to vehicles having a gross weight in excess of 3,500 kilograms. Nor does it extend to the private use of vehicles built primarily for the carriage of passengers, namely cars and mini-buses.

The standard charge of £500, £350 or a proportion of those amounts where vehicles are shared, will be reduced by any contribution made towards non-business use.

Loan facilities

Loans made available for the benefit of a director or employee may frequently be interest-free, or carry a rate of interest falling below a commercial level. Where these facilities are obtained, the director or employee may derive a taxable benefit representing the difference between the official rate of interest and the actual interest paid, if any. The official rate of interest is changed from time to time. For example, on June 6th, 1992, it was reduced to 10.5 per cent and progressively reduced to 7.75 per cent on March 6th, 1993. This gave rise to an average rate of 9.75 per cent for the whole of 1992–93.

There are alternative methods of calculating the taxable benefit using the official rate. One, "the normal method", is to take the average rate for the entire year, or the period of the loan, if shorter. The other, "the alternative method" which either the employee or HM Inspector of Taxes can require, calculates notional interest on a day to day basis.

No liability will arise if the amount otherwise chargeable does not exceed £300 for 1993–94.

Furthermore, if any interest actually paid on the loan would have qualified for income tax relief (see page 36) liability can usually be avoided at the lower rate and the basic rate for 1993–94. It follows, for example, that should an employee receive an interest-free loan not exceeding £30,000 for the purpose of acquiring his only or main residence, no tax may become chargeable at these rates on the benefit, unless there are other loans which, taken collectively, exceed the £30,000 limit. However, relief for mortgage interest paid is limited to income tax at the basic rate only for 1993–94 and further restricted to 20

34 *INTEREST FREE LOAN*

In 1988 a company provided an employee with an interest free loan of £12,000. The loan remained outstanding throughout 1993–94 and notional interest did not qualify for the relief mentioned on page 36. Using an average rate of, say, 8 per cent for the year, the employee will derive a taxable benefit of £960, calculated as follows:

	£
£12,000 × 8 per cent	960
Less interest paid	NIL
Taxable benefit 1993–94	£960

Note: This illustration has used an assumed average rate of 8 per cent as the actual rate cannot be determined until after April 5th, 1994.

per cent for 1994–95. If the director or employee is liable at the higher rate, the benefit attributable to the loan will be assessed at 15 per cent (basic rate of 25 per cent deducted from higher rate of 40 per cent) for 1993–94 and 20 per cent (lower rate of 20 per cent deducted from higher rate of 40 per cent) for 1994–95.

35 *INTEREST FREE LOAN – HIGHER RATE*

Applying the facts in Example 34, let it be assumed that the entire notional interest qualified for relief on the grounds that it was paid on a loan applied to acquire the employee's residence. The employee was a married man aged 41, with earnings of £37,000 for 1993–94 and entitled to the full married couple's allowance.

Income tax payable becomes:

	£	£
Total income		37,000
Less		
Personal allowance	3,445	
Married couple's allowance	1,720	5,165
Tax chargeable on		£31,835

Tax payable:		
Lower rate:		£
On first £2,500 at 20 per cent		500.00
Basic rate:		
On next £21,200 at 25 per cent		5,300.00
Higher rate:		
On balance of £8,135 at 40 per cent		3,254.00
On benefit	£	
Higher rate of 40 per cent on £960	384	
Less Basic rate of 25 per cent on £960	240	144.00
		£9,198.00

Where a loan provided for a director or employee is subsequently released or written off, in whole or in part, the amount involved will be treated as part of the individual's remuneration. No liability will, however, arise where the release or writing off occurs on or after the borrower's death.

Directors or employees may sometimes be permitted to acquire shares for a consideration falling below market value. Arrangements of this nature may produce liability to income tax under several headings, including the possibility that the advantage may be treated as representing a notional loan creating a benefit in the manner discussed above.

Other assets

Where an employer provides a director or higher-paid employee with the use of an asset which is neither living accommodation, a motor car, fuel used for private motoring, a mobile telephone nor a loan of money, the annual benefit assessable to tax will comprise the aggregate of:

a the annual value, and

b the expense incurred by the employer in providing the use.

If the employer rents or hires an asset made available for use by the director or employee the rental paid will be substituted for the annual value, should this produce a higher benefit.

For land, including dwelling-houses, located in the United Kingdom the annual value will usually represent the gross annual value used for rating purposes, notwithstanding the successive replacement of rating by the community charge and the council tax. This will not apply to the provision of living accommodation, which is dealt with under a separate heading, (see page 73). In other cases the annual value will be 20 per cent of the asset's value when it was first made available for use by the director or employee.

Should the ownership of such an asset subsequently be transferred to the director or employee, an additional benefit may arise. This will represent the difference, if any, between the market value of the asset when it was first made available and the aggregate of:

a the consideration given to acquire the asset by the director or employee, and

b the amount of taxable benefits arising during the employer's period of ownership.

This basis only applies if it produces a greater taxable benefit than the excess of current market value, at the time of acquisition by the director or employee, over the price paid by him or her.

Redundancy payments

REDUNDANCY AND LOSS of employment are matters of great concern to those affected. An outgoing director or employee may be entitled to benefit from, or to pursue, several statutory rights which are outside the scope of the present work. The individual may also receive certain payments as a result of redundancy or dismissal and the taxation liability of these sums is discussed below.

STATUTORY REDUNDANCY PAYMENTS

On leaving an employment a director or employee may well receive a statutory redundancy payment. The amount of this payment is tax-free and will not involve the recipient in any liability to taxation.

PAYMENTS DUE BY AGREEMENT

In addition to the statutory redundancy payment, if any, an outgoing director or employee may also receive other terminal payments, often described as "golden handshakes", from his or her former employer. The treatment of these additional sums will be governed by the circumstances in which they are paid. For example, some service agreements contain a provision that, in the event of premature termination, a lump sum will be payable to the employee. Payments of this nature may well represent rewards arising from the contract of service and become assessable to income tax under Schedule E, although the Inland Revenue will not attempt to proceed if "genuine" redundancy occurs. For this purpose a redundancy will be regarded as "genuine" if:

a payment is made only on account of redundancy and is not made to selected employees only;

b the employee has been continuously in the employment of the employer for at least two years; and

c the payment is not excessively large in relation to earnings and length of service.

OTHER TERMINAL PAYMENTS

The majority of lump sum terminal payments made by an employer to an outgoing director or employee will not relate to services rendered or become due under a contract of service which fails to satisfy the requirements of "genuine redundancy". The treatment of these terminal payments will then be governed by a number of complex rules, some of which came into operation on March 1st, 1991.

First, an ex gratia payment made solely by reason of death or disablement by accident will not be directly assessable to income tax. Nor will severance payments made on redundancy or loss of office be assessable. These payments are subject to the £30,000 exemption rule mentioned later.

Secondly, lump sum payments made under the terms of an approved occupational pension scheme (see page 27) will not be treated as income.

Thirdly, other lump sum payments which are not made under the terms of an approved scheme may be exempt from tax if:

a there is only one lump sum payable to the director or employee;

b the director or employee is not a member of an approved scheme conferring benefits other than those attributable to death in service; and

c the lump sum payment does not exceed the limit placed on lump sums payable from approved schemes.

Finally, other ex gratia payments made on or in connection with an individual's death or retirement may well be chargeable to income tax under Schedule E.

It follows that many ex gratia payments or "golden handshakes" which previously escaped assessment now become liable to income tax where the payment is made on or after March 1st, 1991.

In addition to these lump sum payments, an employer may fund the cost of providing counselling services for employees who have become, or are about to become, redundant. For employees made redundant after March 15th, 1993, and in the case of expenditure incurred subsequently for those made redundant on an earlier date, the counselling costs may be included in the redundancy package giving rise to the £30,000 exemption.

The £30,000 exemption

It remains to examine the treatment of ex gratia or other terminal payments which are neither treated as income and chargeable to income tax nor made exempt from tax under the terms of an approved occupational pension scheme. This will broadly extend to payments made to an employee on severance of an employment due to redundancy or loss of office, or because of death or disability due to accident.

The first £30,000 received is usually exempt from income tax, with any excess remaining fully chargeable. Restrictions may arise where two or more employments held with "associated employers" terminate at the same time, or payments arising from a single termination are payable by instalments. When calculating the amount, if any, by which the terminal payment, or payments, exceed £30,000, the statutory redundancy receipt must be included, although it is not subject to tax.

36 *TERMINAL PAYMENT*

An individual became redundant on September 30th, 1993, and received a statutory redundancy payment of £3,250. In addition he received a voluntary golden handshake of £65,000.

The amount taxable for 1993–94 then becomes:

	£
Statutory redundancy payment	3,250
Golden handshake	65,000
Total terminal payments	68,250
Less exempt	30,000
Taxable	£38,250

Assuming the individual is below the age of 65, a married man living with his wife, entitled to the entire married couple's allowance and in receipt of other income amounting to £43,000 for 1993–94, the tax payable becomes:

		£
Total income:		
Other income		43,000
Golden handshake		38,250
		81,250
Less	£	
Personal allowance	3,445	
Married couple's allowance	1,720	5,165
Tax chargeable on		£76,085

	£
Tax payable:	
Lower rate:	
on first £2,500 at 20 per cent	500.00
Basic rate:	
on next £21,200 at 25 per cent	5,300.00
Higher rate:	
on balance of £52,385 at 40 per cent	20,954.00
	£26,754.00

Other matters

Some terminal payments arising by reason of death, injury or disability, together with those arising under superannuation scheme arrangements or for services rendered outside the United Kingdom, are immune from liability, notwithstanding the sums involved may exceed £30,000.

It will often be found that where an outgoing director or employee fails to obtain alternative employment, some repayment of income tax suffered under PAYE will become available for the year of assessment in which redundancy occurs. However, the ability to obtain immediate repayment during a period of unemployment may be limited (see page 61).

Businesses and professions

TAX ON PROFITS

INCOME TAX is normally levied on an individual by reference to the profits arising from his business or profession for the accounting year ending in the year preceding the year of assessment. For this purpose the accounting period used in the business is accepted by the Inland Revenue. Where, for example, the accounts of a trader are habitually prepared by his accountant each year to December 31st, the assessment on his business profits for 1993–94 (year of assessment commencing on April 6th, 1993) will be based on the profits shown by his accounts for the year to December 31st, 1992.

This basis for assessing business profits is expected to change for 1996–97 and future years. However, the nature of the change and arrangements which may be used to achieve a transition from the existing basis to the new are matters which must await future events. The possibility of any change will therefore be disregarded at present as it is most improbable that the basis used for 1993–94 will be affected.

NEW BUSINESSES

In the case of new businesses the normal preceding year basis cannot apply, since there is no preceding year on which to base the assessment. The rules which must then be followed are set out below.

a For *the first tax year* in which the business is commenced the assessment is based on the profits of the actual income tax year (date of commencement to following April 5th).

b For *the second tax year* the profits for twelve months from the date of commencement are taken as the basis.

c For *the third tax year* it is usual to base the assessment on the profits of the twelve months up to the end of the business accounting period preceding the commencement of the tax year.

d For later years the normal preceding year basis operates.

The application of these rules in the early years of a new business will sometimes result in an injustice to the taxpayer. To avoid this an

37 *NEW BUSINESS – SPECIAL RELIEF*

A shopkeeper commences business on January 1st, 1992. His net profits, calculated as required by the Income and Corporation Taxes Act 1988, are:

	£
Year to December 31st, 1992	16,000
Year to December 31st, 1993	12,000
Year to December 31st, 1994	20,000

The normal income tax assessments for the three opening years will be:

1991–92	Actual results to April 5th, 1992 3/12ths of £16,000	£4,000
1992–93	First accounting year to December 31st, 1992	£16,000
1993–94	Previous accounting year to December 31st, 1992	£16,000

It is clear that the profits for the year ended December 31st, 1992 form the basis of assessment for 1991–92 (part only), 1992–93 and 1993–94. To reduce any hardship which this may cause, an election may be made to adjust the assessments for the second *and* third years to the actual profits of those income tax years as follows:

		£	
1992–93	9/12ths of £16,000	12,000	
	3/12ths of £12,000	3,000	
			£15,000
1993–94	9/12ths of £12,000	9,000	
	3/12ths of £20,000	5,000	
			£14,000

It would be beneficial to make such an election as the assessments for both 1992–93 and 1993–94 are reduced.

---

election may be made, at any time within seven years from the end of the second tax year in which the business is carried on, to have the assessment for the second *and* third years (but not one year only) based on the actual profits of those years ending on April 5th. If the taxpayer wishes, he may withdraw his election within six years of the end of the third year.

Where a wife "living with" her husband commenced business during 1988–89 and the second year of assessment is therefore 1989–90, it is the wife, and not her husband, who must file the election affecting the second and third years. This requirement arose following the introduction of independent taxation as it was previously the husband's responsibility to submit any election for his wife's business.

The new business rules may require modification where there is a change in the persons carrying on business in partnership (see page 92).

CLOSING BUSINESSES

Special provisions apply for determining the assessments which must be raised in the closing years where a business closes down or changes hands. These are as follows:

38 *CESSATION OF BUSINESS*

A builder closes down his business on June 30th, 1993. Profits, as computed under the Taxes Acts, have been:

	£
Year to September 30th, 1990	13,500
Year to September 30th, 1991	15,000
Year to September 30th, 1992	16,500
Nine months to June 30th, 1993	12,600

In the absence of discontinuance the assessments would be:

	£
1991–92 (preceding year)	13,500
1992–93 (preceding year)	15,000
1993–94 (preceding year)	16,500

However, the assessment for 1993–94 (the year of cessation) must be adjusted to:

3/9ths of £12,600	£4,200

The actual profits for the preceding years were:

	£	£
1992–93 (year to April 5th, 1993):		
6/12ths × £16,500	8,250	
6/9ths × £12,600	8,400	
		16,650
1991–92 (year to April 5th, 1992):		
6/12ths × £15,000	7,500	
6/12ths × £16,500	8,250	
		15,750
		£32,400

As the figure of £32,400 exceeds the original aggregate assessments of £28,500 (£13,500 + £15,000) for 1991–92 and 1992–93, the assessments for these two years will be adjusted to:

1991–92	£15,750
1992–93	£16,650

a For the *final period* of a business the assessment must be based on the actual profits of the period from the beginning of the tax year (April 6th) to the date when the business closes or changes hands.

b For each of the *two previous years* the normal basis of assessment is the profits of each preceding year. The Inland Revenue have power, however, to decide that the assessments may be based on the actual profits to April 5th for each of those years (but not one year only) if those assessments produce a higher aggregate tax liability. It is to be assumed this power will be exercised if the liability of the taxpayer is thereby increased.

PARTNERSHIP CHANGES

The above rules, governing the assessments to be raised where a new business is commenced or an existing business closes down, may require modification where changes are made in the individuals carrying on business in partnership. These changes will occur where a sole trader admits a second individual, or individuals, into partnership, an individual joins or leaves an existing partnership, or a business carried on in partnership reverts to a sole trader. Special adjustments and elections will apply if at least one individual continues to be involved in the business both before and after the change.

First, all individuals affected by the change may file a written election to treat the business as continuing. The normal preceding year basis of assessment will then apply to determine the profits for each year of assessment. Profits assessable in this manner will be shared between the partners by reference to their actual profit sharing arrangements in each year of assessment.

Secondly, if no continuation election is made the business will be treated as discontinued and a new business commenced at the time of the change in proprietorship. This will require the application of the closing down and new business rules discussed on pages 90 and 91 to establish the assessments both before and after the change. However, some modifications will be necessary where at least one individual engaged in the partnership before the change continues to be so engaged subsequently. This will commonly be the situation where a partner retires from, or a new partner is introduced to, an existing partnership.

These modifications do not affect the normal closing down rules used to establish assessments on the old partnership (see page 91). However, the assessments raised on the new partnership will be as follows:

a For the first tax year in which the change occurs the assessment is based on the actual profits from the date of change to the following April 5th.

b For each of the second, third and fourth tax years the assessments will be based on the actual profits of the year concerned (April 6th to April 5th).

c For the fifth and subsequent years the assessments will be based on the profits of the twelve months up to the end of the business accounting period preceding the commencement of the tax year (the normal preceding year basis).

An election may be made to have the assessments for the fifth and sixth years (but not one year only) based on the actual profits of those years ending on April 5th.

There will be many current partnership changes where the six year period extends to, or beyond, 1996–97. It will be necessary to review the special provisions which will be announced later to establish the effect a new system of taxing profits may have on events which have already taken place.

LOSSES

Where a loss is incurred in a continuing trade or profession carried on by an individual, or by individuals in partnership, no income tax liability arises for the succeeding tax year, as the assessment for this year must be based on the profits, if any, of the previous base year. A number of special adjustments may be necessary if the new business or cessation rules apply. Subject to these the loss may be utilised in several different ways.

One method, which requires the submission of a claim, is to offset the loss against the individual's income in the same year of assessment. Where income is insufficient the unused loss may often be set against income for the following year also. This method of obtaining relief will frequently result in a repayment of income tax suffered on investment income. It is, however, necessary to show that the loss arose from a trade or business being undertaken on a commercial basis and with a view to the realisation of profits. If there is any balance of loss in respect of which tax cannot be repaid, this may be carried forward. In those cases where losses have been incurred in farming or market gardening for five consecutive years the ability to offset future losses against income may be restricted.

Following the introduction of independent taxation on April 6th, 1990, it is no longer possible for the losses of one spouse to be offset against income of the other.

39 *OFFSETTING LOSSES*

A dealer sustains a trading loss of £23,000, in an old-established business, during the accounting year to March 31st, 1994.

He has an income for the year of assessment 1993–94 of £17,000 arising from investments, on which he has suffered, or is deemed to have suffered, income tax by deduction at the basic rate.

The taxpayer may claim to set the loss against investment income of £17,000, with tax suffered on that income being repaid. If such a claim is agreed, the balance of the loss (£6,000) may be carried forward and set against future trading profits arising from the same trade, used in a similar loss claim for 1994–95 or perhaps set against chargeable gains in 1993–94. The claim must be made in writing not later than April 5th, 1996 (namely, within two years following the end of the year of assessment to which the claim relates).

As the results for the year ended March 31st, 1994, form the basis of assessment for 1994–95, the assessment for that year becomes nil.

A second method may be available where there is insufficient income to absorb the loss under the first method. This enables the unused business loss for a year of assessment to be set against chargeable gains otherwise assessable to capital gains tax in the same year. Relief is available only on unused business losses arising in 1991–92 and future years. This relief is explained more fully on page 178.

A third method is to carry the loss forward year by year and offset it against subsequent profits arising from the same business. This process continues until the loss has been fully used or the business ends. Losses can only be carried forward to the extent that they have not been relieved under methods one and two above.

LOSSES AND NEW BUSINESSES

Where a loss arises in the first year of assessment during which a new

40 *CARRYING LOSSES FORWARD*

A trader preparing accounts to October 31st annually has the following profits and losses, as adjusted for income tax purposes:

		£
Year ended October 31st 1991	Loss	10,000
Year ended October 31st 1992	Profit	6,400
Year ended October 31st 1993	Profit	22,100

If the loss of £10,000 is carried forward the results become:

	£	Assessable profit £
Year ended October 31st 1991		NIL
Year ended October 31st 1992 – Profit	6,400	
Less loss brought forward (part)	6,400	NIL
Year ended October 31st 1993 – Profit	22,100	
Less loss brought forward (balance)	3,600	18,500

41 *CARRYING LOSSES BACKWARDS*

An individual commenced a manufacturing business on July 1st, 1992. The actual results for the first four years of assessment, ending on April 5th, were as follows:

		£
1992–93	Loss	7,100
1993–94	Loss	3,400
1994–95	Profit	9,200
1995–96	Profit	15,400

If a claim is made the loss of £7,100 arising in 1992–93 may be carried back and set against income in the following order:

- **a** Income for 1989–90
- **b** Income for 1990–91
- **c** Income for 1991–92

Should a separate claim be made for the loss of £3,400 arising in 1993–94 this will be set against income in the following order:

- **a** Income for 1990–91
- **b** Income for 1991–92
- **c** Income for 1992–93

business is carried on, or in any of the three following years, a claim may be made to set that loss against income for the three years preceding the year in which the loss occurs. The amount of any loss may usually be increased by capital allowances on business assets, but restrictions are necessary if the business is that of leasing. This claim is a further alternative to methods one, two and three outlined above.

FARMERS AND MARKET GARDENERS

The above rules for charging profits apply also to individuals who carry on the trade of farming or market gardening. However, these individuals may claim to average the results of two consecutive years of assessment if the difference between the profits of each year is at least 30 per cent, or one year produces a loss. The claim must be submitted within two years following the end of the second year and cannot apply to the first year of a new business or the last year of a discontinued business. A limited claim may also be available if the difference in profits between the two years is a little less than 30 per cent.

42 *FARMERS AND AVERAGING*

For several years Mr D has carried on the business of farming. His profits for 1992–93 and 1993–94 were as follows:

	£
1992–93	40,000
1993–94	15,000

In the absence of any claim for averaging these profits are chargeable to tax in the normal manner. However, if a claim is made the results for the two years may be averaged as follows:

	£
Profit for 2 years (£40,000 + £15,000)	55,000
1992–93 – one-half	27,500
1993–94 – one-half	27,500

Should a similar claim be made for the two years 1993–94 and 1994–95, the averaged profit of £27,500 must be used for 1993–94 and not the actual profit of £15,000.

DEDUCTIONS FROM BUSINESS PROFITS

Proper accounts are essential if business profits are to be correctly calculated and charged to tax. The absence of proper accounts may result in an overcharge, or perhaps in an undercharge which may later have serious consequences, as failure to disclose the full profits assessable to tax can involve a potential liability to interest and penalties. Many traders use the services of qualified accountants who are expert in this work. They will prepare accounts and negotiate with the Inland Revenue the most favourable assessment which the law permits.

Business and professional profits assessable under Schedule D are not usually the profits shown by the financial accounts. For income tax purposes certain items which commonly appear as expenses in the accounts are not allowed. These have to be added to the profits shown. On the other hand, there are sometimes receipts in the accounts which should not be taxed, or are chargeable to tax under some other heading. These must be deducted from the profits shown.

EXPENDITURE NOT ALLOWED

The following list provides an illustration of some items of expenditure which may appear in the financial accounts of a business, but which are *not* allowed in computing income tax liability and therefore have to be added to profits, or deducted from losses, disclosed by the accounts to arrive at the profit or loss for income tax purposes.

a Expenses not wholly and exclusively laid out for the purpose of the business.

b Expenses for domestic or private purposes.

c The cost of business entertaining, including many gifts. Certain gifts made to charity may be allowed (see page 145).

d The rent of property which is not used for business purposes. The deduction allowed in respect of any dwelling-house or domestic office is not normally to exceed two-thirds of the rent, but a larger proportion may be given in such cases as hotels and boarding houses.

e Provisions for the repair of premises occupied for the business or for implements or utensils, unless sums have actually been expended.

f Any capital sums used in or withdrawn from the business.

g The cost of improvements to premises.

h Debts, other than bad debts or those estimated to be doubtful.

i Any royalty or other sum paid for the use of a patent, where tax is deducted from the payment.

j Income tax, capital gains tax, capital transfer tax or inheritance tax paid.

k Depreciation (capital allowances will usually be available, however – see page 104).

l Withdrawals by proprietors.

m Penalties for breaking the law and legal expenses in connection therewith.

n Reserves (except for discounts or for *specific* doubtful debts).

EXPENDITURE WHICH IS ALLOWED

Any sums expended wholly and exclusively for the purpose of the business may usually be included in the computation of profits, unless the outlay is of a capital nature. Among the deductions allowable are the following:

a Advertising expenditure (but *not* the original cost of permanent signs).

b Bad and doubtful debts.

c Costs of raising business loan finance.

d Interest incurred for business purposes.

e Insurance for business purposes. Note that recoveries under the policies must usually be included in assessable profits.

f Legal expenses for recovering debts or incurred in connection with other non-capital business matters.

g National insurance contributions paid in respect of employees.

h Reasonable payments for the hire of assets. Some restriction may be necessary for the cost of hiring motor cars having a retail price exceeding £12,000 when new.

i Redundancy payments made to former employees.

j Rent of business premises. (A restriction may be necessary as shown under head **d** at the top of page 97 where domestic premises are involved.)

k Repairs to premises, excluding improvements and alterations.

l Subscriptions and donations; where the society to which payment is made has agreed with the Inland Revenue to pay tax on its profits; where purely to maintain the business; or where the staff of the business benefit.

m Wages, salaries and pensions paid to employees and past employees or their dependants (but note the time limit below).

The above list is not intended to be comprehensive but is indicative of the type of expenditure which may be charged against business profits to arrive at the figure on which income tax will be imposed.

Example 43 on the opposite page shows how the adjustments mentioned above are made.

TRADING STOCK AND WORK IN PROGRESS

Unsold trading stock or work in progress retained at the end of an accounting period is usually valued at the lower of original cost or market value and included as a receipt in the financial accounts. Unless the value has fallen, this will effectively eliminate the cost and transfer that cost to the next accounting period in which individual items are sold. If market value has fallen when compared with original cost, the fall will reduce the profits of the business.

REMUNERATION

Remuneration paid to directors and employees may usually be subtracted in the calculation of business profits where the "wholly and exclusively" requirements outlined above are satisfied. However, remuneration attributable to a period for which accounts are made up may only be deducted if it is "paid" within nine months following the end of that period. The date on which "payment" is treated as taking place will be identical to that which governs the time of "receipt" (see page 65). Although any remuneration paid after the expiration of the nine-month period will usually be deductible in arriving at the profits of a later period in which "payment" takes place, this can result in the taxable profits of the earlier period being unnecessarily inflated.

43 *ADJUSTING ACCOUNTS*

The following Profit and Loss Account is prepared by a retail tradesman, using a van for the delivery of goods and living over his shop premises. It will be observed that certain items appearing in the Account are not allowable deductions for tax purposes and have to be added back to arrive at the assessable profit, while adjustment has to be made in respect of the trader's living accommodation.

Profit and Loss Account

	£		£
Wages	15,200	Gross trading profit	74,988
Rent	6,400	Dividends	1,024
Business rates	4,720		
Lighting and heating	1,274		
Repairs to premises	737		
Post and telephone	1,549		
Stationery and printing	726		
General expenses	1,002		
Income tax	5,260		
Electric name sign	1,540		
Depreciation of van	1,927		
Van running costs	4,072		
Extension of garage	7,500		
Net profit	24,105		
	£76,012		£76,012

Adjustment for Tax Purposes

	£	£
Net profit as Profit and Loss Account		24,105
Add Items not allowable:		
Income tax		5,260
Electric name sign		1,540
Depreciation of van		1,927
Extension of garage		7,500
Add For living accommodation (say ⅓rd):		
Rent	2,133	
Rates	1,573	
Lighting and heating	425	
Repairs to premises	246	4,377
		44,709
Less Dividends		1,024
Profit for tax purposes		£43,685

Capital allowances should be available for capital expenditure on the motor van and electric sign. These allowances will be set against the assessment of adjusted business profits. (See page 105 for Example.)

For periods of account ending not later than April 5th, 1990, the nine-month period was extended to one of eighteen months. No restriction applies to remuneration for periods of account ending before April 6th, 1989.

Should accounts and supporting tax computations be submitted to the Inland Revenue before remuneration is paid and in advance of the nine-month deadline, the remuneration cannot be deducted. However, if the remuneration is subsequently paid before the deadline is reached, the remuneration can be restored as a deduction, but only if a special claim is made.

ENTERPRISE ALLOWANCE

To provide some encouragement for unemployed individuals to set up in business, an enterprise allowance may be claimed. This is provided at the rate of £40 per week throughout the initial twelve months of the business. Although the allowance is taxable it does not enter into the calculation of business results. The recipient is separately taxed under Case VI of Schedule D by reference to the amount arising in each year of assessment.

SMALL BUSINESSES

Most proprietors of a business must usually submit proper accounts to the Inland Revenue in support of tax computations, but an exception arises in the case of some small concerns. From April 1990 it became unnecessary to submit detailed accounts where the annual turnover of a business did not exceed £10,000. This limit was increased to £15,000 for accounts submitted after April 5th, 1992.

Where this limit is not exceeded it will be sufficient to disclose the following three factors:

Turnover	A
Less Purchases and expenses . .	B
Net profit	C

Tax returns now contain a box where these factors can be entered.

PARTNERSHIPS

Assessments to income tax made on individuals carrying on business in partnership are raised in the name of the firm. From the joint income, effect is given to all the allowances to which the individual partners are entitled, and for this purpose the profits are apportioned among the partners according to their profit-sharing ratios during the year of assessment. The tax is collectable from the firm but, failing payment, may be recovered by proceedings against any one of the partners. The special rules which must be applied where a change occurs in the members of a partnership are discussed on page 92.

OVERSEAS ENTERTAINERS AND SPORTSMEN

A large number of non-resident entertainers and sportsmen visit the United Kingdom each year, to undertake performances or to compete at a sporting event. These individuals include pop and film stars, actors, musicians, tennis players, golfers, boxers and motor racing drivers, among others. Whether sums arising from performances and other activities in the United Kingdom become liable to taxation will be governed by the personal circumstances of each individual and perhaps by the terms of a Double Taxation Agreement concluded between the United Kingdom and some overseas territory. However, there may well be liability to United Kingdom tax which the Inland Revenue are sometimes unable to collect.

To resolve this difficulty special collection rules apply. These require that when making certain payments to a non-resident entertainer or sportsman for services performed in the United Kingdom the promoter or other person will deduct income tax at the basic rate of 25 per cent. Deductions will also extend to associated income from sponsorship, advertising and endorsements. There will be no deductions for payments arising from record sales, nor will the deduction procedure usually apply to payments not exceeding £1,000. Any deductions made from payments must be accounted for to the Inland Revenue. The requirement to deduct income tax at the basic rate is not affected by the 20 per cent lower rate band.

Deductions made at the basic rate will not necessarily fully exhaust liability to United Kingdom income tax. Any additional liability arising at the higher rate must be recovered by direct assessment on the individual concerned.

The above rules have no application to entertainers and sportsmen who are resident in the United Kingdom for taxation purposes. Those rules are confined to non-residents, which will include both nationals of overseas territories and nationals of the United Kingdom also, if they are not resident in this territory.

SUB-CONTRACTORS

The PAYE scheme of tax deduction applies to emoluments paid to the holder of an office or employment. Certain workers employed by agencies are treated as holding an office or employment and the PAYE scheme is of application to emoluments paid to such persons. However, the PAYE scheme does not apply where payments are made to others for the supply of services. This could result in some loss of tax as the Inland Revenue may experience difficulty in tracing the persons to whom payments are made and collecting tax from those persons.

To avoid this potential loss, arrangements have been made to collect tax from payments to non-resident entertainers and sportsmen, as noted earlier. In addition, a wide ranging tax deduction scheme is in operation for persons engaged in the construction industry and this applies where a contractor makes a payment to a sub-contractor under a contract relating to construction operations.

The expression "contractor" is widely defined and incorporates any person carrying on a business which includes construction operations, a local authority, a development corporation or New Town Commission and certain other persons. Private householders having work done on their own premises are not contractors and a business which is not normally involved in construction operations is unlikely to be treated as carried on by a contractor. A "sub-contractor" includes any person engaged in carrying out construction operations for a business or a public body which is a contractor, and includes companies, individuals and partnerships in addition to other persons.

"Construction operations" extend to almost anything that is done to a permanent or temporary building, structure, civil engineering work or installation. This includes site preparation, construction, alteration, many forms of repair, dismantling and demolition, but excludes some forms of installation.

Sub-contractors may apply to the Inland Revenue for a tax certificate. There are three types of certificate, namely the C certificate which is for certain companies, the P certificate which is for other companies and partnerships and the I certificate which is for use by individuals trading on their own account. Certificates are only issued to individuals, partnerships and companies who satisfy a lengthy list of requirements.

Before making any payment to a sub-contractor, the contractor must establish whether a current tax certificate is held. If a suitable certificate can be produced by the sub-contractor, the contractor will make the payment in full. In the absence of a certificate the contractor is obliged to deduct income tax at the rate of 25 per cent when making payment. This requirement is unaffected by the 20 per cent lower rate band.

The deduction will be made from the full amount of the payment, less the direct cost of materials used, or to be used, in carrying out the construction operations to which the contract relates.

Income tax deducted by a contractor must be paid over to the Inland Revenue. Payment usually falls due fourteen days after the end of each income tax month. Therefore deductions made for the period ending on the fifth of a month should be accounted for to the Inland Revenue by the nineteenth of that month. However, some contractors are permitted to account for deductions on a quarterly basis. If this basis is to be used it must be shown that PAYE, national insurance contributions and deductions made from payments to sub-contractors do not exceed on average £450 per month. Where the quarterly procedure applies the contractor must account for his deductions fourteen days following July 5th, October 5th, January 5th and April 5th respectively. Failure on the part of the contractor to operate correctly the sub-contractors' deduction scheme can have serious repercussions and perhaps lead to the commencement of criminal proceedings. There may also be a liability to discharge interest for late payment where payment is made more than 14 days following the end of the year of assessment in which the deduction was made.

At the end of each year of assessment the sub-contractor will calculate the total amount of deductions suffered on payments received by him. This total amount may then be offset against the sub-contractor's liability to income tax. Should the sums deducted exceed the liability, the surplus can be reclaimed from the Inland Revenue. If the deductions fall below the full liability the sub-contractor must satisfy the excess in the normal manner.

VOLUNTEER DRIVERS – MILEAGE ALLOWANCES

Individuals who drive for the hospital car service and other volunteer organisations usually receive mileage allowances. Any "profit element" in these allowances will be treated as income chargeable to income tax. The profit may be calculated, at the individual's option, by

a using figures taken from the Fixed Profit Car Scheme used by employees (see page 70); or

b taking the actual mileage receipts and the actual expenses.

Profits, if any, arising before October 6th, 1991, are ignored. To avoid the imposition of sudden liabilities after this date the charge is being phased in over a period, with only part of the profits assessable in the transitional years. The proportion of profits assessable is as follows:

	Taxable part
a Period October 6th, 1991 to April 5th, 1992	one-quarter
b Year to April 5th, 1993	one-quarter
c Year to April 5th, 1994	one-half
d Year to April 5th, 1995	three-quarters
e From April 6th, 1995	the whole

This arrangement has no application to taxi, minicab and similar operators who carry on a business.

COMPANIES

Profits, gains and income accruing to companies are chargeable to corporation tax. The assessment of companies to this tax is dealt with on page 187.

Capital expenditure

CAPITAL EXPENDITURE incurred by an individual carrying on a trade, profession or vocation cannot usually be subtracted when calculating business profits. However, many items of capital expenditure enable the individual to obtain capital allowances which are set against business profits or perhaps absorbed against other income. Similar allowances may be available to others not carrying on business, but the ability to utilise such allowances is somewhat limited.

It should be recognised that the system of granting capital allowances has been drastically amended in recent years. In earlier times substantial initial allowances or first-year allowances were granted immediately many items of expenditure were incurred, leaving only limited, or perhaps no, annual allowances to be obtained subsequently. These accelerated allowances were largely withdrawn throughout a two-year transitional period and, with very few exceptions, ceased to apply entirely for expenditure incurred after March 31st, 1986. However, following an interval in excess of six years both initial and first-year allowances were reintroduced for expenditure incurred between November 1st, 1992, and October 31st, 1993.

PLANT AND MACHINERY

Capital allowances are available for the capital cost of providing plant and machinery wholly and exclusively for the purposes of a business. These assets comprise many items commonly used for trading or other activities, including industrial equipment, tractors, motor cars, typewriters, desks, chairs and machinery, among others. They also include most items of computer software.

First-year allowances

A first-year allowance of 100 per cent was generally available for expenditure incurred before March 14th, 1984. This effectively enabled the entire cost to be fully relieved in a single year. The first-year allowance of 100 per cent was rapidly reduced in amount and ceased to apply entirely for expenditure incurred after March 31st, 1986.

The first-year allowance has been reintroduced for expenditure incurred in the twelve-month period commencing on November 1st, 1992, and ending on October 31st, 1993. No allowance of this nature is available for expenditure on ordinary motor cars, with the exception of those operated as taxis, used for short-term hire or comprising mobility allowance vehicles for the disabled. The first-year allowance is given at the rate of 40 per cent, although it remains possible to disclaim part of that allowance.

Annual writing-down allowances

An annual writing-down allowance is available for expenditure incurred when acquiring plant and machinery. This allowance, given at the rate of 25 per cent, is calculated on the reduced balance of unrelieved expenditure remaining after subtracting allowances for earlier years.

In those cases where the first-year allowance is obtained for expenditure incurred in the twelve-month period ending on October 31st, 1993, no writing-down allowance is available in the same year. The balance of the expenditure, usually representing 60 per cent of the outlay, remains available for the 25 per cent writing-down allowance in the second and succeeding years.

44 POOLING – WRITING-DOWN ALLOWANCES

A manufacturer prepares accounts to March 31st annually. The balance of expenditure remaining in the pool of plant and machinery on March 31st, 1992, was £12,500. He incurred expenditure of £12,000 when acquiring new plant on June 24th, 1992, and further expenditure of £10,000 was incurred on February 19th, 1993. £6,500 was received from the sale of obsolete plant. No further expenditure was incurred, or sales made, in the year ending March 31st, 1994.

Capital allowances may be claimed as follows:

	Pool £
Balance brought forward	12,500
Additions – pre November 1st, 1992	12,000
	24,500
Less sales	6,500
	18,000
Writing-down allowance 1993–94: 25 per cent of £18,000	4,500
	13,500
Additions – post October 31st, 1992	10,000
	23,500
First-year allowance 1993–94: 40 per cent of £10,000	4,000
	19,500
Writing-down allowance 1994–95: 25 per cent of £19,500	4,875
Balance carried forward	£14,625

The total allowances for 1993–94 are £8,500 (£4,500 + £4,000).

Pooling
Most items of plant and machinery, with the exception of motor cars, acquired by an individual enter into a "pool". Adjustments must be made to the expenditure remaining in this pool where a new asset is added or an existing asset sold. The 25 per cent annual writing-down allowance is applied to the "pool" as a whole and it is unnecessary to identify each separate asset. Should the sale, or other proceeds, of an asset exceed the balance of unrelieved expenditure remaining in the pool, a balancing charge will be imposed to recoup allowances obtained in earlier periods.

Election for non-pooling
The 25 per cent reducing balance approach enables some 90 per cent of the cost of an asset to be relieved throughout a period of approximately eight years. Many items of plant and machinery have a lifespan falling below eight years and where assets acquired have a limited life expectation the taxpayer may elect to exclude these assets from the common pool. The advantage of the election is that when the excluded asset is sold a balancing adjustment will arise which is not distorted by entries in the common pool.

In those cases where plant and machinery is used only partly for business purposes a suitable restriction in the allowances granted must be made.

45 *ELECTION FOR NON-POOLING*

Let it be assumed that the manufacturer in Example 44 also acquired a further asset at a cost of £25,000 on January 5th, 1993. An election was made to exclude this asset from the common pool. The asset realised £4,000 when sold on March 15th, 1995.

Capital allowances for this asset only are calculated as follows:

	£
Cost	25,000
First-year allowance 1993–94:	
40 per cent of £25,000	10,000
	15,000
Writing-down allowance 1994–95:	
25 per cent of £15,000	3,750
	11,250
Sale proceeds March 15th, 1995	4,000
Balancing allowance 1995–96	£7,250

If the asset had been included in the common pool the aggregate allowances for 1995–96 would be considerably smaller.

MOTOR CARS
Writing-down allowances are available at the rate of 25 per cent for the cost of acquiring motor cars, where the vehicles are used for business

purposes. However, a restriction must be imposed for motor cars costing more than £12,000, as the annual allowance is not to exceed £3,000 on these vehicles. If the vehicle was purchased before March 11th, 1992, the restriction applies to motor cars costing more than £8,000, with the annual allowance limited to £2,000. This restriction does not apply to taxis, short-term hire cars and mobility allowance vehicles for the disabled.

Should a car costing more than £12,000 (or £8,000 where appropriate) when new be leased to a business proprietor, the lessee may suffer some restriction in the hire or rental charge which can be deducted when calculating profits assessable to tax.

Only part of the available allowance may be obtained where a car is used partly for business and partly for private motoring.

46 *MOTOR CARS*

A doctor purchased a motor car for use in his practice on August 15th, 1993, at a cost of £23,500. Assuming the vehicle is used exclusively for business purposes and that accounts are made up to October 31st annually, the calculation of capital allowances will proceed as follows:

	£
Cost	23,500
Writing-down allowance, 1994–95:	
25 per cent of £23,500 – but restricted to	3,000
	20,500
Writing-down allowance, 1995–96:	
25 per cent of £20,500 – but restricted to	3,000
	17,500
Writing-down allowance, 1996–97:	
25 per cent of £17,500 – but restricted to	3,000
	14,500
Writing-down allowance, 1997–98:	
25 per cent of £14,500 – but restricted to	3,000
	11,500
Writing-down allowance, 1998–99:	
25 per cent of £11,500 (no restriction necessary)	2,875
Available for future writing-down allowances	£8,625

INDUSTRIAL BUILDINGS

Allowances are available for expenditure incurred on the construction of buildings or structures used, or to be used, for industrial purposes. These include buildings or structures used for the purpose of the following, among others:

a a trade carried on in a mill, factory or similar premises;

b a transport, dock, inland navigation, water, electricity, or hydraulic undertaking;

c a tunnel undertaking;

d a bridge undertaking;

e a trade consisting of the manufacture of goods or materials, or the subjection of goods to a process;

f a trade which consists in the storage of certain goods;

g a trade which consists in the catching or taking of fish or shell fish;

h a trade which consists in the repairing and servicing of goods.

Relief is also available for the cost of constructing toll roads.

The allowances do not apply to expenditure on retail shops, offices and other non-industrial buildings.

Where part of a building is, and some other part is not, used for a qualifying purpose, allowances must usually be restricted to the cost of constructing the qualifying part. Some relaxation in this approach is, however, available where the cost of constructing the non-qualifying part does not exceed 25 per cent of the cost of constructing the entire building. In this situation, allowances may be obtained on the aggregate cost.

Initial allowances

Initial allowances were previously available for expenditure incurred on the construction of a qualifying building. For expenditure incurred after March 10th, 1981, the initial allowance was 75 per cent, although an increased allowance of 100 per cent could be obtained for expenditure on small industrial workshops. The allowance was reduced throughout a transitional period and, subject to a single exception, was withdrawn completely for expenditure incurred after March 31st, 1986. The exception concerned expenditure on buildings located in enterprise zones where a 100 per cent initial allowance remained available.

The initial allowance was reintroduced at the rate of 20 per cent for expenditure incurred on the construction of a building under the terms of a contract entered into between November 1st, 1992, and October 31st, 1993. It remains a requirement that the building is brought into use for the purposes of a qualifying trade not later than December 31st, 1994. The initial allowance may also be forthcoming for existing unused buildings completed, or in course of construction, before November 1st, 1992, if they are acquired under a contract entered into during the year ended October 31st, 1993, and brought into use by the end of 1994.

Annual writing-down allowances

An annual writing-down allowance of 4 per cent is available for qualifying construction expenditure. This allowance will be given for the first year in which the building is brought into use. It is therefore possible that the 20 per cent initial allowance and the first annual allowance of 4 per cent may be available in the same year, although in many cases there will be an interval between the two allowances.

In the absence of any initial allowance, the annual writing-down allowance of 4 per cent will exhaust all construction costs once a period of 25 years has elapsed. This period will be shortened where a 20 per cent initial allowance is obtained, as the aggregate of initial and writing-down allowances cannot exceed the construction cost.

Where an industrial building, for which initial and/or annual writing-down allowances have been obtained, is sold, a balancing charge may arise. This will represent the difference between the written-down tax value of the expenditure and the disposal proceeds. However, any balancing charge cannot exceed the aggregate allowances previously granted. No balancing charge will arise should the sale take place more than 25 years, or 50 years for older buildings, following the date expenditure was incurred.

A balancing allowance may arise should the sale proceeds fall below the written-down tax value.

A person who acquires an existing building from the previous owner cannot base annual writing-down allowances on the price paid, unless the building is bought unused. However, some future annual writing-down allowances will usually be available, based on the previous owner's "residue of expenditure".

47 *INDUSTRIAL BUILDINGS*

On February 27th, 1993, a manufacturer entered into a contract for the construction of an industrial building. The cost was £200,000 and the completed building was first used in November of the same year. Accounts are prepared to December 31st annually and the allowances available are as follows:

		£
Cost (during accounting year to December 31st, 1993)		200,000
Allowances 1994–95:		
Initial – 20 per cent of £200,000	40,000	
Writing-down – 4 per cent of £200,000	8,000	48,000
		152,000
Allowances 1995–96:		
Writing-down – 4 per cent of £200,000		8,000
		£144,000

Annual writing-down allowances of £8,000 will continue until the expenditure has been exhausted, unless the building is sold or ceases to be used for a qualifying purpose.

SMALL INDUSTRIAL WORKSHOPS

Where expenditure was incurred on the construction of a small industrial workshop, comprising an industrial building as defined above, an initial allowance of 100 per cent could be obtained. A building was regarded as "small" if the gross internal floor space did not exceed 2,500 square feet. Where a larger building was divided into parts, each part qualified as a separate building only if it was permanently separated from the remainder of the building and intended for separate occupation. The increased initial allowance applied only to expenditure incurred in the three-year period ending on March 26th, 1983. However, for a further period of two years, ending on March 26th, 1985, the 100 per cent allowance remained available if the internal floor space did not exceed 1,250 square feet. In the case of converted large buildings, it was sufficient if the average size of each unit within the building did not exceed 1,250 square feet.

The special 100 per cent initial allowance for small industrial workshops cannot apply to construction expenditure incurred after March 26th, 1985.

HOTELS

Expenditure incurred on the construction, extension or improvement of hotels may qualify for capital allowances. It is a necessary requirement that the hotel has at least ten letting bedrooms, is not normally in the same occupation for more than one month, regularly provides guests with breakfast and evening meals and is open for at least four months between April and October. Additionally, all sleeping accommodation offered at the hotel must consist wholly or mainly of letting bedrooms. Any expenditure on that part of the premises occupied by the proprietor or his family must be disregarded but accommodation used by employees may usually be included.

Qualifying expenditure incurred before April 1st, 1986, produced an initial allowance of 20 per cent and an annual writing-down allowance of 4 per cent until the expenditure had been exhausted. No initial allowance was available for expenditure incurred after March 31st, 1986, but an annual writing-down allowance could be obtained at the rate of 4 per cent until the expenditure had been entirely written off.

An initial allowance at the rate of 20 per cent was reintroduced for expenditure incurred between November 1st, 1992, and October 31st, 1993. The annual writing-down allowance may also be obtained until the expenditure is exhausted.

Should an hotel for which allowances have been obtained be sold, the vendor may be taxed on a balancing charge, or receive relief for a balancing allowance, and the purchaser may obtain future writing-down allowances, in a manner similar to that which applies for industrial buildings.

Where an hotel is located in an enterprise zone, it is advisable to claim the alternative allowances discussed below.

ENTERPRISE ZONES

Substantially increased capital allowances are available for expenditure incurred on assets located in enterprise zones. The cost of constructing an industrial building, a qualifying hotel or a commercial building or structure qualifies for an initial allowance, which unlike other allowances, was not withdrawn for expenditure incurred after March 31st, 1986. It is a requirement that the expenditure must be incurred, or a contract entered into, within a period of ten years following the date on which the area first became designated as an enterprise zone.

An initial allowance of 100 per cent can be obtained to absorb the entire expenditure. Alternatively, the initial allowance may be reduced to some smaller amount with annual writing-down allowances, not exceeding 25 per cent of original cost, until the expenditure has been fully used. Where a building located in an enterprise zone is sold, balancing adjustments must be calculated on a basis similar to that applied on the sale of an industrial building.

48 *ENTERPRISE ZONES*

During the year ended on April 5th, 1994, Mr X incurred £100,000 on the construction of a commercial building in an enterprise zone. He decided to claim an initial allowance of £50,000 in 1993–94 which resulted in annual writing-down allowances of £25,000 for both 1994–95 and 1995–96.

In 1993–94 Mr X received rent of £10,000 from letting the building to a tenant. This rent must be set against the initial allowance of £50,000, leaving a balance of £40,000.

The other income of Mr X for 1993–94 was £85,000. Assuming he was a married man aged 47 entitled to the full married couple's allowance, and made a claim to set the unused initial allowance against other income, the tax payable for 1993–94 becomes:

		£
Total income		85,000
Less	£	
Personal allowance	3,445	
Married couple's allowance	1,720	
Surplus initial allowance	40,000	45,165
Tax chargeable on		£39,835

Tax payable:	
Lower rate:	£
On first £2,500 at 20 per cent	500.00
Basic rate:	
On next £21,200 at 25 per cent	5,300.00
Higher rate:	
On balance of £16,135 at 40 per cent	6,454.00
	£12,254.00

AGRICULTURAL BUILDINGS

Expenditure incurred by the owner or tenant of agricultural land on the construction of farm buildings, fences, cottages and other works, such as ditches and drains, will usually qualify for capital allowances. The cost of constructing a farmhouse will also be included but must be restricted to one-third of the capital cost, or a smaller fraction where the amenities of the farmhouse are considered excessive in relation to the agricultural holding.

The calculation of allowances and the effect on those allowances where property is subsequently demolished or sold differs substantially for expenditure incurred before April 1st, 1986, and that incurred subsequently.

Expenditure incurred on or before March 31st, 1986

For expenditure incurred before April 1st, 1986, an initial allowance of 20 per cent could be claimed and usually granted in the year of assessment following that in which the outlay took place. At the taxpayer's option, the initial allowance could be reduced to some smaller amount. An annual writing-down allowance of one-tenth of the expenditure was also granted for the year of assessment following that in which expenditure was incurred and each of the succeeding years until the cost had been fully relieved. Where the maximum initial allowance of 20 per cent was claimed, aggregate allowances of 30 per cent were available in one year and allowances of 10 per cent in each of the seven following years.

Once qualifying expenditure has been incurred allowances remain available and cannot subsequently be withdrawn. Nor will any balancing charge or balancing allowance arise on the sale of an interest in agricultural property. Where an interest in such property changes hands before all allowances have been obtained the benefit of remaining future allowances accrues to the purchaser.

Expenditure incurred after March 31st, 1986

For several years no initial allowance was forthcoming to absorb expenditure incurred after March 31st, 1986. However, an initial allowance of 20 per cent is available for expenditure incurred between November 1st, 1992, and October 31st, 1993.

Writing-down allowances are given at the rate of 4 per cent annually for the year of assessment in which expenditure is incurred and succeeding years. These allowances are given in addition to the initial allowance, although the aggregate allowances obtained cannot exceed the cost incurred.

Subject to the election mentioned below, no balancing charge or allowance will arise if the property is sold or assets cease to exist. Any purchaser of property will become entitled to the annual writing-down allowance at the rate of 4 per cent annually throughout the remaining part of the 25-year period or, where an initial allowance has been obtained, throughout a shorter period. This writing-down allowance is based on the vendor's original cost and not on the purchase price paid by the purchaser.

However, an election may be submitted where a building, fence or other work on which expenditure has been incurred is demolished, destroyed or otherwise ceases to exist. This election will establish a balancing allowance arising at the time of the event and representing the balance of unused expenditure. No future annual writing-down allowances will then be available.

An election may also be made, jointly by the vendor and purchaser, where property on which qualifying expenditure has been incurred is sold. Where such an election is made the disposal proceeds must be compared with the written-down tax value. Should the proceeds exceed this value a balancing charge will be made on the vendor to recoup previous writing-down and initial allowances. If the proceeds fall below the written-down tax value the vendor will receive a balancing allowance. The effect on the purchaser is that he will then receive future annual writing-down allowances throughout the remaining twenty-five year, or shorter, period based on the "residue of expenditure".

Broadly stated, the effect of submitting an election is similar to that which applies to industrial buildings and structures. It does, however, remain a matter for decision by the parties whether or not to take advantage of the election procedure.

49 *AGRICULTURAL BUILDINGS*

On April 12th, 1990, A incurred capital expenditure of £50,000 on the construction of a farm building. He sold the farm to B on October 6th, 1993, with £47,000 being allocated to the building.

If *no election is made* annual allowances will be granted at the rate of £2,000 (4 per cent × £50,000) for 1990–91 and each of the next twenty-four years. These will be allocated as follows:

A

1990–91, 1991–92 and 1992–93	£2,000 annually
1993–94 (to October 5th)	Half × £2,000

B

1993–94 (from October 6th)	Half × £2,000
1994–95 and the following twenty-one years	£2,000 annually

If *an election is made* the effect on A will be:

	£
Cost	50,000
Less writing-down allowances:	
1990–91, 1991–92 and 1992–93 (3 × £2,000)	6,000
	44,000
Sale price	47,000
1993–94 balancing charge	£3,000

B may obtain annual writing-down allowances calculated on the "residue of expenditure" of £47,000 (£44,000 + £3,000), which represents that part of A's original cost not covered by allowances. These allowances will be available to B throughout the remaining part of the twenty-five year period, namely twenty-one and a half years, at the annual rate of £2,186. No initial allowance is available to B as he incurred no cost of construction.

FORESTRY LAND AND BUILDINGS

Capital expenditure incurred by the owner or tenant of commercial forestry land on the construction of forestry buildings, fences and other structures previously produced an entitlement to capital allowances. These allowances were calculated on a basis similar to those for expenditure on agricultural buildings. It was necessary to demonstrate that an election had been made for the occupation of woodlands to be assessed under Case I of Schedule D. Liability to assessment in this manner generally terminated in 1988, although it continued until April 5th, 1993, where an election had been made. No capital allowances are available after the date on which commercial woodlands cease to be within the charge under Case I of Schedule D. It inevitably follows that all entitlement to capital allowances ceased once the special transitional period ended on April 5th, 1993.

OTHER CAPITAL EXPENDITURE

Other expenditure for which allowances are available includes the cost of acquiring patents, "know-how", expenditure on scientific research, ships, and the capital outlay incurred in working mines and sources of mineral deposits.

PARTNERSHIPS

The allowances mentioned earlier are also available to individuals carrying on business in partnership.

COMPANIES

Capital expenditure incurred by companies will enable the various capital allowances to be claimed, but different rules apply for determining the basis periods into which those allowances fall.

NON-TRADERS

Many of the capital allowances discussed on the previous pages are available to individuals who incur expenditure on investment assets leased or used by others. This includes expenditure on industrial buildings, hotels, agricultural property and property located in enterprise zones. Allowances must be primarily offset against income arising from the investment, but it is usually possible to absorb surplus allowances against other income. A non-trader who incurs capital expenditure on plant and machinery leased to others may obtain the appropriate capital allowances, but these are generally only available to be offset against income arising from leasing and cannot be used against other forms of income.

Treatment of income

Property Income

RENT AND OTHER INCOME from land, buildings and other property in the United Kingdom is chargeable to income tax under Schedule A. Liability extends to:

a rents under leases of land;

b rent-charges, ground annuals and feu-duties and any other annual payments reserved in respect of, charged on, or issuing out of, land; and

c any other receipts arising to a person from his ownership of an estate or interest in, or right over, land.

Liability does not extend to yearly interest, mortgage interest, building society interest, or rents and royalties payable in respect of the exploitation of mines, quarries and similar undertakings. These matters are dealt with under different headings. The exemptions and options available for income from furnished lettings and the treatment of furnished holiday lettings is reviewed on page 118.

CALCULATION OF LIABILITY

The income chargeable to tax is that to which the landlord becomes *entitled*, but does not necessarily receive, in the year of assessment. There can be some departure from the "entitlement" rule where rent is payable in arrears by a tenant closely associated with the landlord.

A deduction may be made, from the rent or other income, for expenditure incurred in respect of the following:

a maintenance, repairs, insurance and management;

b services which the landlord is obliged to provide but for which he receives no separate payment;

c rates or other charges on the occupier which the landlord is obliged to pay;

d any rent-charge, ground annual, feu-duty or other periodical payment in respect of the land, or charged on or issuing out of the land.

Relief cannot be obtained for expenditure relating to a period before the landlord acquired the property, or for expenditure incurred by reason of dilapidations which accrued in such a period. Thus, a person who purchases property in a dilapidated condition and incurs substantial expenditure on repairs to the premises cannot obtain relief for the cost of those repairs, if the necessity to repair arose on some earlier date.

The more usual items qualifying for deduction from income will include expenditure on the following:

a normal repairs and redecorations;

b maintenance of common parts of blocks of offices or flats;

c upkeep of gardens of flats, where an obligation to do this is imposed on the landlord by the lease;

d upkeep of private roads, drains, ditches and embankments on an estate containing property let by the taxpayer, where it is incurred for the benefit of the tenants;

e cost of rent collecting;

f legal and accountancy costs of preparing tax statements relating to the property;

g premiums on policies of insurance against the risk of damage by flood, fire and other causes;

h water and other rates, including the council tax where it is attributable to let property;

i rent paid by the landlord;

j upkeep of estate offices;

k cost of valuation for insurance, other than for purchase, sale or probate.

Expenditure which cannot be deducted will include that incurred in carrying out improvements, additions and alterations to property.

EXCESS EXPENDITURE

It will sometimes happen that expenditure incurred by the landlord in respect of a single property exceeds, in any year, the rental income for that year. This excess can usually be set against rental income accruing to the landlord from other properties in the same year. However, the right of set-off may be precluded where properties are let under abnormal conditions. Where expenditure is not offset against other rental income, the excess may be carried forward to succeeding years and set against income subsequently arising from property. Owners of agricultural property may elect to set excessive expenditure against income generally (see page 121) but other landlords cannot relieve expenditure in this manner.

ASSESSMENT

Income tax due by an individual in respect of rental and other income arising from land or buildings is payable on January 1st during the year of assessment. Thus, the tax due in respect of income for the year ended April 5th, 1994, will be payable on January 1st, 1994.

It is apparent that in many cases accurate details of the annual incomings and outgoings cannot be ascertained until after the end of the year of assessment. At the same time, if tax otherwise due on January 1st was held over, considerable delay in collection would inevitably result. This problem is overcome by using the agreed figures of net income for the immediately preceding year. For example, income tax payable on January 1st, 1994, will be provisionally based on net income for the year ended April 5th, 1993. When the final results for the year ended April 5th, 1994, are known the original assessment will be adjusted, thereby producing either a repayment of tax or additional liability. The necessity to estimate income on this basis can only be avoided if, since the beginning of the previous year, property has been sold or ceased to produce income.

Rental income accruing to companies is chargeable to corporation tax in the manner discussed on page 187.

50 *ASSESSMENT OF RENT*

Mrs C owns a single property and the rent received, less outgoings, for the year ended April 5th, 1993, was £5,000. A new lease was negotiated during 1993–94 and the net income for the year ended April 5th, 1994, was eventually found to be £8,450.

An assessment in the sum of £5,000 will be raised on Mrs C for 1993–94 and the appropriate income tax paid on or before January 1st, 1994.

When accurate details are available, following the end of the tax year, Mrs C will receive an additional assessment of £3,450 (£8,450 less £5,000) on which income tax must be paid.

LOST RENTS

The charge to income tax under Schedule A is based on the rents or other receipts to which the landlord was *entitled* during the year of assessment. Failure to obtain payment will not necessarily provide sufficient grounds for avoiding liability to satisfy tax becoming due. However, if the person entitled to receive rents or other sums can show that:

a the non-receipt was attributable to the default of the person liable to pay and all reasonable steps have been taken to enforce payment; or

b the payment has been waived without consideration and to avoid hardship,

the landlord may claim that the sum outstanding should be disregarded. If this claim is accepted no liability to tax will arise on the "lost" rents.

PREMIUMS

Premiums received on the grant of a lease for a term not exceeding fifty years in duration are liable to taxation. The amount of the premium received must be reduced by 2 per cent for every complete twelve months of the lease, excluding the first twelve months, and only the balance remaining will produce liability.

Any part of a premium excluded from assessment under Schedule A may enter into other calculations of income or gains requiring assessment to income tax or capital gains tax.

51 *PREMIUMS ON LEASES*

On June 25th, 1993 Mr T granted a 21 year lease of property in return for a premium of £40,000. That part of the premium which must be treated as income for 1993–94 will be calculated as follows:

	£
Number of complete years of the lease	21
Less first year	1
	20

	£
Premium received	40,000
Less	
20 years at 2 per cent = 40 per cent	16,000
Taxable "rent" for 1993–94	£24,000

FURNISHED LETTINGS

Profits from furnished lettings, calculated after deducting expenses including rent, rates, lighting and wages paid for household assistance, do not arise from a trade. The actual profits for a year of assessment will be assessed, at the taxpayer's option, under Schedule A or Case VI of Schedule D. The selection of the proper charging provision may be important where some deficiency can be relieved against amounts chargeable under one heading only. The special treatment of income arising under the "rent a room" scheme or from letting furnished holiday accommodation is discussed below.

FURNISHED LETTINGS – RENT A ROOM SCHEME

A new tax exemption – introduced on April 6th, 1992 – applies to individuals who receive rent from letting rooms in their own homes. This scheme, known as the "rent a room" scheme, extends to owners and tenants who let rooms furnished in their only or main residence. It is a necessary requirement that all income from this activity is either attributable to the letting of furnished accommodation assessable to income tax under Case VI of Schedule D or represents profits from a trade chargeable under Case I of the same Schedule. The scheme is confined to the letting of rooms and accommodation in an individual's only or main residence and has no application to similar activities undertaken in some other property.

Gross rents up to a maximum of £3,250 received in a tax year may qualify for complete exemption, but this figure is halved to £1,625 if two or more individuals each receive income from lettings in the same property. This could arise, for example, where an owner lets part of his home to a tenant who sub-lets to a sub-tenant. Both the owner and the tenant may each obtain a maximum exemption of £1,625, if of course each individual can treat the property as his or her only or main residence.

Complete exemption

Where gross rents do not exceed £3,250 (or £1,625 where appropriate) in a tax year both receipts and expenses will be disregarded and the rent received incurs no liability to taxation. It remains possible to file an election to avoid taking advantage of this exemption. An election may be beneficial where the expenses incurred exceed rental income, as it will then be possible to carry forward surplus outgoings to a subsequent year or years.

52 *RENT A ROOM SCHEME – EXEMPTION*

David owns "Fairways" and resides in the property with his wife and family as their only residence. He lets part of the property furnished to a lodger, and information for 1993–94 was as follows:

	£
Gross rents	2,700
Expenses	600

Apart from David, no other person receives any income for letting "Fairways".

As the gross rents do not exceed £3,250 there will be no taxable profit, nor can relief be obtained for the expenses of £600.

Partial exemption

Gross rents arising in a tax year may exceed the ceiling of £3,250 (or £1,625). The taxpayer is then provided with a choice, namely:

a The individual may elect to suffer tax on that proportion of the gross rents which exceeds the ceiling of £3,250 (or £1,625). No relief will then be available for outgoings.

b In the absence of an election the individual will incur liability to tax on the difference between gross rents received and expenses paid with no relief under the "rent a room" scheme.

The election must be made within a period of twelve months following the end of the year to which it relates.

In most situations the calculation of gross rents and outgoings will be based on transactions taking place in the actual tax year. There may be some departure from this approach where the preceding year basis of assessment is adopted. In this situation it is the income and expenditure for the basis year and not that of the tax year which must be used.

FURNISHED HOLIDAY ACCOMMODATION

A relaxed approach is available for individuals deriving income from the commercial letting of furnished holiday accommodation. Several

53 *RENT A ROOM SCHEME – PARTIAL EXEMPTION*

Using the basic facts in Example 52, let it be assumed that the figures for 1993–94 were:

	£
Gross rents	8,000
Expenses	4,100

David is now provided with a choice, namely:

a He may file an election and pay tax on the following, without obtaining any relief for expenses:

Gross rents	8,000
Less basic exemption	3,250
Taxable profit	£4,750

b He may decline to file an election and pay tax on the following:

Gross rents	8,000
Actual expenses	4,100
Taxable profit	£3,900

It would be advisable not to file any election.

---

requirements must be satisfied before these relaxations can apply, including the following:

a the property must be located in the United Kingdom;

b there must be a letting on a commercial basis and with a view to the realisation of profits;

c the tenant or occupier must be entitled to the use of furniture;

d accommodation must be available for commercial letting as holiday accommodation to the public generally for periods which aggregate at least 140 days;

e the property must actually be so let for at least 70 days; and

f in a period of seven months the property must not normally be in the same occupation for a continuous period exceeding 31 days.

Special rules must be applied to determine whether these requirements are satisfied in a year of assessment. It also remains possible to submit a claim for averaging where some properties in the same ownership would, and others would not, satisfy the requirements.

Once the existence of qualifying lettings has been established, there are several taxation advantages. Income remains chargeable under Case VI of Schedule D but for all practical purposes that income is deemed to be derived from a trade. Income is treated as "earned", losses may be relieved against other income, profits will be calculated by applying trading principles and income can be used to provide cover for personal pension or retirement annuity premiums.

An additional benefit from establishing qualifying furnished holiday lettings is that the disposal of property used for this purpose may enable roll-over relief and retirement relief to be obtained when calculating capital gains tax liability.

The relaxed treatment of furnished holiday lettings is confined to property in the United Kingdom and has no application to property situated overseas, perhaps in Spain, Portugal or France.

SAND AND GRAVEL QUARRIES

Rents and royalties for the use and exploitation of quarries of sand and gravel, sand-pits and brickfields are payable after deduction of income tax at the basic rate of 25 per cent. Deduction at this rate is not affected by the 20 per cent lower rate band.

It is often possible for the recipient of mineral royalties to divide the sums received into two equal parts. One part will be regarded as a chargeable gain assessable to capital gains tax and the other remains assessable to income tax. This does not affect the deduction of income tax at the rate of 25 per cent from the aggregate gross sum received.

FARMERS

Farmers who carry out farming on a commercial basis and with a reasonable expectation of profit, and persons who occupy land managed on a commercial basis and with a view to profit, are chargeable in the same manner as other persons who carry on a trade (see page 90). A claim may be made to average profits from farming between two consecutive years. Relief for farming losses may be obtained by setting those losses against other sources of income derived by the farmer, but there may be some limitations in the relief available where losses have been sustained for five consecutive years.

The allowances in respect of plant and machinery referred to on page 104 are available to farmers, and other allowances will frequently be obtained for capital expenditure on agricultural buildings and works (see page 111).

Owners of agricultural land let to tenants are entitled to special relief for expenses. In the ordinary case where the cost of repairs, maintenance and other outgoings of a property exceeds the income from that property in a year of assessment, the excess must be carried forward and set against income accruing from the same property in future years, unless relief can be obtained by setting the excess against rental income from some other property. However, if the expenditure was incurred on land, houses or other buildings used for agricultural purposes, the excess may be set against any income of the landlord for the same year. When calculating the amount of any excess, an appropriate proportion of the expenditure attributable to a farmhouse may be included by owner–occupiers.

FORESTRY AND WOODLANDS

In earlier times the occupation of woodlands did not give rise to a tax liability unless the woodlands were managed on a commercial basis and with a view to the realisation of profit. If woodlands were managed in this manner the occupier was provided with a choice. He could either choose to be assessed under Schedule B on an assumed annual value or elect to be assessed under Case I of Schedule D as a person carrying on a trade. Persons having the use of woodlands for the purpose of felling and removing timber in connection with an actual trade could not be assessed under Schedule B.

This basis for dealing with commercial woodlands was substantially amended and has now been withdrawn entirely as shown by the following timetable:

a Schedule B cannot apply after April 5th, 1988.

b Subject to **d** below, no new election for assessment under Case I of Schedule D can be made after March 14th, 1988.

c Elections for assessment under Schedule D and made before March 15th, 1988, continued until April 5th, 1993.

d Persons who had entered into commitments or made applications for grants received from the Forestry Commission before March 15th, 1988, could also elect to be assessed under Case I of Schedule D until April 5th, 1993.

The effect of these measures is that from April 6th, 1993, the occupation of commercial woodlands has been entirely removed from income tax liabilities, reliefs and commitments, unless those woodlands are occupied for the purpose of felling and removing timber in connection with a bona fide trade.

Investment Income

INDIVIDUALS retaining surplus funds, or maintaining an investment portfolio, will be concerned to obtain the maximum income or capital yield from the investment of capital. There are many investment opportunities and the eventual choice will also be influenced by tax considerations. Income from certain investments, notably National Savings Certificates and Children's Bonus Bonds, is exempt from liability to income tax. Exemption also extends to dividends and other revenue arising from Personal Equity Plans and interest from TESSA arrangements. However, most other forms of income are liable to tax where the investor's income is sufficiently substantial.

Following the introduction of independent taxation it is necessary to allocate income between husband and wife, particularly where income-producing assets are jointly owned. Caution must be taken to ensure that any attempt to transfer future income from one spouse to the other cannot be set aside by the Inland Revenue.

These and other matters affecting investment income are discussed below.

TAXATION OF INVESTMENT INCOME

Income arising on many investments may be received "net" after deduction of income tax at the basic rate of 25 per cent. Examples include interest received from debentures, loan interest payable by a company and interest on many Government stocks. Depositors with building societies and banks also receive interest after deduction of income tax, although those not liable to tax can arrange to receive income gross. Where the recipient is liable to income tax at the basic rate only, the income has been fully taxed by deduction and no further tax is due. Recipients who are not liable, or not wholly liable, to tax at the basic rate may obtain a partial or complete repayment of the tax deducted as shown on page 158. The gross income, calculated before deduction of income tax, must be included in the figure of total income where the recipient is liable to income tax at the higher rate of 40 per cent, but tax will only be charged at the rate in excess of the basic rate suffered, namely at 15 per cent.

Certain income, such as interest on holdings of 3½ per cent War Loan, Income Bonds and Deposit Bonds issued by the National Savings movement, together with interest on National Savings Investment Accounts and Government stocks purchased through the National Savings Stock Register, is received gross, without deduction of income tax, and the recipient is taxed directly on the basis of the previous year's income. In the early years of ownership of every new source of income, and also in the closing years, a special basis of assessment applies.

There are complex rules for dealing with certain forms of indirect income. For example where an investment in an offshore "roll-up" fund is realised, surplus proceeds may be treated as income. Accrued income may also arise on the realisation of deep-discounted stock, namely stock issued at a large discount. The special rules which affect interest on National Savings Capital Bonds are reviewed later.

DIVIDENDS

Dividends paid by United Kingdom companies are not subject to deduction of income tax. However, each dividend is treated as having attached to it a "tax credit". The amount of this tax credit and the effect on the liability of individual shareholders changed significantly on April 6th, 1993. It is therefore advisable to examine the system in operation before that date and then to review the new system introduced on April 6th, 1993.

Dividends paid on or before April 5th, 1993

For 1992–93 the tax credit was equal to one-third of the dividend paid. When calculating the total income of an individual who received such a dividend, the tax credit was added to the dividend received. For example, a cash dividend of £75 would have a tax credit of £25 thereby creating gross income of £100.

The tax credit was regarded as income tax suffered on the aggregate dividend at the rate of 25 per cent, with the following results:

a An individual who was not liable to income tax, due to an insufficiency of income, could obtain a repayment of the tax credit in full.

b An individual who only became liable following the receipt of dividends could recover part of the tax credit.

c An individual liable to tax at the lower rate of 20 per cent could also recover part of the tax credit.

d An individual liable at the basic rate only would neither pay nor recover tax on the dividend unless the dividend increased taxable income beyond the basic rate band of £23,700.

e An individual liable to tax at the higher rate of 40 per cent would be assessed on the aggregate of the dividend and the tax credit, but received a reduction in the tax otherwise payable equal to the amount of the tax credit. This involved an effective higher rate liability of 15 per cent on the gross sum.

Dividends paid on or after April 6th, 1993

Dividends paid on or after April 6th, 1993, also have a tax credit but for 1993–94 this is equal to one-quarter (and not one-third) of the dividend paid. Here also an individual receiving such a dividend will calculate total income by adding the tax credit to the dividend received. Thus a dividend of £75 will have attached to it a tax credit of £18.75 which gives rise to a gross sum of £93.75.

The tax credit will be regarded as income tax suffered on the aggregate dividend at the rate of 20 per cent. However, the dividend is not liable at the basic rate of 25 per cent and will only involve an individual in liability to income tax at the higher rate of 40 per cent to the extent that the dividend increases taxable income above the basic rate band of

54 *DIVIDENDS RECEIVED*

The personal and married couple's allowance available to Andrew for 1993–94 amounted to £5,165. During the year he received dividends of £1,600 (tax credit £400).

Using these basic facts, it will be assumed that other income chargeable to income tax was £5,300, £10,000, £27,500 and £40,000 respectively.

Other income £5,300

Total income:	£
Other income	5,300
Dividends – gross	2,000
	7,300
Less allowances	5,165
Tax chargeable on	£2,135

Tax payable:	£
On £2,135 at 20 per cent	427.00
Less tax credit	400.00
	£27.00

Other income £10,000

Total income:	£
Other income	10,000
Dividends – gross	2,000
	12,000
Less allowances	5,165
Tax chargeable on	£6,835

	£
Tax payable:	
On first £2,500 at 20 per cent	500.00
On next £2,335 at 25 per cent	583.75
On dividends of £2,000 at 20 per cent	400.00
	1,483.75
Less tax credits	400.00
	£1,083.75

The dividends have been taxed in full and no further tax is due.

Other income £27,500

	£
Total income:	
Other income	27,500
Dividends – gross	2,000
	29,500
Less allowances	5,165
Tax chargeable on	£24,335

	£
Tax payable:	
On first £2,500 at 20 per cent	500.00
On next £19,835 at 25 per cent	4,958.75
On dividends:	
On first £1,365 at 20 per cent	273.00
On balance of £635 at 40 per cent	254.00
	£5,985.75
Less tax credits	400.00
	£5,585.75

This calculation ensures that only to the extent that total income exceeds the basic rate band of £23,700 by £635 will the excess gross dividend of £635 give rise to liability at 40 per cent.

Other income £40,000

	£
Total income:	
Other income	40,000
Dividends – gross	2,000
	42,000
Less allowances	5,165
Tax chargeable on	36,835

	£
Tax payable:	
On first £2,500 at 20 per cent	500.00
On next £21,200 at 25 per cent	5,300.00
On balance of £13,135 at 40 per cent	5,254.00
	£11,054.00
Less tax credits	400.00
	£10,654.00

It is clear that the entire gross dividend of £2,000 is fully taxable at the higher rate of 40 per cent.

£23,700. To achieve this result the dividend is treated as comprising the higher slice of the taxpayer's income.

This will support the following conclusions:

a An individual who is not liable to income tax, due to an insufficiency of income, may obtain a repayment of the tax credit in full.

b An individual who only becomes liable following the receipt of dividends may recover part of the tax credit.

c An individual liable to tax at the lower rate of 20 per cent will neither pay additional tax nor recover any part of the tax credit.

d An individual liable at the basic rate only will neither pay nor recover tax on the dividend unless the dividend increases taxable income beyond the basic rate band.

e An individual liable to tax at the higher rate of 40 per cent will be assessed on the aggregate of the dividend and the tax credit but will receive a reduction in the tax otherwise payable equal to the amount of the credit. As the tax credit is now given at the reduced rate of 20 per cent, this will involve a higher rate liability of 20 per cent on the gross sum.

BUILDING SOCIETY INTEREST

When making payments of interest, or crediting interest to a depositor's account, after April 5th, 1991, a building society will deduct income tax at the basic rate of 25 per cent, leaving only the net sum payable or to be credited. Depositors not liable, or not fully liable, to income tax at the basic rate may recover part, or all, of the tax deducted. Those incurring liability at the higher rate will be assessed to further tax on the gross sum. The 20 per cent lower rate band has no effect on the requirement to deduct income tax at the basic rate of 25 per cent. Nor does the tax credit system, which applies to dividends, have any application to interest payments.

It is apparent that substantial administrative problems would arise if small savers received interest after deduction of income tax at the basic rate and in the absence of tax liability had to reclaim the tax suffered from the Inland Revenue. This problem has been recognised and investors who do not expect to pay income tax may complete a simple registration form. Once this form has been completed and forwarded to the building society concerned, interest will subsequently be paid or credited gross without any deduction of income tax. Should the circumstances of the investor change, the building society must be notified immediately to ensure that in future income tax is deducted from interest. It is possible that some investors may fraudulently complete the registration form or fail to notify the building society of changed circumstances. This is a serious matter as following detection a penalty of up to £3,000 may be incurred.

Many minor children have building society accounts into which pocket money, gifts or earnings are deposited. If sums deposited in a minor child's account by that child's parents, but not by grandparents or others, produce interest in excess of £100 the interest may well be treated as that of the parents. In this situation no registration should be made in an attempt to receive interest gross.

A considerable number of individuals entitled to receive interest gross have failed to register. There will be others having anticipated income close to, or a little in excess of, the threshold at which income tax liability commences who subsequently find there is no liability. These individuals may apply for repayment of excess income tax deducted from payments made in 1993–94 shortly after April 5th, 1994. However, very large numbers of repayment claims must be processed and to avoid undue delay repayments of £50 or more can be claimed at any time in the year of assessment on application to the Inland Revenue.

No tax is deducted from building society TESSAs (see page 133).

BANK DEPOSIT AND OTHER INTEREST

With limited exceptions, which include National Savings Ordinary Accounts, Investment Accounts and Income Bonds, items of interest paid or credited on bank deposits after April 5th, 1991, are discharged net after deduction of income tax at the basic rate of 25 per cent. Those investors unlikely to incur income tax liability may complete a simple registration form which will enable the bank or other person to discharge interest gross. The formalities of registration, the penalties for false declarations

55 *BUILDING SOCIETY INTEREST – BASIC RATE*

A married woman aged 42 earns a salary of £8,500 for 1993–94. She receives interest of £342 on an ordinary building society deposit account and has not registered to receive interest gross. An election has been made to transfer one half of the married couple's allowance.

Total Income:	£	£
Salary		8,500
Building society interest received	342	
Add Tax deducted at 25 per cent	114	
		456
		8,956
Less		
Personal allowance	3,445	
Married couple's allowance – one half	860	4,305
Tax chargeable on		£4,651

Tax payable:	£
On first £2,500 at 20 per cent	500.00
On balance of £2,151 at 25 per cent	537.75
	1,037.75
Less Tax deducted on building society interest	114.00
Tax payable	£923.75

The total tax due is £1,037.75 of which £114 has been suffered by deduction from interest received, leaving the balance to be collected from the salary under the PAYE deduction scheme.

56 BUILDING SOCIETY INTEREST – HIGHER RATE

A single man receives building society interest of £1,245 on a non-TESSA account in 1993–94. His other income for the year amounts to £30,000.

	£	£
Total income:		
Other income		30,000
Building society interest received	1,245	
Add Tax deducted at 25 per cent	415	
		1,660
		31,660
Less Personal allowance		3,445
Tax chargeable on		£28,215

	£
Tax payable:	
Lower rate:	
On first £2,500 at 20 per cent	500.00
Basic rate:	
On next £21,200 at 25 per cent	5,300.00
Higher rate:	
On balance of £4,515 at 40 per cent	1,806.00
	7,606.00
Less Tax deducted on building society interest	415.00
Tax payable	£7,191.00

and procedures for the recovery of excessive basic rate income tax deductions are identical to those which affect building society deposits (see page 126). Banks also may take deposits within the TESSA arrangements and interest credited under these arrangements is not subject to income tax (see page 133).

Individuals over the age of 64 may obtain an increased personal allowance and married couple's allowance. The amount of any increase will require restriction, or perhaps elimination, where total income exceeds £14,200 in 1993–94. When calculating income for this purpose it should not be overlooked that the gross amount of bank, building society or other interest must be included and not only the net sum received or credited.

NATIONAL SAVINGS BANK INTEREST

Interest received on deposits with the National Savings Bank is chargeable to income tax. The assessment for any tax year is based on income received in the preceding year, but special adjustments must be made where a new source arises or an existing source is discontinued.

However, when calculating the total income of an individual for 1993–94, the first £70 of interest received from deposits, other than investment deposits, with the National Savings Bank, is disregarded. If husband and wife each receive interest, both may obtain the £70 exemption. This applies also where husband and wife have a joint holding. Should interest received by one spouse fall below £70 the unabsorbed balance cannot be used to increase the other's exemption limit above £70.

57 *BANK INTEREST RECEIVED AND INCREASED PERSONAL ALLOWANCE*

A married man aged 78 receives pensions amounting to £14,100 in 1993–94. He also receives net building society interest of £1,650 in the same year. No TESSA account was involved and the man is entitled to the full married couple's allowance.

Total income:		£
Pensions		14,100
Building society interest received	1,650	
Add Tax deducted at 25 per cent	550	2,200
		16,300
Less		
Personal allowance	4,370	
Married couple's allowance	2,505	
Maximum	6,875	
Deduct one-half of excess over £14,200 (£16,300 – £14,200)	1,050	5,825
Tax chargeable on		£10,475

Tax payable:	£
On first £2,500 at 20 per cent	500.00
On balance of £7,975 at 25 per cent	1,993.75
	2,493.75
Less Tax deducted on building society interest	550.00
Tax payable	£1,943.75

The gross building society interest of £2,200 has been included to calculate total income. This has had the effect of reducing allowances by £1,050.

NATIONAL SAVINGS CAPITAL BONDS

National Savings capital bonds offer a guaranteed return of interest throughout a five-year period. Interest is not paid out but added, without deducting income tax, to the value of the bond. However, the amount of interest added is liable to income tax as if it was actually received by the bond holder. Liability arises by reference to the interest added in the previous year of assessment, with special adjustments for the opening years of a new source and the closing years of a discontinued source.

GOVERNMENT AND OTHER SECURITIES

A special scheme applies for dealing with interest arising on large holdings of securities. The scheme has no application to shares but extends to Government securities, together with most securities issued by companies and local authorities, among others.

Normally, the price paid to acquire securities, together with proceeds arising from the disposal of those assets, will be calculated by inserting an adjustment for accrued interest. This adjustment has no effect for income tax purposes as the holder actually receiving interest is liable to bear tax on the entire amount of that interest at his or her appropriate rate.

However, the position is otherwise for securities brought within the scheme as interest is treated as accruing on a day to day basis and this will determine the individual's liability to tax where securities are purchased and sold. For example, where securities are purchased between interest payment dates the purchaser will only bear tax on that part of the interest for the period from the purchase date to the end of the interest period. Similarly, where securities are sold the vendor will bear tax on interest from the commencement of the interest period to the date of settlement.

The scheme will only apply if the nominal value of all securities held by an individual in the year of assessment during which the interest period

58 *SAVINGS BANK INTEREST*

A married man receives a salary of £16,000 for 1993–94 and his wife has business profits of £4,850 assessable in the same year. Both have ordinary deposits with the National Savings Bank and the amounts of interest from these deposits otherwise assessable for 1993–94 are as follows:

	£
Husband	90
Wife	37

Assuming neither spouse has reached the age of 65 and the husband is entitled to the full married couple's allowance, the tax payable by the husband will be:

	£	£
Total income:		
Salary		16,000
Interest	90	
Less exemption	70	
		20
		16,020
Less		
Personal allowance	3,445	
Married couple's allowance	1,720	5,165
Tax chargeable on		£10,855

Tax payable:	
On first £2,500 at 20 per cent	500.00
On balance of £8,355 at 25 per cent	2,088.75
	£2,588.75

The liability of the wife will become:

	£	£
Total income:		
Profits		4,850
Interest	37	
Less exemption	37	–
		4,850
Less Personal allowance		3,445
Tax chargeable on		£1,405

Tax payable:	
On £1,405 at 20 per cent	£281.00

ends, or in the previous year, exceeds £5,000. The threshold of £5,000 applies separately to a husband and to his wife. Personal representatives are brought within the scheme if the nominal value of securities held in the deceased person's estate exceeds £5,000.

Individuals and personal representatives who do not retain holdings of this magnitude remain unaffected by the special scheme and continue to suffer income tax on the actual amount of interest received.

59 *GOVERNMENT SECURITIES*

Mr A acquired a holding of securities on May 1st, 1993. Interest at the rate of £6,000 was payable half-yearly on July 1st and January 1st. Interest of £6,000 (less tax) was received by Mr A on July 1st, 1993. He sold his holding, with settlement on December 15th, 1993. If Mr A is not within the special scheme his income for 1993–94 will comprise £6,000, representing the gross equivalent of interest actually received.

However, if, as seems probable, the special scheme applies, Mr A's income will be calculated as follows:

	£
Interest period to July 1st, 1993 – 181 days	
Period of ownership – 61 days	
Taxable $^{61}/_{181} \times$ £6,000	2,022
Interest period to January 1st, 1994 – 184 days	
Period of ownership – 167 days	
Taxable $^{167}/_{184} \times$ £6,000	5,446
Taxable income	£7,468

PURCHASED LIFE ANNUITIES

Life annuities can be purchased from insurance companies and other financial institutions. Each annuity, which may be paid on an annual or some other periodic basis, contains two elements, namely a capital element and an income element. The amount of each element will be determined by the insurance company or institution responsible for the arrangement.

The capital element is effectively a return of the purchase price and will not be liable to income tax. However, the income element is taxable and payments will be received after deduction of income tax at the basic rate. Only the income element will enter into the calculation of the annuitant's total income. The use of the basic rate is not affected by the 20 per cent lower rate band.

SAVE AS YOU EARN

Save As You Earn contracts enable monthly investments to be made throughout a period of five years. At the end of this period, or at the investor's option two years later, the investment may be withdrawn together with a terminal bonus. The bonus is not liable to income tax. Share option related Save As You Earn contracts enable employees to purchase shares in their employing company with the proceeds arising on maturity. Here also the terminal bonus is not liable to income tax.

60 *PURCHASED LIFE ANNUITY*

A widow aged 67 receives a social security retirement pension and a pension from her late husband's former employers aggregating £8,400 for 1993–94. She also receives £1,500 (gross) annually from a purchased life annuity. The annuity contains a capital element of £850 and an income element of £650.

The actual sum received from the annuity in 1993–94 will be:

	£	£
Capital element		850.00
Income element	650.00	
Less Tax at 25 per cent	162.50	487.50
Cash received		£1,337.50

The tax payable will be:

	£
Total income:	
Pensions	8,400
Annuity (income element only)	650
	9,050
Less Personal allowance	4,200
Tax chargeable on	£4,850
Tax payable:	£
On first £2,500 at 20 per cent	500.00
On balance of £2,350 at 25 per cent	587.50
	1,087.50
Less Deducted on annuity	162.50
	£925.00

Save As You Earn contracts are issued by building societies, banks and the Department of National Savings.

PERSONAL EQUITY PLANS

As an incentive to encourage wider share ownership, personal equity plans have been available for several years. Individual plans are managed by plan managers, usually financial institutions, which must be approved by the Inland Revenue. Investment is confined to individuals aged 18 years and above who must be either resident and ordinarily resident in the United Kingdom, or performing duties on behalf of the Crown in some territory overseas.

There are basically two kinds of available plan, namely a general plan and a single company plan. For 1993–94 the maximum permitted cash investment capable of being made by an individual in a general plan is £6,000. The entire sum may be invested in investment or unit trusts. It remains a condition that at least one-half of the investments made by the investment or unit trusts are in United Kingdom ordinary shares or comparable shares in companies incorporated within a Member State of the European Community. Where this 50 per cent level is not achieved the maximum amount of investment capable of being made in unit or investment trusts is limited to £1,500. From April 6th, 1993, it is a further condition that this limited investment will only be recognised if the underlying unit or investment trust holds at least one-half of its investments in shares, which need not necessarily be issued by a United Kingdom company or one in the EC.

It is also possible for an individual to invest up to £3,000 in a single company plan during 1993–94. This is in addition to an investment in a general plan. However, an individual cannot invest in more than one general plan during the year of assessment.

The attraction of a personal equity plan is the exemption from taxation offered to investors. Any dividends paid on investments made by plan managers will have the usual tax credit attached. Managers may obtain repayment of the tax credit from the Inland Revenue on behalf of investors. This ensures that dividend income received by the plan will effectively be realised "gross" without suffering the inroads of income tax. Some relief may also be available for interest on investments made within the plan. Should gains arise from the disposal of assets held by the plan no liability to capital gains tax will arise.

Plan managers charge a fee for their services and the investor cannot obtain any tax relief for this outlay.

Since their introduction in 1986 personal equity plans have grown in popularity and now provide many investors with a convenient method of achieving tax-free investments.

TAX EXEMPT SPECIAL SAVINGS ACCOUNT

A further facility conferring taxation benefits became available on January 1st, 1991. This facility, the Tax Exempt Special Savings Account (TESSA), is operated by authorised banks and building societies. Among the conditions which must be discharged before the account will be recognised for taxation purposes are the following:

a the account holder must be an individual aged at least 18 years;

b the account must be identified as a TESSA;

c the holder of the account must not have any other TESSA;

d the account must not be held on a joint basis;

e the account must not be held for the benefit of any person except the holder;

f the account must not be connected with any other account.

A maximum is placed on the amount which can be deposited in a TESSA throughout a five-year period. Deposits must not exceed £3,000 in the first year or £1,800 in each of years two, three, four and five. In addition, the total deposited must be limited to £9,000.

Where these conditions are satisfied, any interest or bonus added to the account will not become liable to income tax if the account is maintained throughout a full five-year period, or until the death of the account holder, whichever event occurs first. Once the five-year period has come to an end any future interest will become chargeable to income tax but the account holder may close the account and open another TESSA attracting similar tax advantages.

It is possible to contemplate the withdrawal of some interest during the five-year period. The amount withdrawn is not to exceed the interest credited less income tax at the basic rate. However, should interest in excess of the amount calculated on this basis be withdrawn, or any extraction of capital take place, the tax advantages will be lost. All interest will then be treated as the depositor's income, with that interest deemed to arise at the date exemption is abandoned.

INCOME FROM ABROAD

A taxpayer may receive income from abroad which must suffer United Kingdom taxation. As this income has probably been taxed in a foreign country also, it is effectively taxed twice. To avoid the problems of double taxation, agreements have been entered into between the United Kingdom and many foreign countries. These agreements contain a variety of features. Some exempt income from tax in either the foreign country or the United Kingdom and others provide that the foreign tax suffered shall be deducted from the United Kingdom tax due on the same income.

Even where no double tax agreement has been concluded a taxpayer who would otherwise pay tax on the same slice of income both here and abroad is entitled to similar relief.

No relief from double taxation will be granted unless it is claimed by the taxpayer, who must be resident in the United Kingdom. A person not liable to United Kingdom taxation, where, for example, personal allowances exceed income, cannot claim any repayment of foreign tax from the United Kingdom authorities.

Dividends received from overseas companies are not within the United Kingdom "tax credit" system discussed on page 123. However, the income tax charge on those overseas dividends is reduced from 25 per cent to 20 per cent from April 6th, 1993. Increased liability will arise for individuals liable at the higher rate.

HUSBAND AND WIFE –

Joint property

A husband and wife "living together" may jointly retain the ownership of income-producing assets. It is then necessary to allocate any income arising between each party. The general rule is that the income from jointly held assets must be apportioned equally between each spouse. This does not apply to earned income, income from a partnership or to some special types of income where the legislation requires a specific allocation.

Where equal apportionment is appropriate it remains possible for this to be varied by making a joint declaration. The declaration does not enable the parties to impose their own allocation but requires income to be apportioned on the basis of each individual's beneficial interest in the asset.

A declaration could be made at any time before June 6th, 1990, and applied to income arising on any previous date. If a declaration is made after June 5th, 1990, it will only apply to income arising after the date on which the declaration is made.

A separate declaration is required for each jointly owned asset. For example, a husband and his wife may jointly own perhaps five assets.

The declaration may apply to any number between one and four, extend to all assets, or the parties may choose not to make any declaration whatsoever. A declaration is only valid if it reaches HM Inspector of Taxes within a period of 60 days from when it is made.

A declaration once made cannot subsequently be withdrawn and will only cease to apply where the couple separate, one spouse dies or there is a change in the beneficial interests.

61 *JOINT ASSETS*

Mr and Mrs X are the joint owners of commercial property with the husband retaining a beneficial interest of two-thirds and his wife the remaining one-third. Net rental income taxable under Schedule A amounted to £3,000 for 1993–94.

In the absence of a declaration the income will be allocated as follows:

	£
Mr X – one-half	1,500
Mrs X – one-half	1,500
	£3,000

If a declaration is made before the commencement of the year of assessment on April 6th, 1993, the allocation becomes:

	£
Mr X – Beneficial ownership two-thirds	2,000
Mrs X – Beneficial ownership one-third	1,000
	£3,000

A finding that the declaration was only made on, say, October 6th, 1993, and income accrued evenly throughout the year would support the following allocation:

	Mr X £	Mrs X £
Income to October 5th, 1993 – £1,500		
Mr X – one-half	750	
Mrs X – one-half		750
Income from October 5th, 1993 – £1,500		
Mr X – two-thirds	1,000	
Mrs X – one-third		500
	£1,750	£1,250

HUSBAND AND WIFE –

Transfer of assets

A deceptively simple method of transferring future income from one spouse to the other is to transfer the ownership of the asset producing that income. Where the transfer is made by way of outright gift, and without any strings attached, the transfer should achieve the required objective. The position will, however, be otherwise if the transferee does not obtain an interest in all income arising, is bound to apply that income for the benefit or advantage of the transferor, or the transferor can benefit from either income or capital in any circumstances whatsoever. Some caution must therefore be exercised when contemplating the transfer of income-producing assets between a husband and his wife.

Social security benefits

WHILST SOME social security benefits are taxable, many do not incur liability to income tax. A list of the main taxable and non-taxable benefits is shown below:

BENEFITS WHICH ARE TAXABLE (see also notes on page 137)

Industrial Injury Disablement Benefit
Invalid Care Allowance
Jobstart Allowance
Maternity Pay
Old Person's Pension
Retirement Pension
Statutory Sick Pay
Unemployment Benefit
Widowed Mother's Allowance
Widow's Pension

BENEFITS WHICH ARE NOT TAXABLE (see also notes on page 137)

Short-term Benefits

Maternity Allowance
Sickness Benefit

Benefits in respect of children

Child Benefit
Child Dependency Additions
Guardian's Allowance

Industrial Injury Benefits

Constant Attendance Allowance

War Disablement Benefits

Age Allowance
Allowance for Lower Standard of Occupation
Clothing Allowance
Comforts Allowance
Constant Attendance Allowance
Disablement Pension
Exceptionally Severe Disablement Allowance
Severe Occupational Disablement Allowance
Unemployability Supplement
War Pensions Mobility Supplement

Other Benefits

Attendance Allowance
Christmas Bonus
Council Tax Benefit
Disability Living Allowance
Disability Working Allowance
Family Credit
Housing Benefit
Income Support
Invalidity Allowance when paid with Invalidity Pension
Invalidity Benefit
One Parent Benefit
Severe Disablement Allowance
War Orphan's Pension
War Widow's Pension
Widow's Payment

Notes on Social Security Benefits

a Unemployment benefit paid to the unemployed is chargeable to income tax. Additions for children, housing and exceptional circumstances remain exempt from liability. The method of collecting tax is discussed on page 61.

b Income support paid to the unemployed or to the partner of a striking worker will be taxable in whole or in part.

c Payments of short term statutory sick pay made by the recipient's employer are taxable through the PAYE deduction scheme, but long term sickness benefit which the employer is not required to pay remains exempt from liability. Statutory maternity pay is also discharged by employers, with PAYE being deducted where required.

d Before April 6th, 1990 a married woman's retirement pension paid on the basis of her husband's contributions was treated as the husband's income only. On and after this date the pension will be regarded as income of the wife. Where a relevant pension includes an adult dependency addition, the entire pension will also be regarded as that of the recipient.

Deeds of covenant

THROUGHOUT A PERIOD of many years payments made under a properly drawn deed of covenant have formed a popular method of transferring income from one person to another. In some cases payments have been made for valuable and sufficient consideration but the great majority have been devoid of any consideration whatsoever. The continuing use of deeds of covenant as a tax efficient arrangement was severely restricted by the withdrawal of relief for many covenants made after March 14th, 1988. This withdrawal has no effect on covenants in favour of recognised charities, nor does it apply to the diminishing list of non-charitable covenants entered into before that date.

To achieve a proper understanding of the effect which payments made under deed of covenant may have on taxation liabilities a distinction must be drawn between:

a charitable covenants; and

b other covenants.

CHARITABLE COVENANTS

Charitable covenants must require payments to be made to a named charity throughout a period capable of exceeding three years. Many deeds drawn in simple form will be suitable but professional advice should be obtained before entering into deeds containing unusual provisions.

If a covenant is capable of being terminated within the initial three-year period it will not be recognised for tax purposes. To avoid this some covenants are drawn in a form which enables termination to occur after the end of three years. Previously such covenants ceased to be recognised immediately the power arose, but in 1992 a change was made enabling this type of covenant to continue, should the parties so require, without the need for a fresh deed.

When making payments under a deed of covenant drawn in favour of a charity the payer should deduct income tax at the basic rate. This will involve a deduction at the rate of 25 per cent for payments made in 1993–94. The rate at which tax must be deducted is not influenced by the 20 per cent lower rate band. If the payer has taxable income equal to, or in excess of, the gross sum payable, and chargeable at the basic rate, he or she may retain the income tax deducted. This effectively provides relief from income tax at the basic rate if, but only if, the payer exercises the right to deduct tax.

Where the payer's taxable income is not sufficiently substantial to incur liability at the basic rate on an amount equal to payments made under deed of covenant, income tax similar to the amount of tax deducted must be accounted for to the Inland Revenue. This situation may arise where income is exceeded by allowances and reliefs, or occasionally where liability arises at only the lower rate of 20 per cent. The possibility of such a development should not be overlooked particularly following the introduction of independent taxation. For years up to and including that ending on April 5th, 1990, it was possible to aggregate the income of a husband and wife "living together" for the purpose of establishing whether covenanted payments made by either spouse were covered by taxable income. This can no longer be achieved as both husband and wife are now independently assessed. A married woman with insufficient income may be well advised to refrain from entering into any deed of covenant as this might involve an unexpected commitment to taxation.

Some married couples enter into joint covenants. The Inland Revenue will treat payments made under such covenants as discharged in equal proportions by each spouse, unless there is evidence supporting a different conclusion.

62 *CHARITABLE COVENANTS*

Mr W is a married man aged 54 earning an annual salary of £21,000 and entitled to the full married couple's allowance. During 1993–94 he made a payment of £500, less tax, to a charity as required by a properly drawn deed of covenant.

The actual payment made will be:

	£
Gross sum	500
Less Income tax at 25 per cent	125
Actual payment	£375

The income tax payable by Mr W in 1993–94 will be:

	£	£
Total income		21,000
Less		
Personal allowance	3,445	
Married couple's allowance	1,720	5,165
Tax chargeable on		£15,835

Tax payable:	
On first £2,500 at 20 per cent	500.00
On balance of £13,335 at 25 per cent	3,333.75
	£3,833.75

As Mr W suffers tax at the basic rate on an amount of income in excess of the gross covenanted payment, he may retain the tax deducted of £125.

63 RESTRICTION OF RELIEF

Mrs P, a married woman aged 40 living with her husband has earnings of £3,200 for 1993–94. During the year she makes an annual payment of £300, less tax, under a charitable covenant. The actual payment made will be:

	£
Gross sum	300
Less tax at 25 per cent	75
Actual payment	£225

The income tax payable will be:	£
Total income	3,200
Less Personal allowance	3,445
Tax chargeable on	NIL
Tax payable:	
On £300 at 25 per cent	£75.00

Although income is fully covered by the personal allowance, income tax must be charged at the basic rate of 25 per cent on £300. This ensures that tax of £75 deducted from the annual payment is fully accounted for.

In those cases where the payer's income is sufficiently substantial to incur income tax liability at the higher rate of 40 per cent, covenanted payments may be offset against income otherwise chargeable at that rate.

Thus an individual having suffered sufficient tax on income at the top rate of 40 per cent and making payments of, say, £10,000 (less tax) to a charity obtains the following tax reliefs for 1993–94:

a £2,500 (£10,000 at 25 per cent) by deduction; and

b £1,500 (£10,000 at 40 per cent less 25 per cent) against higher rate liability.

The net cost of the payments becomes £6,000 (£10,000 less £2,500 plus £1,500).

The charity receiving payments under a properly drawn deed of covenant may expect to recover income tax suffered at the basic rate.

Further matters relating to payments made under charitable deeds of covenant are discussed on page 143. In addition, single donations made under the Gift Aid scheme are effectively treated as discharged in a manner similar to payments under deed of covenant (see page 145).

OTHER COVENANTS

Payments made under a non-charitable deed of covenant entered into before March 15th, 1988, continue to be recognised for taxation purposes. It remains a condition, however, that the deed of covenant was examined by H M Inspector of Taxes not later than June 30th, 1988. In the absence of such an examination the deed will not be accepted and payments made after April 5th, 1988 must be entirely disregarded for taxation purposes.

Where a non-charitable covenant is accepted by the Inspector the

64 COVENANTS – HIGHER RATE RELIEF

A married man has business profits of £70,000 assessable for 1993–94. During the year he made payments under deed of covenant aggregating £20,000 (gross) to several charities.

The actual aggregate payments made to charity in 1993–94 will be:

	£
Gross sums	20,000
Less income tax at 25 per cent	5,000
Actual payments	£15,000

The income tax payable, assuming the husband is entitled to the full married couple's allowance, will be calculated as follows:

		£
Total income		70,000
Less		
Personal allowance	3,445	
Married couple's allowance	1,720	5,165
Tax chargeable on		£64,835

	£
Tax payable:	
Lower rate:	
On first £2,500 at 20 per cent	500.00
Basic rate:	
On next £21,200 at 25 per cent	5,300.00
On next £20,000 at 25 per cent (re covenanted payments)	5,000.00
Higher rate:	
On balance of £21,135 at 40 per cent	8,454.00
Tax payable	£19,254.00

Note:
Relief at the basic rate on £20,000 has been obtained by deducting, and retaining, tax at 25 per cent on payment. It is therefore necessary to ensure that the above calculation confines relief to rates in excess of 25 per cent on this outlay. This has been achieved by imposing tax of 25 per cent on £20,000 of taxable income.

payer will deduct and retain or account for income tax at the basic rate of 25 per cent for 1993–94 in a manner identical to that which applies to a charitable deed of covenant. However, relief is restricted to the deduction of income tax at the basic rate on payment. It is not possible to obtain relief at the higher rate of 40 per cent.

Payments made under a non-charitable deed of covenant will have no effect for taxation purposes where the covenant was entered into after March 14th, 1988. The payer cannot deduct income tax at the basic rate and must satisfy payments "gross". The recipient will not treat the amount received as taxable income, nor can any attempt be made to recover income tax allegedly deducted. Shortly stated, payments under a non-charitable deed of covenant executed after March 14th, 1988, have no effect whatsoever for income tax purposes. Similar comments apply to non-charitable deeds executed before that date for payments made after April 5th, 1988, if the document was not inspected by H M Inspector of Taxes before July 1st in the same year.

65 OTHER COVENANTED PAYMENTS

A father receives a salary of £25,000 in 1993–94 and makes an annual payment of £2,500, less tax, to his 24-year-old son who is attending university. The covenant was made before March 15th, 1988 and has been accepted as qualifying by the Inland Revenue.

The actual payment made in 1993–94 will be:

	£
Gross sum	2,500
Less Income tax at 25 per cent	625
Actual payment	£1,875

On the assumption the father is entitled to the married couple's allowance, his tax liability becomes:

	£	£
Total income		25,000
Less Personal allowance	3,445	
Married couple's allowance	1,720	5,165
Tax chargeable on		£19,835
Tax payable:		
On first £2,500 at 20 per cent		500.00
On balance of £17,335 at 25 per cent		4,333.75
		£4,833.75

As tax is chargeable at the basic rate on a sum in excess of £2,500, the father may retain the tax of £625 deducted when making the annual payment. If the income of the father had been sufficient to incur liability at the higher rate of 40 per cent, the covenanted payment would not support any further relief.

It may well be possible for the son to obtain a complete or partial repayment of the tax deducted on application to the Inland Revenue.

Charitable bodies

GENERAL EXEMPTION

RECOGNISED CHARITIES are provided with a general exemption from tax where income is applied for charitable purposes. This exemption extends to rents and other receipts from land, together with dividends and interest, among others. Therefore a charity may invest surplus funds and obtain a return which is not eroded by taxation liabilities. Where income is received after deduction, or deemed deduction, of tax, for example interest and dividends, the charity may obtain a repayment of tax suffered from the Inland Revenue.

Trading profits earned by a charity are, however, exempt only where either:

a the trade is exercised in the course of the actual carrying out of a primary purpose of the charity; or

b the work in connection with the trade is mainly carried out by beneficiaries of the charity.

Failure to satisfy one of these conditions will result in the trading profits remaining liable to tax, notwithstanding that the proprietor of the business is a charity.

INDUCEMENTS FOR CHARITABLE FUNDING

In addition to exemptions from tax for income arising on investments made, or profits earned, by a charity, several reliefs are available to encourage charitable funding.

Deeds of covenant

On making payments under deed of covenant to a charity an individual may deduct and usually retain income tax at the basic rate of 25 per cent for 1993–94. Additionally, the charity may obtain repayment of the tax deducted from the Inland Revenue. Where the payer is liable to tax at the higher rate of 40 per cent he or she may obtain further relief as shown on page 140. Thus the cost to the covenantor is reduced and the charity obtains the full benefit of the gross payment. If the donor merely made a cash gift equal to the gross sum, no deduction of income tax could be made and the cost to the donor would be correspondingly increased.

The position may be otherwise if sufficiently large gifts are made to qualify for relief under the Gift Aid arrangements outlined on page 145.

The advantages of making payments under deed of covenant are not confined to individuals, as similar payments may be made by companies. These payments enable the corporate payer to obtain relief for corporation tax and also confer an entitlement on the recipient charity to recover tax suffered by deduction.

Deeds of covenant often provide for the payment of a fixed annual sum which must be grossed up at the basic rate prevailing at the time of payment. The advantage of this arrangement is that the covenantor may continue to make the same cash payment annually, notwithstanding any change in the basic rate of income tax.

As a general rule, payments made under deed of covenant will only be recognised for tax purposes if they produce no benefit for the payer and place no obligation on the payee to provide some advantage. Small benefits or advantages may be disregarded but those of any substance may not. This prevents subscriptions being paid in the form of covenanted payments and qualifying for tax relief. However, a relaxation affects payments made to a limited range of charities whose sole or main purpose is the preservation of property or the conservation of wildlife for the public benefit. This also includes museums and supporters' organisations having charitable status. For payments made to these charities, any right of entry to view property or perhaps a collection will not be treated as a benefit which may otherwise disqualify a deed, if the right is limited to the covenantor, or members of the covenantor's family.

Company donations

Although payments made under covenant provide the payer with tax relief, there is no general relief for isolated donations. An exception concerns donations made by a limited range of companies. The maximum amount of qualifying donations is not to exceed 3 per cent of the ordinary dividends paid by the company concerned. Closely controlled companies are excluded from this arrangement, which is therefore confined to larger public companies. On making a qualifying donation the paying company will deduct income tax at the basic rate of 25 per cent and account for the deduction to the Inland Revenue. This will usually enable the company to subtract the gross sum when calculating liability to corporation tax. The recipient charity may then claim repayment of the tax deducted in a manner similar to that available for tax suffered on payments under deeds of covenant. An alternative and substantially more widely used method of obtaining relief is available under the Gift Aid arrangements (see page 145).

Payroll deduction scheme

Limited income tax relief will be available where charitable donations are made under an approved payroll deduction scheme. These schemes must be operated by an employer through an approved charity agency. Membership is voluntary but those employees who join may contribute up to £900 in 1993–94. Contributions are subtracted from each employee's earnings and the aggregate sums collected paid to an approved agency which is responsible for distributing those funds to the required charities. The qualifying contributions are also deducted from earnings when calculating the net sum chargeable to income tax. This effectively provides contributing employees with tax relief for payments made under the payroll deduction scheme.

Costs incurred by an employer when operating the scheme may be subtracted when calculating the employer's liability to taxation. In addition, relief can be obtained where the employer contributes towards the costs of a charitable agency administering the employer's scheme.

Gift Aid scheme

As a further inducement to charitable giving, a Gift Aid scheme was launched on October 1st, 1990. This scheme encourages individuals to make lump sum donations to charity and obtain income tax relief. If the donations are to qualify the following conditions, among others, must be discharged:

a There must be a payment in money.

b The payment must not be subject to any condition leading to repayment.

c The payment must not comprise a covenanted payment to charity.

d The payment must not fall within the payroll deduction scheme.

e No benefit of any substance must be receivable by the donor in return for the donation.

f The sum paid must not be less than £250. An increased threshold of £400 applied for payments made before March 16th, 1993.

Where the above conditions are satisfied the donor is provided with a choice. He or she may decline to make any attempt to obtain tax relief, in which eventuality the transaction is entirely disregarded for taxation purposes. However, the individual may provide a certificate confirming that the above conditions have been satisfied and that any tax liability will be discharged. This certificate will identify the donation made as a net sum after deduction of income tax at the basic rate of 25 per cent for 1993–94. The donor must treat the payment on a basis identical to payments made under deed of covenant. The tax deemed to have been deducted can usually be retained and relief may be available at the higher rate of income tax on the gross equivalent. Should the donor have insufficient income to absorb the gross payment he or she will be required to account to the Inland Revenue for the income tax deemed to have been deducted.

Companies also may make single donations under the Gift Aid scheme. Income tax will be deducted at the basic rate on payment and accounted for to the Inland Revenue, if of course the required certificate is forthcoming. The gross amount of donations can then be set against profits chargeable to corporation tax.

No upper limit is placed on the maximum lump sum which individuals or companies may contribute under Gift Aid, providing the minimum of £250 (or £400 where appropriate) is exceeded.

66 *GIFT AID SCHEME*

A married man aged 42 has business profits of £70,000 assessable for 1993–94. During the year he made a single donation of £15,000 to a recognised charity. The payment satisfied the requirements of the Gift Aid scheme and a certificate was provided.

The actual payment of £15,000 must be treated as a net sum calculated as follows:

	£
Gross sum	20,000
Less Income tax at 25 per cent	5,000
Actual payment	£15,000

The income tax payable, assuming the full married couple's allowance can be obtained, will be calculated as follows:

	£	£
Total income		70,000
Less Personal allowance	3,445	
Married couple's allowance	1,720	5,165
Tax chargeable on		£64,835

	£
Tax payable:	
Lower rate:	
On first £2,500 at 20 per cent	500.00
Basic rate:	
On next £21,200 at 25 per cent	5,300.00
On next £20,000 at 25 per cent	5,000.00
Higher rate:	
On balance of £21,135 at 40 per cent	8,454.00
Tax payable	£19,254.00

Note:
Relief at the basic rate on £20,000 is deemed to have been obtained by deducting, and retaining, tax at 25 per cent on payment. It is therefore necessary to ensure that the above calculation confines relief to rates in excess of 25 per cent on the outlay. This is achieved by imposing tax at the basic rate of 25 per cent on £20,000.

It will be noted that the tax liability in this case is identical to that shown by Example 64 on page 141 which involved payments of £20,000 made under deed of covenant.

Gifts of business equipment

A novel form of relief is made available for business gifts to educational establishments where the gift is made after March 18th, 1991. The relief is available to individuals, partnerships and companies carrying on a trade. Only the transfer of "equipment" is brought within this relief, with "equipment" comprising plant and machinery.

Where the equipment is either manufactured or sold by the business the gift of that equipment will not require any adjustment in the calculation of trading profits. However, as the cost of the equipment, or the raw materials and other costs involved in manufacture, will be included in the computation of profits, relief is effectively obtained. In those cases where the equipment has qualified for capital allowances, its transfer will be treated as taking place for no consideration.

The transfer must be made to a recognised educational establishment, including a university, polytechnic, college and school.

Company dividends

The tax credit of one-third attaching to dividends paid by United Kingdom companies in 1992–93 was reduced to one-quarter in 1993–94. Charities able to reclaim the amount of the tax credit from the Inland Revenue therefore suffered a reduction in income. For example, the tax credit on a dividend of £75 paid in 1992–93 was £25. The credit on the same dividend in 1993–94 has been reduced to £18.75. Charities receiving a great deal of dividend income would therefore suffer a substantial reduction in aggregate receipts.

To offset this reduction, special claims may be made by charities in 1993–94 and each of the three following years. In addition to claims for repayment of the tax credit, charities may recover from the Inland Revenue an amount representing:

a one-fifteenth of dividends received in 1993–94;

b one-twentieth of dividends received in 1994–95;

c one-thirtieth of dividends received in 1995–96; and

d one-sixtieth of dividends received in 1996–97.

These special payments will have no effect whatsoever on companies paying the dividends involved.

Other reliefs

Wide-ranging reliefs from capital gains tax and inheritance tax are also available where assets are transferred to charitable bodies.

Husband and wife

Marriage

FOR THE YEAR of assessment in which a couple marry, each will receive the normal personal allowance, suitably increased for those over the age of 64.

A married couple's allowance of £1,720 will be available for 1993–94 if the ceremony takes place before May 6th, 1993. The married couple's allowance may be increased to some higher figure for those over the age of 64 or 74 years.

However, the amount of the married couple's allowance will be reduced by one-twelfth for each complete month after April 5th until marriage occurs. In those cases where the amount of the increased married couple's allowance for older persons must be restricted by reason of the husband's income exceeding £14,200 the restriction must firstly be applied and the one-twelfth limitation then made applicable to the reduced married couple's allowance only.

It is possible that the husband will be entitled to the additional personal allowance for a child or children in the year of marriage. He may then choose whether to retain that allowance or abandon the allowance and obtain the married couple's allowance. This choice applies for the year of marriage only. Whilst the additional personal allowance will be greater, when making the choice it should not be overlooked that any part of this allowance which cannot be used by the husband is incapable of being transferred to the wife. In contrast, any unused part of the married couple's allowance can be transferred.

The wife may retain the additional personal allowance for the year of marriage if the qualifying child was resident with her before the ceremony took place. Any unused blind person's allowance can be transferred between the couple in that year.

It is possible that a married man already entitled to the married couple's allowance for a year of assessment re-marries in the same year, perhaps following the death of his first wife. In such a situation there will be no restriction to the married couple's allowance, which may be obtained in full. However, only one married couple's allowance can be obtained and not a separate allowance for each wife.

Although a husband may have more than one wife as permitted by his religious or other beliefs, only a single married couple's allowance will be available for each year.

67 *RESTRICTED HIGHER PERSONAL ALLOWANCE*

Janet and Mark, both aged 24, were married on November 14th, 1993. The married couple's allowance for 1993–94 is £717, calculated as follows:

	£
Full married couple's allowance	1,720
Deduct period before marriage 7/12ths of £1,720	1,003
Married couple's allowance available	£717

In addition, each individual will obtain a full year's personal allowance of £3,445.

68 *YEAR OF MARRIAGE*

Michael and Sarah were married on October 19th, 1993. Michael earns a salary of £16,000 per annum and Sarah £8,500 per annum. Michael is to obtain the full married couple's allowance. The tax payable for 1993–94 is calculated as follows:

Michael	£	£	£
Total income			16,000
Less			
Personal allowance		3,445	
Married couple's allowance	1,720		
Deduct period before marriage ½ of £1,720	860		
		860	
			4,305
Tax chargeable on			£11,695
Tax payable:			
On first £2,500 at 20 per cent			500.00
On balance of £9,195 at 25 per cent			2,298.75
			£2,798.75

Sarah	£
Total income	8,500
Less Personal allowance	3,445
Tax chargeable on	£5,055
Tax payable:	
On first £2,500 at 20 per cent	500.00
On balance of £2,555 at 25 per cent	638.75
	£1,138.75

The wife may elect to obtain one-half of the basic married couple's allowance. Husband and wife may jointly elect that the entire basic allowance should be transferred to the wife (see page 13). This election must be made during the year of marriage.

Death of spouse

WHERE A HUSBAND and wife are "living together" and the husband dies, no apportionment of allowances is made. A full year's personal allowance will be granted when calculating the liability of the deceased husband. In addition, a full year's married couple's allowance will be available. It is possible for the personal representatives administering the estate of the deceased husband to transfer any unused married couple's allowance for 1993–94 to the widow.

In the year of her husband's death the widow will obtain the normal personal allowance. In addition, she will qualify for a widow's bereavement allowance. This allowance will be available for the following year also, unless she re-marries in the year of her husband's death. If the widow has a qualifying child she should be entitled to receive the additional personal allowance.

On the death of his wife the surviving widower is entitled to a full year's married couple's allowance for the year in which death occurs, unless an election has been made to transfer any part of that allowance to the wife. The allowance will not be available for later years unless the widower re-marries. Although a widow may obtain a widow's bereavement allowance, usually for two consecutive years, no similar allowance is available to a widower.

PENSIONERS AND ELDERLY PERSONS

Pensioners and elderly persons are liable to tax in exactly the same manner as other individuals but the increased personal allowance and increased married couple's allowance mentioned on pages 8 and 9 may be available to those who are in receipt of income falling below, or not substantially exceeding, £14,200 for 1993–94.

Retirement pensions payable under the state scheme and those received from a former employer are subject to tax. A state retirement pension received by a married woman is treated as her income, whether or not it arises from contributions made by the wife or by her husband. Where only small sums of tax are involved on retirement pensions and other income the Inland Revenue may refrain from raising assessments (see page 64).

CHILDREN'S INCOME

Income accruing to a child will not usually be treated as that of the child's parents. Special rules apply, however, where a parent creates a settlement for, or makes gifts to, such a child. Income arising from the

69 DEATH OF HUSBAND

Mr and Mrs G had been married for many years but the husband died on August 7th, 1993. Income assessable in 1993–94 was as follows:

Before death	
Mr G	£
Earnings	8,700
Investment income (gross)	390
Mrs G	
Earnings	3,750
Investment income (gross)	220
After death	
Mrs G	£
Pension and taxable social security benefits	4,900
Earnings	6,800
Investment income (gross)	350

Neither individual was over the age of 64 and no election had been made to transfer the married couple's allowance.

Tax payable will be calculated as follows:

Deceased husband (to date of death)		
Total income:	£	£
Own earnings		8,700
Own investment income		390
		9,090
Less		
Personal allowance	3,445	
Married couple's allowance	1,720	
		5,165
Tax chargeable on		£3,925
Tax payable:		
On first £2,500 at 20 per cent		500.00
On balance of £1,425 at 25 per cent		356.25
		£856.25

Mrs G		
Total income:	£	£
Pension and social security benefits		4,900
Own earnings (£3,750 + £6,800)		10,550
Own investment income (£220 + £350)		570
		16,020
Less		
Personal allowance	3,445	
Widow's bereavement allowance	1,720	
		5,165
Tax chargeable on		£10,855
Tax payable:		
On first £2,500 at 20 per cent		500.00
On balance of £8,355 at 25 per cent		£2,088.75
		£2,588.75

settlement or gift may then be treated as that of the parent until the child reaches the age of 18 or marries, whichever event first occurs. This only arises if the income exceeds £100 in 1993–94.

A minor child can obtain the benefit of a personal allowance of £3,445 for 1993–94 if income received is chargeable to income tax as the child's income.

Divorce and separation

MARRIAGE BREAKDOWN

Where a husband and wife are separated under an order of a court of competent jurisdiction, by deed of separation, or are in fact separated in such circumstances that the separation is likely to be permanent, the couple will be treated as not "living together" for income tax purposes. The loss of this status may affect the future availability of allowances. It may also have some application for capital gains tax purposes on the treatment of assets transferred between the parties.

Year of separation

For the year of assessment in which separation occurs the husband will obtain a full year's married couple's allowance. There will be no reduction in the amount of the allowance, providing the couple were "living together" at some time during the year of assessment. It will remain possible for the husband to transfer any unused part of the married couple's allowance to his separated wife for the year of separation.

The wife will receive the normal personal allowance for 1993–94, perhaps increased to some higher amount if she is over the age of 64. In addition, where a wife has a qualifying child living with her after the date of separation she may obtain the additional personal allowance of £1,720.

Exceptionally, a husband who was separated from his wife on April 5th, 1990, may obtain the married couple's allowance if he is wholly maintaining the wife but obtains no relief for his outlay (see page 23).

MAINTENANCE PAYMENTS

Payments will frequently be made by a husband to his separated wife, or by a former husband to his divorced wife, under a binding legal agreement recorded in a separation deed or similar document or under the terms of a United Kingdom court order. The nature and treatment of these and other payments for taxation purposes will be governed by the date on which the order or agreement was concluded. It is therefore necessary to examine separately:

a payments made under "old" orders and agreements, and

b payments made under "new" orders and agreements.

70 *YEAR OF SEPARATION*

Mr and Mrs H, both in their thirties, were living together until July 1993 when they permanently separated. There were two children, aged 10 and 7 years, who continued to reside with their mother after the separation. Both parents were employed, with Mr H receiving earnings of £20,000 and his wife earnings of £9,500 in 1993–94. No maintenance payments were made and the husband was entitled to the full married couple's allowance.

The tax payable by Mr H will be:

	£	£
Total income		20,000
Less		
Personal allowance	3,445	
Married couple's allowance	1,720	5,165
Tax payable on		£14,835

Tax payable:	
On first £2,500 at 20 per cent	500.00
On balance of £12,335 at 25 per cent	3,083.75
	£3,583.75

The tax payable by Mrs H becomes:

	£	£
Total income		9,500
Less		
Personal allowance	3,445	
Additional personal allowance	1,720	5,165
Tax payable on		£4,335

Tax payable:	
On first £2,500 at 20 per cent	500.00
On balance of £1,835 at 25 per cent	458.75
	£058.75

As the husband was living with his wife during part of the year, a full year's married couple's allowance is available. The wife can obtain the additional personal allowance as she has a qualifying child.

OLD ORDERS AND AGREEMENTS

The first group incorporates payments made under:

a court orders made before March 15th, 1988;

b court orders applied for before March 16th, 1988 and made not later than June 30th in the same year;

c maintenance agreements made before March 15th, 1988; and

d court orders or maintenance agreements made on or after March 15th, 1988, which vary or replace earlier orders or agreements.

The maintenance agreements referred to in **c** and **d** must be binding documents concluded between the parties. Not only is it necessary for these agreements to have existed before March 15th, 1988, but they must also have been examined by H M Inspector of Taxes not later than June 30th in the same year if they are to be recognised for taxation purposes. Failure to achieve recognition destroys relief for payments made after April 5th, 1988.

To obtain relief for payments in 1993–94 under "old" orders or agreements it must be shown that the payments were made:

a to one of the parties of a marriage, including a marriage which has been dissolved or annulled, to or for the benefit of the other party to the marriage and for the maintenance of the other party; or

b to any person under 21 years of age for his own benefit, maintenance or education; or

c to any person for the benefit, maintenance or education of a person under 21 years of age.

All payments falling in the "old" group will be made gross without deducting income tax.

The payer will obtain income tax relief for payments made in each year of assessment up to an amount not exceeding the payments qualifying for relief in 1988–89 (12 months ending on April 5th, 1989).

71 *PAYMENTS UNDER "OLD" ORDERS*

A husband and wife were divorced in 1983. Under the terms of a pre-1988 court order the former husband was required to pay maintenance at the rate of £500 per month. His income for 1993–94 was £27,500. The former wife had no other income.

The tax liability of the former husband will be as follows:

	£	£
Total income		27,500
Less		
Personal allowance	3,445	
Maintenance payments	6,000	9,445
Tax chargeable on		£18,055
Tax payable:		
On first £2,500 at 20 per cent		500.00
On balance of £15,555 at 25 per cent		3,888.75
		£4,388.75

The tax liability of the former wife becomes:

	£
Total income	6,000
Less Exempt	1,720
	4,280
Less Personal allowance	3,445
Tax chargeable on	£835
Tax payable:	
On £835 at 20 per cent	£167.00

These limits will take account of any amending court order or agreement made before April 6th, 1989, but subject to this any future increase will not obtain relief.

The recipient will be taxable on the amount received, or if lower, the amount taxable in 1988–89, after subtracting an amount equal to the married couple's allowance for the year of receipt.

An election may be made to adopt the "new" rules outlined on page 156. This could be beneficial where the level of payments made in 1988–89 falls below the married couple's allowance for a future year.

72 *VARIATION OF ORDER*

Using the basic facts in Example 71, let it be assumed that in September 1988 the former wife obtained an order increasing the monthly payments from £500 to £700, with the first revised payment falling due in October of that year.

The payments made by the former husband in 1988–89 then became:

	£
6 × £500	3,000
6 × £700	4,200
	£7,200

The aggregate amount payable in 1988–89, namely £7,200, will establish the amount which can be recognised for future years. The revised calculation of tax payable then becomes:

Former husband

	£	£
Total income		27,500
Less Personal allowance	3,445	
Maintenance payments restricted	7,200	10,645
Tax chargeable on		£16,855
Tax payable:		
On first £2,500 at 20 per cent		500.00
On balance of £14,355 at 25 per cent		3,588.75
		£4,088.75

Former wife

	£
Total income:	
Maintenance payments – restricted	7,200
Less Exempt	1,720
	5,480
Less Personal allowance	3,445
Tax chargeable on	£2,035
Tax payable:	
On first £2,035 at 20 per cent	£407.00

Although the actual maintenance payments made in 1993–94 were £8,400 (£700 × 12), the amount in excess of payments due in 1988–89 must be disregarded.

NEW ORDERS AND AGREEMENTS

The second group incorporates payments made under "new" court orders and maintenance agreements concluded after March 14th, 1988, other than:

a Court orders applied for before March 16th, 1988, and made not later than June 30th in the same year; and

b Court orders or maintenance agreements varying orders or agreements made before March 15th, 1988, or falling within **a**.

All payments made under orders and agreements of this nature will be discharged gross in 1993–94 without deducting income tax.

Where a divorced former spouse or separated spouse is required to make payments to the other spouse income tax relief can be obtained on the smaller of:

a the payments made in 1993–94, and

b £1,720, which is equal to the married couple's allowance for the year.

This relief continues to apply, subject to an adjustment for the appropriate married couple's allowance, until the recipient re-marries, if at all. In the somewhat unusual case where an individual is making payments to more than one divorced former spouse or separated spouse all payments must be aggregated when establishing the £1,720 limitation.

73 *PAYMENTS UNDER "NEW" ORDERS*

Mr J separated from his wife in 1989–90. Under a court order made on August 12th, 1990, Mr J was required to make monthly payments of £500 to his separated wife; the first payment falling due on August 15th, 1990.
Mr J received a salary of £25,500 for 1993–94 but his separated wife received no other income.

Payments made under the court order in 1993–94 will aggregate £6,000 (12 × £500). Mr J will obtain relief on £1,720, which is less than the payments made. His liability for 1993–94 becomes:

		£
Total income		25,500
Less	£	
Personal allowance	3,445	
Maintenance payments	1,720	5,165
Tax chargeable on		£20,335
Tax payable:		
On first £2,500 at 20 per cent		500.00
On balance of £17,835 at 25 per cent		4,458.75
		£4,958.75

The separated wife has no taxable income as the payments received from her husband are ignored. There is no liability to tax, nor can the wife obtain any tax repayment as no tax has been suffered.

Apart from limited relief where payments are made to a divorced former spouse or a separated spouse, no other tax relief whatsoever will be available to the payer. It follows that relief cannot be obtained for payments made to a child or those falling due under an affiliation order.

The relief based on the smaller of **a** or **b** is available at the payer's top rate suffered for 1993–94. Relief will be limited to the lower rate of 20 per cent only for 1994–95.

In the case of all payments falling within the second group and made under a court order or maintenance agreement, the recipient is immune from any taxation liability.

CHILD SUPPORT AGENCY

In April 1993 the Child Support Agency became responsible for a great deal of work associated with child maintenance. Included in this work is the collection of certain maintenance payments which are then forwarded to the person entitled. This function will not affect the treatment of maintenance payments for tax purposes, notwithstanding the involvement of an "intermediary".

RECONCILIATION

It is possible that a separated couple achieve a reconciliation. For the year of assessment in which this occurs a full year's married couple's allowance will be available.

Administration

Repayment of tax

SOME ITEMS OF investment income are received after deduction of income tax at the basic rate of 25 per cent for 1993–94. These may include interest on building society and bank deposits, although many depositors not liable to income tax may arrange to receive interest gross. Other examples of income received after deduction of income tax include interest on many Government securities and annuities. Income tax is not strictly deducted from dividends paid by United Kingdom companies but each dividend has a tax credit equal to one-quarter of the sum received which effectively represents income tax at the rate of 20 per cent on the aggregate amount.

Where tax has been suffered by deduction it may be possible to obtain a complete or partial repayment. This may arise where the recipient is exempt from income tax and does not receive the full benefit of personal and other allowances from direct assessment on other income, or is not fully liable to tax on the amount deducted or that treated as deducted. Repayment situations are not confined to income tax suffered on investment income but may arise where excessive deductions have been made under the PAYE scheme, where there are claims for loss relief or claims are submitted for some other relief.

74 *REPAYMENT CLAIM*

The total income of a widower, aged 72, for 1993–94, was as follows:

	£	£
Retirement pension		2,917
Dividends received	960	
Add Tax credits at ¼th	240	
		1,200
Total income		£4,117

The taxpayer is entitled to a personal allowance of £4,200 and as total income does not exceed this amount no tax is due. The tax credits of £240 on dividends received may be reclaimed from the Inland Revenue.

75 *REPAYMENT CLAIM*

A single woman, aged 58, receives an annuity of £6,000 (tax deducted £1,500), building society interest of £600 (tax deducted £150) and cash dividends of £1,200 for 1993–94.

Total income:	£	£
Annuity (gross)		6,000
Dividends received	1,200	
Add Tax credits at ¼th	300	
		1,500
Building society interest (gross)		600
		8,100
Less Personal allowance		3,445
Tax chargeable on		£4,655

Tax payable:		£
On first £2,500 at 20 per cent		500.00
On next £655 at 25 per cent		163.75
On dividends of £1,500 at 20 per cent		300.00
		963.75
Less		
Tax on annuity	1,500.00	
Tax credits	300.00	
Tax on interest	150.00	
		1,950.00
Repayment due		£986.25

For 1992–93 and earlier years the tax credit attaching to a dividend effectively represented tax suffered at the basic rate of 25 per cent. The credit has been reduced to 20 per cent for 1993–94 and shareholders entitled to any repayment will only receive the appropriate sum at the rate of 20 per cent.

Stringent time limits apply for submitting claims and exemptions and there is a wide range of different limits which must be observed. However, claims for the repayment of income tax suffered may be forwarded within a period of six years following the end of the year of assessment to which the claim relates. Such claims cannot strictly be submitted until after the end of the year of assessment. However, where tax in excess of £50 has been suffered on building society interest or bank interest and that tax is available for repayment, claims can be submitted at any time in the year of assessment. Before submitting such repayment claims the claimant should consider whether it is possible to arrange for interest to be received "gross", or indeed that a claim for repayment is justified.

The effect of claims for the repayment of tax suffered by deduction is shown by the examples on pages 158–160.

Where a repayment of tax claimed for a year of assessment has not been made within twelve months after the end of that year, the taxpayer may become entitled to receive a repayment supplement. The amount of this supplement is amended from time to time but rates used in the last six years are as follows:

From		To	Per cent
April 6th, 1987	–	June 5th, 1987	9
June 6th, 1987	–	September 5th, 1987	8.25
September 6th, 1987	–	December 5th, 1987	9
December 6th, 1987	–	May 5th, 1988	8.25
May 6th, 1988	–	August 5th, 1988	7.75
August 6th, 1988	–	October 5th, 1988	9.75
October 6th, 1988	–	January 5th, 1989	10.75
January 6th, 1989	–	July 5th, 1989	11.5
July 6th, 1989	–	November 5th, 1989	12.25
November 6th, 1989	–	November 5th, 1990	13
November 6th, 1990	–	March 5th, 1991	12.25
March 6th, 1991	–	May 5th, 1991	11.50
May 6th, 1991	–	July 5th, 1991	10.75
July 6th, 1991	–	October 5th, 1991	10
October 6th, 1991	–	November 5th, 1992	9.25
November 6th, 1992	–	December 5th, 1992	7.75
December 6th, 1992	–	March 5th, 1993	7
March 6th, 1993	–		6.25

76 *REPAYMENT CLAIM*

A married man, entitled to the full married couple's allowance, receives interest on investments of £2,400 gross (tax deducted £600) in 1993–94. He has National Savings Bank interest of £90 on an ordinary deposit account, National Savings Income Bonds interest (paid gross) of £275 and business profits of £3,700 chargeable in the same year.

	£	£
Total income:		
Business profits		3,700
Investment income (gross)		2,400
National Savings Bank interest	90	
Less Exempted	70	
		20
Deposit Bond interest		275
		6,395
Less		
Personal allowance	3,445	
Married couple's allowance	1,720	5,165
Tax chargeable on		£1,230
Tax payable:		£
On £1,230 at 20 per cent		246.00
Less Tax suffered by deduction		600.00
Repayment due		£354.00

Schedules and Cases

TO FACILITATE the collection of income tax each *source* of income is allocated to a Schedule. The scope of each Schedule is given below but it must be borne in mind that there is only one income tax and the use of the various Schedules in no way affects this principle.

Schedule	***Source of income includes***
A	Income from land and property in the United Kingdom.
B	Previously woodlands managed on a commercial basis and with a view to the realisation of profit but this Schedule has now been abolished.
C	Interest and dividends on Government or public authority funds and certain payments made out of the Public Revenues of overseas countries.
D	This Schedule is divided into the following Cases: Case I – trades; Case II – professions and vocations; Case III – interest, annuities, annual payments and discounts; Case IV – securities located outside the United Kingdom; Case V – possessions located outside the United Kingdom; Case VI – annual profits or gains not chargeable under any other Case or Schedule.
E	This Schedule includes three Cases and extends to emoluments from offices and employments of profit and also to pensions arising in the United Kingdom.
F	Company distributions.

INCOME LIABLE TO ASSESSMENT

In general, liability to United Kingdom income tax extends to all income arising in England, Scotland, Wales and Northern Ireland. Additionally, persons who are regarded as resident in the United Kingdom are usually liable to income tax on income arising overseas. However, in the case of persons resident in the United Kingdom but either domiciled abroad, or, being British subjects, ordinarily resident abroad, only overseas income actually remitted to, or received in, the United Kingdom will suffer income tax.

RESIDENCE

Liability to United Kingdom income tax may arise on overseas income if an individual becomes resident here and this is of particular importance to visitors and other persons whose stay is only intended to be temporary. In the absence of residence no part of the visitor's income arising overseas will be subject to United Kingdom taxation, whether remitted here or retained abroad.

A visitor is regarded as resident for any income tax year (commencing on April 6th) if he or she is present in the United Kingdom for periods amounting to six months or more during that year. There are no exceptions to this rule.

Difficult cases arise where an individual is in the United Kingdom for a period falling short of six months, but if visits are made year after year, and are for substantial periods, residence will be acquired. For this purpose visits are usually regarded as substantial if they average three months or more per annum over a four-year period. When establishing the duration of visits for this purpose, days spent in the United Kingdom which were beyond the individual's control may be ignored. This may arise in the case of illness and also in the case of individuals affected by the outbreak of hostilities overseas. Where an individual comes to the United Kingdom to commence permanent residence or with the intention of remaining for at least three years, he or she will be treated as becoming resident from the date of arrival.

The retention of a place of abode in the United Kingdom could sometimes be sufficient to indicate residence for any year during which visits, however short, were made. The existence of such a place was disregarded if the individual worked full-time in a trade, profession or vocation, no part of which was carried on in the United Kingdom, or if that individual worked full-time in an office or employment, all the duties of which were performed overseas. From April 6th, 1993, the existence of a place of abode will no longer influence the determination of an individual's residential status.

An individual's status of residence strictly applies throughout a full year of assessment. In practice, however, where an individual comes to the United Kingdom and acquires the status of "resident" this will apply only from the date of arrival. A similar approach is adopted where an individual leaves the United Kingdom and ceases to be both resident and ordinarily resident in this territory.

Following the introduction of independent taxation the residence status of a wife must be determined separately from that of her husband. However, where the husband leaves the United Kingdom to take up employment overseas and is accompanied by his wife at or about the time of departure, the residential status of the husband may extend to the wife also.

The significance of "splitting" a year of assessment is that certain items of income arising in the "non-resident period" may be exempt from United Kingdom taxation.

Date tax payable

WAGES, SALARIES and other remuneration arising from an office or employment will usually be paid after deduction of income tax under the PAYE scheme. The deductions will extend to tax at the lower rate, the basic rate, and the higher rate also where earnings are sufficiently substantial. Pensions paid by a former employer will frequently be subject to PAYE deductions. The PAYE deduction scheme is also extended to include the taxation of statutory maternity and short-term sick benefits payable by an employer.

Many payments of interest, together with various annual payments, will be received net after deduction of income tax at the basic rate of 25 per cent for 1993–94. No deduction of income tax will be made from dividends paid by United Kingdom resident companies, but each dividend carries a tax credit and the recipient will not be assessed to income tax at the lower or basic rates.

In those cases where the recipient of income is assessable direct the tax will generally fall due for payment on whichever is the later of:

a January 1st in the year of assessment; or

b thirty days after the date on which an assessment is made.

The income tax assessable in this manner will include tax at the lower rate, the basic rate and the higher rate.

Income arising from a trade, profession or vocation is payable by two equal instalments, namely on:

a January 1st in the year of assessment; and

b July 1st following.

Here also the tax will extend to the lower rate, the basic rate and the higher rate.

Any higher rate tax attributable to the following income will be separately charged and become payable on December 1st following the end of the year of assessment to which the charge relates, or on the expiration of thirty days from the date of making the assessment, whichever is the later:

a Dividends from United Kingdom companies.

b Investment income taxed at source at the basic rate of 25 per cent.

Where an assessment is under appeal an application may be made to defer payment of some, or all, of the tax, pending determination of the disputed liability. This application must usually be made within a period of thirty days from the issue of the notice of assessment and it is necessary to specify the grounds for believing there has been an overcharge of tax.

From 1996–97 some taxpayers will be provided with the option of "self-assessment". The use of this option will remain at the discretion of the taxpayer but where it is exercised different arrangements will be introduced governing the payment of tax.

REMISSION OF TAX

Where arrears of tax have accumulated, due to failure by the Inland Revenue to make proper and timely use of information supplied by a taxpayer, the collection of those arrears may, by concession, be waived. This will not normally apply where notification of the arrears is made by the end of the tax year following that in which the arrears arose. In other cases, the amount of tax waived will be governed by the income of the taxpayer. The income limits have been changed from time to time, but where arrears are notified after February 16th, 1993, the following limits apply:

a Where gross income is not greater than £15,500, no attempt will be made to recover the arrears.

b Where the income exceeds £15,500 but is not greater than £18,000, only one-quarter of the arrears will be recovered.

c If the income exceeds £18,000 but is not more than £22,000, one-half of the arrears will be recovered.

d If the income exceeds £22,000 but is not greater than £26,000, three-quarters of the arrears will fall due for payment.

e If the income exceeds £26,000 but is not greater than £40,000, nine-tenths of the arrears will be collected.

f Where the gross income exceeds £40,000 no remission of tax will be granted.

When applying this concession (based on previous figures) to a husband and wife "living together" where notification of the arrears took place before April 6th, 1990, the joint income of the couple had to be taken. With the introduction of independent taxation consideration is now confined to the taxpayer's own income, without reference to that of his or her spouse.

INTEREST AND PENALTIES

Failure to discharge, or disclose, tax liabilities promptly may have serious repercussions resulting in an obligation to satisfy interest and penalties. The law on this subject is extremely complex and the comments made below provide little more than broad guidelines. Individuals should never disregard the possibility of additional obligations arising where there is a failure to comply with statutory requirements.

INTEREST ON OVERDUE TAX

When tax falls due for payment, it must be satisfied not later than the due and payable date. Overdue tax incurs a liability to interest, calculated from the "reckonable date" to the date of payment. The reckonable date is broadly that on which tax falls due, but may be affected by such matters as an appeal against an assessment and the increase of an estimated assessment which is adjusted to the proper amount later.

The rate of interest has changed on numerous occasions in recent years and is calculated at the percentage rates shown by the table on page 165. Any interest paid cannot be subtracted when calculating the payer's income chargeable to income tax.

INTEREST ATTRIBUTABLE TO OFFENCES

If an assessment is raised to make good a "loss of tax" due to failure on the part of a taxpayer to provide notice, complete a tax return or to supply proper accounts or other information, a liability to satisfy interest may also arise. This situation often develops where a taxpayer has failed to disclose details of taxable income in sufficient time for assessments to be raised before the normal due and payable date. Interest runs from the date on which tax ought to have been satisfied, and not from the date when an assessment is issued, to the date of payment. It is by no means uncommon for interest calculated on this basis to extend over several years, and it may actually exceed the tax payable which must be satisfied in addition.

In the last six years interest has been calculated at the rates shown by the following table:

From		To	Per cent
April 6th, 1987	–	June 5th, 1987	9
June 6th, 1987	–	September 5th, 1987	8.25
September 6th, 1987	–	December 5th, 1987	9
December 6th, 1987	–	May 5th, 1988	8.25
May 6th, 1988	–	August 5th, 1988	7.75
August 6th, 1988	–	October 5th, 1988	9.75
October 6th, 1988	–	January 5th, 1989	10.75
January 6th, 1989	–	July 5th, 1989	11.5
July 6th, 1989	–	November 5th, 1989	12.25
November 6th, 1989	–	November 5th, 1990	13
November 6th, 1990	–	March 5th, 1991	12.25
March 6th, 1991	–	May 5th, 1991	11.50
May 6th, 1991	–	July 5th, 1991	10.75
July 6th, 1991	–	October 5th, 1991	10
October 6th, 1991	–	November 5th, 1992	9.25
November 6th, 1992	–	December 5th, 1992	7.75
December 6th, 1992	–	March 5th, 1993	7
March 6th, 1993	–		6.25

The Revenue have powers to mitigate the interest charged. Interest arising under this alternative heading displaces interest otherwise chargeable where overdue tax is satisfied late. Here also, any interest paid cannot be subtracted when calculating income chargeable to tax.

PENALTIES

The Taxes Acts provide a wide range of penalties for failure to notify the Inland Revenue of tax liabilities and other matters. This broadly involves the commission of fraud, wilful default or neglect.

Among the offences is failure to complete properly an income tax return within a reasonable time, or to provide notification of liability where no return form has been received. There may also be a failure to provide many other returns required by the legislation. A much more serious offence giving rise to penalties is the deliberate understatement or omission of profits, gains or income.

The maximum amount of penalties chargeable may vary considerably between relatively nominal sums and 100 per cent of the under-assessed tax. In very serious situations a criminal prosecution may result.

Where penalties fall due, these must be satisfied in addition to tax and interest, but the Inland Revenue retain wide powers to mitigate amounts otherwise payable. Like interest, penalties incurred cannot be deducted when calculating the payer's income chargeable to income tax.

How to appeal

APPEALS AGAINST income tax assessments must be made in writing to H M Inspector of Taxes within thirty days of the date appearing on the notice of assessment. The required notice of appeal must state the grounds on which the appeal is made, for example, "on the grounds that the assessment is excessive".

Most appeals can be settled by agreement with the local Inspector, but it is as well to be represented professionally if the appeal is to be heard personally by the General (Local) or Special Commissioners.

If no appeal is made against an assessment, or if an assessment is confirmed on appeal, it cannot afterwards be reopened unless, exceptionally, it was made on the basis of an error or mistake in the taxpayer's return.

No award of costs is currently made at the conclusion of appeal hearings before the General or Special Commissioners; nor are details of the hearings made available for examination by the public. However, it is anticipated that the Special, but not the General, Commissioners will be given powers to make an award of costs where either party has acted "unreasonably" in pursuing the appeal. The Special Commissioners are also likely to obtain powers to publish details of important decisions.

Rates of Income Tax for earlier years

FOR THE CONVENIENCE of those readers who may wish to know the rates of income tax for earlier years, the following tables show the rates for the past six years.

1987–88 Basic rate 27 per cent

Higher rates (*payable on taxable income exceeding £17,900*)

On the next £2,500	40%	On the next £7,900	55%
On the next £5,000	45%		
On the next £7,900	50%	On the remainder	60%

1988–89 Basic rate 25 per cent

Higher rate (*payable on taxable income exceeding £19,300*)
40%

1989–90 Basic rate 25 per cent

Higher rate (*payable on taxable income exceeding £20,700*)
40%

1990–91 Basic rate 25 per cent

Higher rate (*payable on taxable income exceeding £20,700*)
40%

1991–92 Basic rate 25 per cent

Higher rate (*payable on taxable income exceeding £23,700*)
40%

1992–93 Basic rate 25 per cent

Lower rate (*payable on first £2,000 of taxable income*)
20%

Higher rate (*payable on taxable income exceeding £23,700*)
40%

Capital gains tax

WHERE A SURPLUS arises from the disposal of land, securities or other assets it is necessary to establish whether that surplus forms part of the profits from a business. A finding that the surplus is derived from a business of dealing will require that the profit must be assessed to income tax in a manner identical to that applicable for other business profits as illustrated on page 90. In those cases where surplus proceeds do not represent business profits and are not otherwise chargeable to income tax, those proceeds may be chargeable to capital gains tax.

Capital gains tax was introduced in 1965 and its application has been amended on numerous occasions subsequently. The most recent significant amendment affected transactions taking place after April 5th, 1988, as not only was the method used to calculate gains and losses altered but the calculation of tax payable was radically reformed.

The following comments are of application to events taking place after April 5th, 1988 and have only limited application to those occurring previously.

DISPOSAL OF ASSETS

Liability to capital gains tax may be incurred where chargeable gains arise on the disposal of assets. The expression "disposal" usually involves a change of ownership but certain "deemed" disposals are treated as having taken place and these also may produce liability to capital gains tax. "Assets" include nearly all forms of "property"; an expression which extends to stocks, shares, unit trust holdings, land, buildings, jewellery and antiques, among others.

EXEMPTIONS AND RELIEFS

The potential scope of liability to capital gains tax is extremely wide but numerous exemptions are available. For example, gains arising on the disposal of private motor vehicles, National Savings Certificates and Premium Savings Bonds, together with sums received on the maturity or surrender of normal policies of life assurance and sums received from the sale of most chattels which have a predictable life of less than fifty years, are exempt. Gains arising on the disposal of goods and chattels not otherwise exempted, usually those with a life expectation of more than fifty years, will be exempt if the disposal proceeds, but not the gains, do not exceed £6,000. Should the proceeds exceed £6,000 by a small amount, the gains otherwise arising on disposal may be reduced. The disposal of gilt edged securities, marketable securities issued by public corporations and guaranteed by the government, together with most fixed interest stocks, are also exempt.

No liability to capital gains tax arises on assets retained at the time of an individual's death. However, personal representatives, legatees and others taking assets on death are deemed to acquire those assets for a consideration representing market value at the time of death. This use of market value will establish the notional cost of acquisition should the personal representatives, or other persons, subsequently undertake the disposal of assets in circumstances requiring the calculation of chargeable gains.

The disposal of assets to a recognised charity, or to certain national institutions, will incur no liability to capital gains tax. Further, a claim may be made to exclude from liability gains arising on the disposal of works of art, historic houses, and other assets of national interest, if a number of conditions are satisfied.

These exemptions are given in addition to the annual exemption of £5,800 which applies for 1993–94.

TRANSFERS BETWEEN HUSBAND AND WIFE

Transfers of assets between a husband and wife "living together" will incur no liability to tax. This is achieved by applying the assumption that assets are transferred for a consideration which produces neither gain nor loss to the transferor. It is immaterial whether the transfer has taken place before or after the introduction of independent taxation.

In those cases where the parties are not "living together", for example by reason of separation, liability to tax will arise in the normal manner.

PRIVATE RESIDENCES

An exemption which is of considerable interest to many individuals arises on the disposal of a private residence. Where the property has been used as an individual's only or main residence throughout the period of ownership, or from March 31st, 1982 if later, no chargeable gain will arise on disposal by that individual. In other situations, involving such use throughout part only of the ownership period, some portion of the gain may be chargeable. However, where a property has been occupied for a qualifying purpose at some time in the ownership period, it will be treated as so occupied in the closing years whether occupied or not. This previously extended to the final twenty-four months of ownership but in recognition of the difficulty experienced by many when attempting to find a buyer of property, this was increased to thirty-six months for disposals taking place after March 18th, 1991.

An individual can have only one qualifying residence at any time. If two or more main residences are held simultaneously, perhaps a town house and a seaside cottage, the individual may select which property should qualify for exemption. In the case of husband and wife "living together", the couple cannot each have a qualifying residence simultaneously.

In addition, where an individual derives gains from the disposal of a private residence previously occupied by a dependent relative, rent-free and without other consideration, exemption from capital gains tax may be forthcoming. This exemption cannot be obtained where the dependent relative first commenced to occupy the property after April 5th, 1988.

Employees occupying job-related accommodation and self-employed individuals required to occupy accommodation in connection with their business may also establish a qualifying residence which is either used or intended to be used on some future occasion.

RETIREMENT RELIEF

Where an individual undertakes the disposal of business assets the gain arising may be reduced or eliminated by retirement relief. This relief is available for gains realised on the disposal of:

a the whole or part of a business carried on by a sole trader or by individuals in partnership;

b assets used for the purposes of a business in **a** which has ceased; and

c shares or securities issued by a company where the following requirements are satisfied:

  i the company was a trading company;

  ii the individual retained a sufficient percentage holding of voting rights; and

  iii the individual was a full-time working director or employee of that company or an associated company.

For disposals undertaken before March 16th, 1993, the requirement under **ii** was only satisfied if the individual personally retained at least 25 per cent of the voting rights, or held at least 5 per cent of those rights personally with that individual and members of his or her family having more than 50 per cent. For subsequent disposals it is only necessary for the individual to personally retain at least 5 per cent of the voting rights. A further relaxation taking effect from the same day was the widening of **iii** to include employees in addition to directors.

For disposals made after March 18th, 1991, the maximum amount of retirement relief will comprise:

a 100 per cent of gains up to £150,000, plus

b 50 per cent of the gains between £150,000 and £600,000.

This formula may produce maximum retirement relief of £375,000 calculated as follows:

	£
On first £150,000 at 100 per cent	150,000
On balance of £450,000 at 50 per cent	225,000
	£375,000

In many situations the total gains arising on disposal will fall substantially below £600,000. However, the above approach must be used to establish the available retirement relief.

Maximum relief will only be forthcoming where the business has been carried on, or the shares retained, throughout a minimum ten-year period. If those conditions are satisfied for less than ten years, but more than twelve months, the available retirement relief will be reduced. Relief is then governed by the "appropriate percentage", which represents that part of the ten-year period throughout which the conditions are satisfied and comprises the aggregate of:

i the appropriate percentage of £150,000 plus

ii one half of the gains exceeding the product of **i** but which do not exceed the appropriate percentage of £600,000.

Retirement relief cannot exceed the gains less losses arising on disposal, as it merely serves to reduce or eliminate the net gains. However, apart from premature retirement on the grounds of ill-health,

77 *RETIREMENT RELIEF*

On December 12th, 1993 Mr Y realised gains of £320,000 from the disposal of business assets. At the time of disposal Mr Y was 58 years of age and had carried on business for more than 10 years.

As the maximum 10 year period is satisfied the appropriate percentage becomes $^{10}/_{10}$ths. The chargeable gain assessable to capital gains tax will be calculated as follows:

Aggregate gains	£320,000

Maximum relief $^{10}/_{10}$ths × £600,000 = £600,000

Available relief:	£
On first £150,000 at 100 per cent	150,000
On balance of £170,000 at 50 per cent	85,000
Total relief	£235,000

	£
Aggregate gains	320,000
Less retirement relief – maximum	235,000
Assessable chargeable gains, 1993–94	£85,000

A finding that Mr Y had only carried on the business for exactly 4 years would limit retirement relief to the following:

Appropriate percentage = $^{4}/_{10}$ths	£
Maximum relief $^{4}/_{10}$ths × £600,000 = £240,000	
Available relief:	
On $^{4}/_{10}$ths of £150,000 = £60,000 at 100 per cent . . .	60,000
On £240,000 *less* £60,000 = £180,000 at 50 per cent . .	90,000
Total relief	£150,000

	£
Aggregate gains	320,000
Less retirement relief	150,000
Assessable chargeable gains, 1993–94	£170,000

physical retirement is usually unnecessary and "retirement relief" may be available for two or more separate disposals until maximum relief has been obtained. In most cases involving disposals after March 18th, 1991, it is only necessary to show that the individual was at least 55 years of age on the disposal date. Retirement relief may also be available for disposals made by an individual before reaching this age if the individual was compelled to retire from business early on the grounds of ill-health.

ROLL-OVER RELIEF

Gains arising from the disposal of many assets used for the purpose of a business may be "rolled over" and offset against the cost of acquiring a replacement asset. This avoids any liability on the gain, but as the cost of the replacement asset is reduced a correspondingly increased gain may arise from the eventual disposal of that asset. A written claim must be made if roll-over relief is to be forthcoming.

It remains a requirement that both the old and the replacement assets fall within a restricted list. This list includes land and buildings occupied and used for the purposes of the business, goodwill, fixed (but not moveable) plant and machinery, aircraft, hovercraft and ships. It also includes milk quotas, potato quotas and other agricultural quotas, together with qualifying property used to provide furnished holiday accommodation and commercial woodlands.

If a disposal is to be matched with an acquisition, the replacement

78 *ROLL-OVER RELIEF*

On September 18th, 1993, Mr C sold freehold premises used for the purposes of his business. The chargeable gain arising on disposal was calculated as follows:

	£
Disposal proceeds	150,000
Less cost	60,000
	90,000
Less indexation allowance – say	38,000
Chargeable gain	£52,000

Mr C purchased replacement premises at a cost of £200,000 on July 17th, 1993, and submitted a claim for roll-over relief. The claim was duly accepted with the following results:

	£
Gain arising on disposal	52,000
Less roll-over relief	52,000
Chargeable gain 1993–94	NIL

	£
Cost of replacement premises	200,000
Less roll-over relief	52,000
Deemed cost	£148,000

asset must usually be acquired within a period commencing twelve months before and ending thirty-six months following the disposal of the old asset.

Only limited roll-over relief will be available where the consideration used to acquire the replacement asset falls below the amount of consideration received from the disposal of the old asset.

Where gains arise after March 15th, 1993, from the disposal of shares in unquoted trading companies, it may be possible to defer the payment of capital gains tax, if any, should the proceeds be reinvested in acquiring shares in another unquoted trading company.

GIFTS AND HOLD-OVER RELIEF

Where assets are transferred by way of gift, or for an inadequate consideration, the disposal proceeds actually passing, if any, and the corresponding cost of acquisition to the transferee, will be deleted and replaced by market value. A similar adjustment must be made for all transactions between "connected persons", an expression which applies to near relatives and many other closely associated individuals and companies.

The insertion of market value may well produce chargeable gains accruing to the transferor which are not actually realised gains. However, where the transferor is an individual and the transferee resides in the United Kingdom a claim for hold-over relief may be available. The effect of this claim is that the chargeable gain will be reduced to nil and the amount of the reduction subtracted from the cost of acquisition (namely market value) to the transferee. As the transferee's cost is reduced, he or she may well incur an increased chargeable gain from the

79 *GIFTS AND HOLD-OVER RELIEF*

On October 14th, 1993, a father gifted shares in a family trading company to his son. The shares, which retained a market value of £50,000 at the time of the transfer, had been acquired by the father for £6,000 in 1983 and the transaction satisfied the requirements for hold-over relief.

If no claim is made the chargeable gain accruing to the father will be:

	£
Disposal proceeds (market value)	50,000
Less cost	6,000
	44,000
Less indexation allowance – say	3,900
Chargeable gain 1993–94	£40,100

However, should a claim for hold-over relief be made there will be no chargeable gain accruing to the father. The son's cost of acquisition must be adjusted as follows:

	£
Cost of acquisition (market value)	50,000
Less father's chargeable gain	40,100
Deemed cost of acquisition	£9,900

eventual disposal of the asset. A similar claim is available for assets transferred by trustees residing in the United Kingdom.

Only limited hold-over relief may be available if the transferee provides some consideration for the asset. Any hold-over relief previously granted may be withdrawn should the transferee emigrate from the United Kingdom within the succeeding six-year period before undertaking a disposal of the asset.

For disposals taking place after March 13th, 1989, only a limited range of assets can qualify for hold-over relief. These comprise:

a Assets used for the purposes of a business carried on by the transferor, or by a company in which the transferor retains a significant interest.

b Agricultural property.

c Shares or securities in unquoted trading companies.

d Shares or securities in quoted trading companies and companies dealt in on the Unlisted Securities Market, where the transferor retains a significant interest.

No restriction is placed on the nature of an asset where the transfer is a lifetime transfer, other than a potentially exempt transfer, which is recognised for inheritance tax purposes.

INDEXATION ALLOWANCE

Many capital gains are created or swollen by inflation. This phenomenon will often increase the apparent value of assets and produce substantial paper gains on disposal without creating gains in real terms. For disposals made before April 6th, 1982, there was no relief for the inroads caused by inflation but for disposals taking place on or after this date the gain arising may be reduced by an indexation allowance. The availability, calculation and application of the indexation allowance has changed from time to time and the following comments are confined to disposals taking place after April 5th, 1988.

The indexation allowance is calculated using monthly figures taken from the retail prices index. There are two components, namely:

RI — which represents the figure extracted from the index for the month of March 1982, or the month in which expenditure is incurred, whichever is the later; and

RD — which is the index figure for the month in which the disposal takes place.

The allowance will then comprise:

$$\frac{RD - RI}{RI} \times \text{Expenditure}$$

Where two or more items of expenditure have been incurred in relation to an asset in different months, separate calculations must be prepared for each item.

Recent retail prices index figures used to establish factors RI and RD are shown by the Tables on the following page.

Retail Prices Index 1982–1987

Month	1982	1983	1984	1985	1986	1987
Jan		325.9	342.6	359.8	379.7	394.5
Feb		327.3	344.0	362.7	381.1	100.4
Mar	313.4	327.9	345.1	366.1	381.6	100.6
Apr	319.7	332.5	349.7	373.9	385.3	101.8
May	322.0	333.9	351.0	375.6	386.0	101.9
Jun	322.9	334.7	351.9	376.4	385.8	101.9
Jul	323.0	336.5	351.5	375.7	384.7	101.8
Aug	323.1	338.0	354.8	376.7	385.9	102.1
Sep	322.9	339.5	355.5	376.5	387.8	102.4
Oct	324.5	340.7	357.7	377.1	388.4	102.9
Nov	326.1	341.9	358.8	378.4	391.7	103.4
Dec	325.5	342.8	358.8	378.9	393.0	103.3

Retail Prices Index 1988–1993

Month	1988	1989	1990	1991	1992	1993
Jan	103.3	111.0	119.5	130.2	135.6	137.9
Feb	103.7	111.8	120.2	130.9	136.3	138.8
Mar	104.1	112.3	121.4	131.4	136.7	139.3
Apr	105.8	114.3	125.1	133.1	138.8	
May	106.2	115.0	126.2	133.5	139.3	
Jun	106.6	115.4	126.7	134.1	139.3	
Jul	106.7	115.5	126.8	133.8	138.8	
Aug	107.9	115.8	128.1	134.1	138.9	
Sep	108.4	116.6	129.3	134.6	139.4	
Oct	109.5	117.5	130.3	135.1	139.9	
Nov	110.0	118.5	130.0	135.6	139.7	
Dec	110.3	118.8	129.9	135.7	139.2	

The compilation of the retail prices index was amended by introducing a revised unit of 100 for January 1987. Changes in subsequent months are measured against the new unit of 100. To calculate the indexation allowance for acquisitions taking place before the month of February 1987 and corresponding disposals made in or after that month the procedure is as follows:

a Take factor RD for the month of disposal

b Multiply factor RD by the January 1987 indexed figure of 394.5

c Divide the product of **b** by factor RI, the figure taken from the index for the month of acquisition

d Subtract 100 from the result to produce the required percentage change.

Example 80 below shows how the calculation is made.

The indexation allowance calculated on this basis will be subtracted from the gain arising on disposal. Where a loss occurs the allowance will increase the amount of that loss. In some situations the insertion of an indexation allowance will convert a gain into a loss.

80 INDEXATION ALLOWANCE

Mr A purchased shares at a cost of £10,000 on June 12th, 1982. He realised £42,000 from selling the shares on January 10th, 1993. Figures extracted from the retail prices index were as follows:

June 1982 (RI)	322.9
January 1987	394.5
January 1993 (RD)	137.9

The indexation allowance becomes:

$\frac{137.9 \times 394.5}{322.9} =$	168.5
Less	100
	68.5
£10,000 × .685 per cent	£6,850

The chargeable gain for 1992–93 will be:

	£
Disposal proceeds	42,000
Less Cost	10,000
	32,000
Less indexation allowance	6,850
Chargeable gain 1992–93	£25,150

For most disposals taking place after April 5th, 1988, and involving assets acquired before March 31st, 1982, the computation of the indexation allowance will proceed by applying the assumption that assets were actually acquired for a consideration reflecting market value on the latter date. In the case of assets acquired, or expenditure incurred, subsequently the actual amounts involved will be used as representing cost.

Before an indexation allowance can be calculated the disposal must be matched with the corresponding acquisition of an asset. This should not give rise to difficulty where there is a single acquisition followed by a single disposal. However, problems do arise when dealing with a holding of shares or securities. The holding may have been created by acquisitions made on two or more occasions, only part of the aggregate holding may be realised and many quoted holdings will be affected by bonus issues, rights issues, exchanges and reorganisations. Complex rules must then be followed to identify a disposal with the matching acquisition before the calculation of gain or loss can proceed and the indexation allowance be established.

81 *INDEXATION ALLOWANCE – ASSETS ACQUIRED BEFORE APRIL 1982*

Using the facts in Example 80, let it be assumed that the shares were acquired in 1973. On March 31st, 1982, the holding retained a market value of £20,000.

As the shares were acquired before March 31st, 1982 they will be treated as having been acquired on that date for a consideration representing market value, both for the purpose of calculating the gain (see later) and also when determining the indexation allowance. Factor RI will represent the index figure of 313.4 for March 1982.

The indexation allowance becomes:

$\frac{137.9 \times 394.5}{313.4} =$	173.6
Less	100
	73.6
£20,000 × .736 per cent	£14,720

	£
Disposal proceeds	42,000
Less cost (*i.e. market value at 31.3.82*)	20,000
	22,000
Less indexation allowance	14,720
Chargeable gain 1992–93	£7,280

CALCULATION OF GAINS AND LOSSES

Before the indexation allowance can be subtracted from a gain, or added to a loss, the amount of that gain or loss must be determined. In some cases the calculation used for disposals taking place before April 6th, 1988, will differ from that used for disposals undertaken on or after that date. The following comments apply only to disposals occurring after April 5th, 1988.

The gain or loss will broadly reflect the difference between acquisition cost and the disposal proceeds, with an adjustment for incidental costs of both acquisition and disposal and costs incurred when carrying out improvements to the asset. There is, however, a significant alteration in the computation procedure for assets acquired before March 31st, 1982. These assets are deemed to have been acquired for a "cost" representing market value on that date. The position will only be otherwise where this approach produces an excessive gain or loss exceeding the actual gain or loss incurred, converts a gain into a loss or a loss into a gain. It is, however, possible to file an election to adopt market value at March 31st, 1982, for all assets (but not some only) held on that date. Where such an election is made any distortions in the gain or loss are ignored. The election must be submitted within a period of two years following the end of the first year of assessment, commencing on April 6th, 1988, in which the first disposal of an asset held on March 31st, 1982, is made.

82 *CALCULATION OF GAIN*

Mrs J purchased an asset at a cost of £8,000 on March 27th, 1972. The asset realised £100,000 when sold on October 9th, 1993. Market value at March 31st, 1982 was agreed to be £52,000.

The chargeable gain arising on disposal becomes:

	£
Disposal proceeds	100,000
Less deemed cost – market value at March 31st, 1982	52,000
	48,000
Less indexation allowance – say	36,000
Chargeable gain 1993–94	£12,000

CAPITAL LOSSES

Not all disposals will produce gains and inevitably some will give rise to capital losses. Any capital losses arising in a year of assessment must be set against chargeable gains, if any, realised in the same year. If a surplus of losses remain these may be carried forward to future years.

Capital losses brought forward from a previous year of assessment may be subtracted from the net gains arising in the subsequent year. However, the application of earlier losses in this manner is not to reduce the net gains for the subsequent year below the exempt amount for that year. Any surplus losses brought forward from earlier years which cannot be relieved against net gains in a subsequent year may be carried forward and utilised in future years.

83 *USING CAPITAL LOSSES*

At the end of 1992–93 Mr Z had unused capital losses of £11,800 carried forward to 1993–94.

He realised chargeable gains of £16,000 and capital losses of £7,300 from disposals taking place in 1993–94.

The losses must be dealt with as follows for 1993–94:

	£
Chargeable gains	16,000
Less Capital losses	7,300
	8,700
Less Losses brought forward (part)	2,900
	5,800
Less Exempt amount (see page 179)	5,800
Tax chargeable on	NIL

The capital losses of £7,300 arising in 1993–94 must be set against chargeable gains for that year. It then remains to reduce the net gains remaining by £2,900 to the exemption threshold of £5,800.

The balance of capital losses brought forward from 1992–93, namely £8,900 (£11,800 less £2,900), will be carried forward to 1994–95.

BUSINESS LOSSES

Before April 6th, 1991, it was not possible to set unused losses from a trade, profession or vocation against chargeable gains for the purpose of calculating capital gains tax payable. However, this restriction is relaxed for business losses arising in 1991–92 and future years.

Where business losses arise in a year of assessment a claim can be made to set those losses against income chargeable to income tax in the same year. If surplus losses remain they can be included in a similar claim for the following year only (see page 93). Certain losses from hobby farming and non-commercial activities cannot be relieved in this manner.

If business losses arising in a year of assessment cannot be absorbed against income for the same year, those losses may be set against net gains (chargeable gains less capital losses) for that year. Should surplus business losses remain, these can be set against income for the following year only, but here also if, or to the extent that, income is not sufficiently substantial the balance can be set against net capital gains in the following year only. Any remaining losses can only be carried forward and set against future profits from the same business.

Where a claim is made to set business losses against net capital gains those losses must be used in priority to any capital losses brought forward from an earlier year.

84 *USING BUSINESSES LOSSES*

Mrs A had unused capital losses of £15,000 being carried forward at the end of 1992–93. In 1993–94 she realised chargeable gains of £21,000 and capital losses of £4,500. During the same year Mrs A suffered a loss of £18,400 when carrying on a trade. A claim was made to offset part of this loss against income but £7,260 remained unrelieved. Mrs A then made a separate claim to set this unrelieved balance against her net capital gains for 1993–94.

The result of this claim for capital gains tax purposes is as follows:

	£
Chargeable gains	21,000
Less Capital losses	4,500
Net gains	16,500
Less Business losses	7,260
	9,240
Less Losses brought forward (part)	3,440
	5,800
Less Exempt amount (see below)	5,800
Tax chargeable on	NIL

The business loss of £18,400 has been fully relieved, partly against income and partly against chargeable gains. The balance of capital losses carried forward to 1994–95 will be £11,560 (£15,000 less £3,440).

ANNUAL EXEMPTION

The initial slice of gains (chargeable gains less losses) arising in a year of assessment is exempt from capital gains tax. For 1993–94 the exempt amount is £5,800. The corresponding figure for the six earlier years is shown by the following table:

	£		£
1987–88 .	6,300	1990–91 .	5,000
1988–89 .	5,000	1991–92 .	5,500
1989–90 .	5,000	1992–93 .	5,800

If the exempt amount is not utilised, or fully utilised, any balance remaining cannot be carried forward to succeeding years. It is therefore advisable to use fully the exempt amount wherever possible.

For 1989–90 and earlier years only one combined exempt amount was available to shelter chargeable gains accruing to a husband and wife "living together". However, for 1990–91 and future years each spouse has his or her own exempt amount without reference to the gains, if any, realised by the other.

CALCULATION OF TAX PAYABLE

Where net gains remaining exceed the exempt amount for a year of assessment the excess is chargeable to capital gains tax.

For disposals taking place before April 6th, 1988, the excess was chargeable at the flat rate of 30 per cent. However, the flat rate calculation of capital gains tax payable has no application to net gains arising on and after that date. The first step when calculating liability subsequently is to establish:

a the amount of net gains arising in the year of assessment which exceed the exempt amount; and

b the taxable income of the individual chargeable to income tax for that year. This will determine the amount of income charged at the lower rate, the basic rate or the higher rate.

Liability to capital gains tax is then calculated by reference to the individual's marginal rate of income tax. This requires that the amount of the excess net gains must be added to income chargeable to income tax and income tax rates used to establish liability on the excess. The tax remains a capital gains tax notwithstanding the use of income tax rates.

It will be recognised that where income already incurs liability to the higher rate of 40 per cent for 1993–94 net chargeable gains will be assessed at the rate of 40 per cent. If the individual has not fully utilised the basic rate 25 per cent band of £21,200, the net gains may be wholly assessed at 25 per cent or partly assessed at 25 per cent with the balance taxable at 40 per cent. Where the 20 per cent lower rate band has not been fully used any balance may be applied to calculate the tax due before proceeding to the basic rate or higher rate.

Personal representatives administering the estate of a deceased person will be assessable to capital gains tax at a rate equivalent to the basic rate of 25 per cent.

TAX PAYABLE – HUSBAND AND WIFE

For 1989–90 and earlier years the chargeable gains of a married woman "living with" her husband were assessed on the husband, other than in the year of marriage. Capital losses of one spouse were subtracted from the gains of the other spouse, unless the loss making spouse filed an election to retain the benefit of the losses. Only one combined exempt amount of £5,000 was available.

Capital gains tax liability was calculated by reference to the husband's marginal rate of tax. Where a wife's earnings election was in force the

85 CALCULATION OF TAX PAYABLE

Mr P derived the following chargeable gains and capital losses from the disposal of assets made in 1993–94:

Chargeable gains	£14,800
Capital losses	£3,100

The amount chargeable to capital gains tax becomes:

	£
Chargeable gains	14,800
Less Capital losses	3,100
	11,700
Less exempt amount	5,800
Tax chargeable on	£5,900

To establish the amount of capital gains tax payable for 1993–94, Mr P's marginal rate of income tax must be determined. It was found that he incurred liability at the basic rate on £12,000. As a further £9,200 would produce liability at the basic rate only, capital gains tax will be due as follows:

On £5,900 at 25 per cent	£1,475.00

If the income of Mr P for 1993–94 produced, say, £19,500 liable at the basic rate, capital gains tax due would be:

	£
On first £1,700 (£21,200 less £19,500) at 25 per cent	425.00
On balance of £4,200 at 40 per cent	1,680.00
Capital gains tax payable 1993–94	£2,105.00

If the income of Mr P for 1993–94 was already sufficient to produce income tax liability at the higher rate of 40 per cent, the capital gains tax payable becomes:

£5,900 at 40 per cent	£2,360.00

Finally, a finding that the income of Mr P was only sufficient to produce income tax liability at the lower rate of 20 per cent on income of £750 would support the following liability:

	£
On first £1,750 (£2,500 less £750) at 20 per cent	350.00
On balance of £4,150 at 25 per cent	1,037.50
Capital gains tax payable 1993–94	£1,387.50

86 *TAX PAYABLE – HUSBAND AND WIFE*

Mr and Mrs M are a husband and wife "living together". After agreeing capital gains tax computations for 1992–93, it was found that the following capital losses were being carried forward:

Mr M	£2,000
Mrs M	£18,000

In 1993–94 Mr M realised chargeable gains of £16,500 from the disposal of assets. Mrs M made no disposals at all.

The losses of Mrs M cannot be set against the gains of her husband. The husband must suffer liability on the following:

	£
Chargeable gains	16,500
Less losses brought forward	2,000
	14,500
Less exempt amount	5,800
Tax chargeable on	£8,700

Assuming Mr M incurs income tax liability at the higher rate of 40 per cent for 1993–94, the tax payable becomes:

On £8,700 at 40 per cent	£3,480.00

chargeable gains were effectively treated as "investment income" and added to the husband's income when calculating the marginal rate of income tax.

With the introduction of independent taxation on April 6th, 1990, this system no longer applies. Husband and wife are independently taxed, with each entitled to his or her £5,800 exemption and marginal rate for 1993–94.

RETURNS

Details of disposals, and the resultant chargeable gains, must be entered on the income tax return form, where a form is required for completion. However, where the chargeable gains accruing to an individual do not exceed £5,800 for 1993–94 and the gross proceeds from all disposals do not exceed £11,600, it is sufficient to state this on the return form without submitting calculations.

In the absence of an income tax return requiring completion, liability to capital gains tax should be notified to the Inland Revenue independently to avoid incurring a liability to satisfy interest and perhaps penalties.

TRUSTS

Complex provisions apply to the taxation of chargeable gains accruing to trustees. Where the trustees are resident in the United Kingdom, they will usually suffer capital gains tax at the appropriate rate. Trustees residing overseas are unlikely to be taxed direct but gains accruing to those trustees may be assessed on United Kingdom beneficiaries, or perhaps on the settlor, namely the individual who created the trust.

Making the annual return

EVERY INDIVIDUAL who has profits, gains or income which is chargeable to income tax or capital gains tax must notify the Inspector of Taxes of that fact. If he or she fails to do so a liability to satisfy penalties may be incurred. Many taxpayers will receive income tax returns annually, or at less frequent intervals of time. Should a completed return be delivered late, or contain insufficient or incorrect information, with the result that the issue of assessments is delayed, a liability to interest may also arise. Details of any chargeable gains assessable to capital gains tax must also be recorded on the return, unless the limits mentioned on page 182 are not exceeded.

The first part of the return form should record the income and gains for the previous year of assessment ending on April 5th. The second part is primarily concerned with allowances for the following year.

When completing the 1993–94 return, containing claims for allowances relating to 1993–94, it should not be overlooked that this return

87 *Example*

A 1993–94 return of income and capital gains is required for completion by a taxpayer. This will record details of income and gains for 1992–93 (year ending on April 5th, 1993), and incorporate a claim for allowances for the following year, 1993–94:

Information to be inserted on the return is as follows:

	£
Rents from property (i.e. actual rents less expenses)	4,200.00
Salary as secretary	18,000.00
National Savings Income Bond interest	120.00
War Loan interest	120.00
Building society interest	107.00
Dividend	438.00

Interest is payable on a building society mortgage.

During the year chargeable gains arose from the disposal of shares in D Ltd.

The return of total income will be completed as shown by the abridged illustration on pages 184–185.

Tax return 1993–1994

Income: year ended April 5th, 1993

EARNINGS

Earnings from full time employment Secretary — X Ltd, 99 High Street, Anytown	£ 18,000
Other earnings:	
Profits from a trade or profession	—
Tips	—
Benefits in kind	—
Redundancy or other leaving payment	—
Unemployment benefit or income support	—

PENSIONS

Retirement or old person's pension	£ —
Widow's or other State Benefits	—
Pension from former employment	—

INVESTMENTS, SAVINGS, ETC.

National Savings Bank interest	£ —
Ordinary account	—
Investment account, Income Bonds and Capital Bonds Deposit Bonds	120
Interest from UK banks and UK building societies ABC Society	107
Interest from UK banks not already taxed	—
Interest not already taxed from other UK source War loan interest	120

Maintenance and alimony	—
Company dividends and Unit Trusts T Ltd — Tax credit £146	438
Other dividends and interest	—
Rents from land and property in UK (Details attached)	4,200
Income from abroad	—
Payments from settlements and estates	—
Any other income or gains	—

OUTGOINGS

	£
Work expenses Subscriptions to professional bodies	—
Interest on loans to buy home Joint EFG Society	Not required
Interest on UK property for letting	—
Other loan interest	—
Covenants	—
Maintenance and alimony paid	—
Rent and yearly interest paid to persons abroad	—

CAPITAL GAINS

	£
Description of asset disposed of Shares in D Ltd	
Date of disposal June 27th, 1992	
Amount of Gain or Loss Gain — as attached	12,200

ALLOWANCES — YEAR ENDED APRIL 5th, 1994

(full details will be inserted — see notes on page 25)	

requires the insertion of details of income and gains for the year ended April 5th, 1993. Husband and wife "living together" are independently assessed and a return completed by one spouse will not contain details of income and gains accruing to the other.

It is expected that many self-employed individuals completing tax returns for 1996–97 and future years will be provided with the option to apply self-assessment, without waiting for the Inland Revenue to raise assessments.

Companies

PROFITS AND INCOME accruing to individuals are subject to income tax, and any chargeable gains arising to such persons may be assessable to capital gains tax. In contrast, profits, income and chargeable gains accruing to companies resident in, or carrying on business in, the United Kingdom, are assessed to corporation tax.

Corporation tax is charged on the profits, gains and income of an accounting period and this will usually be the period for which accounts are made up annually. In arriving at assessable profits a deduction may be claimed for capital allowances where expenditure is incurred on the acquisition of plant, machinery, industrial buildings and similar assets.

RATES OF CORPORATION TAX

The rates at which corporation tax must be paid are fixed by reference to a financial year which commences on April 1st and ends on the following March 31st. In those cases where the company accounting year does not end on March 31st the results must be apportioned on a time basis. This apportionment will only assume significance where there is a change in the rate of corporation tax.

In recent years corporation tax has been charged, or is being charged, at the following rates:

	Per cent
April 1st, 1986, to March 31st, 1990	35
April 1st, 1990, to March 31st, 1991	34
April 1st, 1991, to March 31st, 1992	33
April 1st, 1992, to March 31st, 1993	33
April 1st, 1993, to March 31st, 1994	33

SMALL COMPANIES RATE

Where the profits of a United Kingdom resident company do not exceed stated limits, the full rate of corporation tax shown above is reduced to the small companies rate. The application of the reduced small companies rate is governed by the amount of profits and *not* by the size of the company.

The small companies rate for recent years and the immediate future is shown by the following table.

	Per cent
April 1st, 1986, to March 31st, 1987	29
April 1st, 1987, to March 31st, 1988	27
April 1st, 1988, to March 31st, 1994	25

Limits governing the availability of the small companies rate have differed as between one year and another. However, for several years up to and including that ending on March 31st, 1989, the small companies rate could be used where profits did not exceed £100,000. If profits exceeded this figure, but fell below £500,000, marginal relief was available. This relief was calculated by subtracting from the liability determined at the full corporation tax rate a fraction of the difference between profits and £500,000. Marginal relief ceased to apply where profits exceeded £500,000 and the full rate of corporation tax had then to be used.

The lower and upper limits have subsequently been amended as follows:

Year ending March 31st	Lower Limit	Upper Limit
	£	£
1990	150,000	750,000
1991	200,000	1,000,000
1992, 1993 and 1994	250,000	1,250,000

The fraction to be used in the calculation becomes:

Year ending March 31st
1988 – 1/50th
1989 – 1/40th
1990 – 1/40th
1991 – 9/400ths
1992 – 1/50th
1993 – 1/50th
1994 – 1/50th

Some modification to the calculation is necessary where there are associated companies, namely companies under common control, or the accounting period is less than twelve months. Adjustments must also be made for accounting periods overlapping March 31st where a change in

88 *SMALL COMPANIES RATE*

The trading profits, calculated after subtracting capital allowances, accruing to Y Ltd in the twelve-month period ending on March 31st, 1994 were £120,000. These profits fall below the ceiling of £250,000 and the corporation tax payable becomes:

£120,000 at 25 per cent	**£30,000**

rate or rates arises. The small companies rate is not available to close investment-holding companies. These are companies which neither carry on a trade nor derive income from most forms of property letting.

89 *MARGINAL SMALL COMPANIES RATE RELIEF*

X Ltd derived trading profits, calculated after deducting capital allowances, of £460,000 for the twelve-month period ending on March 31st, 1994. Marginal small companies relief applies and the corporation tax payable is as follows:

Trading profits	£460,000
	£
Tax on £460,000 at 33 per cent (full rate)	151,800.00
Less marginal relief:	
£1,250,000 less £460,000 = £790,000 × 1/50th	15,800.00
Tax payable	£136,000.00

CHARGEABLE GAINS

The calculation of chargeable gains and capital losses accruing to companies proceeds on a basis similar to that used for individuals. Here also, the indexation allowance can be subtracted from gains for disposals carried out after March 31st, 1982. In addition, where the disposal of assets acquired before April 1st, 1982, occurs after April 5th, 1988, the calculation may usually proceed by treating the assets as acquired at market value on March 31st, 1982. However, the annual exemption of £5,800, which can be obtained by individuals, has no application to companies.

The calculation of tax payable by a company on chargeable gains was significantly amended for disposals taking place after March 16th, 1987. Before this date only a fraction of the chargeable gains, less capital

90 *CHARGEABLE GAINS*

A Ltd prepares accounts to March 31st annually. Trading profits, suitably adjusted for tax purposes by subtracting capital allowances, amounted to £180,000 for the year ending March 31st, 1994.

On January 12th, 1994, the company derived a chargeable gain of £45,000, after deducting the indexation allowance, from the disposal of an asset.

Aggregate profits do not exceed £250,000 and the small companies rate applies. Corporation tax payable will therefore be calculated as follows:

	£
Trading profits	180,000
Chargeable gain	45,000
Total profits	£225,000
Tax on £225,000 at the small companies rate of 25 per cent	£56,250

losses, were assessable to corporation tax at the full rate. It was not possible to use the small companies rate.

The fractional basis has no application for disposals taking place after March 16th, 1987. The full amount of chargeable gains will be assessable to corporation tax without subtracting any fraction. However, these gains are now treated like other profits or income when calculating corporation tax payable at the small companies rate, the marginal small companies rate or the full rate.

INTEREST PAYMENTS

When making payments of yearly interest and other annual sums (but not dividends), a company will deduct income tax at the basic rate of 25 per cent. Any tax must usually be paid over to the Inland Revenue and cannot be retained by the paying company. Some relief for the outlay is available, however, as the gross interest, or other payment, may usually be deducted from profits chargeable to corporation tax, unless the payment represents a "distribution".

CHARITABLE PAYMENTS

Annual payments made under a properly drawn deed of covenant to a charity are satisfied "net" after deducting income tax at the basic rate of 25 per cent. This tax must be accounted for to the Inland Revenue but the gross sum may be relieved when calculating the paying company's liability to corporation tax. A similar procedure applies to single donations made by larger companies where the requirements outlined on page 145 are satisfied, and also to donations exceeding £250 (or £400 where appropriate) made by all companies under the Gift Aid scheme.

DISTRIBUTIONS

Payments which are treated as distributions cannot be deducted in calculating company profits. The expression "distribution" has a wide meaning and includes dividends paid on shares, benefits provided to shareholders and other advantages.

Dividends and other qualifying distributions are paid in full, without deduction of income tax. However, on making such a distribution the paying company is required to make a payment of advance corporation tax (ACT) to the Inland Revenue. The rates of ACT for recent years and those for the immediate future are shown below.

Distributions made:	**Rate**
April 6th, 1986, to April 5th, 1987	29/71sts
April 6th, 1987, to April 5th, 1988	27/73rds
April 6th, 1988, to April 5th, 1993	1/3rd
April 6th, 1993, to April 5th, 1994	9/31sts
April 6th, 1994, to April 5th, 1995	1/4th

Any ACT paid may usually be offset by the paying company against its liability to corporation tax for the accounting period during which the distribution is made. Therefore, as the title suggests, ACT is really an advance payment of corporation tax, where the company has sufficient profits chargeable to that tax. Should the corporation tax liability be insufficient to absorb payments of ACT, the surplus may be carried forward to future periods or perhaps carried back to earlier periods.

For many years the rate of ACT when added to the distribution produced an amount identical to income tax at the basic rate on the grossed-up equivalent. For example, a distribution of £75 made in the year to April 5th, 1993, would produce £25 ACT, which is 25 per cent when applied to the grossed-up sum of £100.

The tax credit attaching to dividends and other distributions paid after April 5th, 1993, is reduced to one-quarter of the sum received. Therefore a dividend of £75 has attached to it a tax credit of £18.75. The rate of ACT is also being reduced, but in two stages. ACT attributable to dividends and other distributions paid in the year to April 5th, 1994, will be 22.5 per cent of the aggregate of the amount paid and the ACT. This will reduce to 20 per cent for dividends and other distributions made after April 5th, 1994.

The treatment of dividends received by shareholders after April 5th, 1993, is discussed on page 123.

PAY AND FILE

A new system for administering the assessment and collection of corporation tax from companies is being introduced and applies to all accounting periods ending on and after October 1st, 1993. This system is known as "pay and file" and as the title suggests requires companies to discharge corporation tax on a self-assessment basis and to submit both accounts and tax returns at a later date.

All corporation tax will become due and payable nine months following the end of the company's accounting period. Failure to discharge tax on that date will incur a liability to interest, which commences to run from the end of the nine-month period. Supporting accounts and tax returns will have to be filed within a period of twelve months commencing on the annual accounting date. Should this obligation remain undischarged, a company will become liable to satisfy penalties at a rate increasing as the period of failure lengthens.

Value added tax

VALUE ADDED TAX is charged on the value of supplies made by a registered trader and extends both to the supply of goods and also to the supply of services. Special rules must be applied to determine the nature of the supply and also the time at which that supply is made.

For many years value added tax was charged on the value of most goods imported into the United Kingdom, unless the importation was of a temporary nature. However, with the commencement of the European Single Market on January 1st, 1993, value added tax is no longer charged where goods are imported from a Member State of the European Community. Instead of a tax on importation, value added tax will be imposed on the person who "acquires" goods in substitution for liability at the point of importation. Goods arising from suppliers outside the Single Market continue to attract tax on importation.

A registered trader will both suffer tax (input tax) when obtaining or acquiring goods or services for the purposes of a business and charge that tax (output tax) when supplying goods or services to customers and others. It is necessary for the trader to calculate both the input tax suffered and the output tax charged, or chargeable, during a prescribed accounting period. Not all input tax may be included in the calculation as some outgoings, for example supplies involving business entertaining and supplies relating to domestic accommodation provided by a company for use by directors and their families, must be disregarded. Should the output tax exceed the input tax qualifying for relief, the difference must be paid over to Customs and Excise. However, if the input tax exceeds the output tax a repayment will usually be due.

Value added tax returns are usually submitted for prescribed accounting periods of three months, although some repayment traders may submit returns on a monthly basis. Very large traders will also submit returns on a three-monthly basis, although they must account for tax due monthly. An optional scheme is available for traders having an annual taxable turnover falling below £300,000. Such traders may, if they so wish, render returns on an annual basis. Nine equal payments of value added tax will then be made on account, with a final, tenth, balancing payment accompanying submission of the return.

REGISTRATION

The collection and repayment of value added tax is confined to registered traders, an expression which includes individuals, partnerships and companies carrying on a trade, profession or vocation and certain other activities. Mandatory registration is confined to those making taxable supplies exceeding certain thresholds. These thresholds are amended periodically and from March 16th, 1993, an unregistered trader must register:

a at any time, if there are reasonable grounds for believing that the value of taxable supplies in the next thirty days will exceed £37,600; or

b at the end of any month if the value of taxable supplies in the last twelve months then ending has exceeded £37,600.

A person liable to be registered under **a** is required to notify liability, and will be registered with effect from the date he or she becomes so liable. If a person is liable to registration under **b**, he or she must notify liability within thirty days of the end of the month concerned and will be registered with effect from the end of the month in which the thirtieth day falls, unless registration from an earlier date is agreed.

These stringent time limits must be fully recognised when commencing a new business, or where the value of taxable supplies increases, as failure to notify Customs and Excise promptly may result in demands for value added tax which ought to have been paid on earlier occasions.

A trader whose taxable supplies do not reach the mandatory registration threshold may apply for voluntary registration. This may sometimes be thought advisable, as only registered traders can obtain relief for input tax suffered. Persons acquiring an existing registered business as a going concern must usually register immediately.

Racehorse owners obtaining sponsorship or appearance money may register from a date not earlier than March 16th, 1993. This possibility has arisen following a change in the Rules of Racing which enables those owners to carry on a business.

Registered traders may seek cancellation of their registration where the value of taxable supplies does not exceed certain limits. From May 1st, 1993, an application for de-registration can be made if the value of taxable supplies is not expected to exceed £36,000 in the year then beginning.

EXEMPT SUPPLIES

Supplies of certain goods and services which comprise "exempt supplies" are not chargeable to value added tax. These include the provision of finance, insurance and education, together with burial and cremation facilities. The granting of a lease or licence to occupy land will usually represent an exempt supply not chargeable to value added tax, but there are numerous exceptions. In particular, transactions affecting new non-domestic buildings may represent standard rated supplies. It is also possible for the landlord of a non-domestic building to exercise an option to treat rents as standard rated supplies. The purpose of such an election will be to avoid, or to limit, restrictions otherwise arising from the making of partially exempt supplies.

In those cases where a trader makes exempt supplies, no value added tax will be added to the prices charged, and in the absence of sufficient taxable supplies it may not be mandatory to register. A trader who is registered but who makes exempt supplies may be unable to fully recover the input tax suffered when obtaining goods or services. However, where a trader makes some taxable supplies and the input tax attributable to exempt supplies does not exceed £7,200 in a twelve-month period, it may be possible to obtain relief for all input tax suffered.

BAD DEBTS

Tax is charged on the supply of goods or services and not on the amount actually received for the supply, unless the supplier is operating a special scheme. As special schemes only require receipts to be included, those operating these schemes effectively obtain relief for bad debts. The range of special schemes which provide effective relief for bad debts may also extend to registered traders having an annual turnover falling below £350,000 (or £300,000 before April 1st, 1993). Such traders may, at their option, adopt a system of cash accounting which only recognises payments actually made and received. Since the amount of any bad debt will not be "received" traders adopting this scheme are not required to account for tax on that debt.

For other traders not within these schemes relief may be available for bad debts suffered. This relief was previously limited to a genuine debt more than twelve months old and which had been written off in the books of the trader. The waiting period has been reduced from twelve to six months from April 1st, 1993.

RATES OF TAX

Value added tax is levied at two rates, namely:

a a zero, or nil, rate; and

b a standard rate of 17.5 per cent (increased from 15 per cent on April 1st, 1991).

ZERO RATING

Zero rating extends to many supplies, including the following:

a The supply of food and drink for human consumption. This does not include such items as ice cream, chocolates, sweets, crisps and alcoholic drinks. Nor does it include supplies made in the course of catering, for example, at a wedding reception or dinner, or supplies for consumption in a restaurant or cafe. Take-away supplies of "cold" foods for consumption off the supplier's premises are zero rated but the supply of "hot" food and drink, for example, fish and chips or a container of hot tea, are taxable at the standard rate.

b Sewerage and water services, unless supplies are made for non-domestic purposes.

c Books, booklets, brochures, pamphlets, leaflets, newspapers, journals and periodicals.

d Talking books for the blind and handicapped and wireless sets for the blind.

e Electricity, gas and other fuels, excluding supplies made for non-domestic purposes. Zero rating will cease to apply to fuel and power used for domestic purposes on April 1st, 1994. From this date domestic supplies will suffer tax at the reduced standard rate of 8 per cent. The reduced rate will remain for twelve months before being increased to the full standard rate of 17.5 per cent on April 1st, 1995.

f Supplies made in the construction of the following:

i A dwelling, for example, a house or flat. This may include the construction of a garage if work is undertaken at the same time as the construction of the dwelling.

ii New buildings used as children's homes, old people's homes and to provide student accommodation, but not hotels or prisons.

iii New buildings to be used by a charity for non-business purposes, for example, churches.

iv Substantial alterations to listed buildings used for a purpose within i, ii or iii.

The construction of other buildings, for example, offices, shops and factories, is not zero rated.

g Transport of passengers in a vehicle, ship or aircraft designed or adapted to carry not less than twelve passengers.

h Exports, including those to Member States in the Single Market where the required documentation is forthcoming.

i Supply of drugs, medicines, medical and surgical appliances.

j Supply of clothing and footwear suitable for young children.

This list is not intended to be exhaustive but it provides some indication of those supplies which may, and those which may not, be zero rated for value added tax purposes. In addition, a number of supplies made to charities obtain the benefit of zero rating and incur no liability to value added tax.

FARMERS

A new agricultural flat rate scheme was introduced on January 1st, 1993. This scheme is optional and may be used by farmers engaged in crop production, stock farming, forestry, fisheries and processing. It cannot be used by individuals whose primary activity is to buy and sell animals, nor can animal trainers qualify. Persons who purchase dairy products from farmers and those operating sawmills are excluded from the scheme.

Where a farmer uses the flat rate scheme he will not be registered for value added tax purposes. In the absence of registration there will be no right to recover input tax. However, the farmer may add a special addition of 4 per cent to his sales and retain that addition in lieu of relief for input tax. Non-farming activities undertaken by a farmer and which cannot be brought within the flat rate scheme must be dealt with separately. It will not be possible to add the flat rate addition to non-farming supplies of this nature. Where the value of taxable supplies attributable to non-farming activities is sufficiently substantial to require registration, or the farmer registers on a voluntary basis, he can no longer use the flat rate scheme.

Persons to whom supplies are made by a farmer can treat the 4 per cent addition as input tax and obtain relief for that tax in the normal manner.

ADMINISTRATION

Value added tax is administered by H M Customs and Excise and not by the Board of Inland Revenue. The tax performs no role whatsoever in the United Kingdom income tax system.

Registered traders should recognise that the application and administration of value added tax involves the satisfaction of many compliance requirements. Failure to submit value added tax returns, or to account for the proper amount of tax due promptly, may involve liability to penalties and interest.

Inheritance tax

INTRODUCED IN 1974 to replace estate duty, capital transfer tax imposed a wide-ranging liability to tax on lifetime gifts and also on the value of an individual's estate immediately before the time of death. Complex rules were included to deal with settled property held on trust. The potential scope of capital transfer tax was substantially redrafted for events taking place after March 18th, 1986. Whilst much of the former administrative framework remained, the tax was re-named inheritance tax. The following comments outline the nature and scope of inheritance tax but apply only to events occurring on and after March 19th, 1986.

When examining these comments it must be emphasised that the new system of independent taxation, which was introduced on April 6th, 1990, has absolutely no effect on inheritance tax. Independent taxation of husband and wife is limited to income tax and capital gains tax. There was no need for this system to be extended to inheritance tax as husband and wife have been separately taxed since the introduction of capital transfer tax in 1974.

Liability to inheritance tax extends to assets located in the United Kingdom. The tax also applies to assets located overseas if the person concerned was domiciled in the United Kingdom at the time of the transfer or other event. There are two main occasions of charge, one affecting a limited range of lifetime transfers and the other of application to the value of an estate immediately before death.

LIFETIME TRANSFERS

Lifetime gifts and other transfers which deplete the value of an individual's estate may fall into four broad categories, namely transactions to be disregarded, exempt transfers, potentially exempt transfers and chargeable transfers.

Transactions disregarded

Some lifetime gifts and dispositions are entirely disregarded and incur no liability to inheritance tax, notwithstanding the value of the transferor's estate is reduced. These include dispositions not intended to confer any gratuitous benefit, the provision of family maintenance, the waiver of the right to receive remuneration and dividends, and the grant of agricultural tenancies made for full consideration.

Exempt transfers

Transfers of value which can be treated as "exempt transfers" also avoid liability to inheritance tax. These include the following:

a A transfer by an individual to his or her spouse. This is subject to modification if the transferee is not domiciled in the United Kingdom.

b The first £3,000 of transfers made in a year ending on April 5th. If the total value of transfers taking place in any year falls below £3,000 the excess may be carried forward for one year only and utilised in that year.

c Transfers of value made by a transferor to any person in a year ending on April 5th if the value transferred does not exceed £250.

d A transfer made as part of the transferor's normal expenditure and satisfied out of income.

e Outright gifts in consideration of marriage to the extent that the value transferred by any one transferor in respect of a single marriage does not exceed:

i £5,000 if the transferor is the parent of either party to the marriage

ii £2,500 if the transferor is a party to the marriage or a grandparent or remoter ancestor of either party;

iii £1,000 if the transferor is any other person.

f Transfers made to a charity where the assets transferred become the property of a charity or are held in trust for charitable purposes only.

g The transfer of property to a political party. If this exemption is to apply it must be shown that at the most recent General Election at least two members of the party were elected to the House of Commons. Alternatively, the requirement will be satisfied if a single member is elected with not less than 150,000 votes being cast for members of that party.

h Transfers made to an extensive list of institutions, including the National Museum, the National Trust for Places of Historic Interest or Natural Beauty, a local authority, and many others.

i Transfers of heritage property and other assets of value to the nation made to an approved body not established or conducted for profit.

Potentially exempt transfers

If a transfer is neither to be disregarded nor an exempt transfer it may comprise a potentially exempt transfer. This represents a transfer made by an individual to:

a a second individual;

b trustees administering an accumulation and maintenance trust; or

c trustees administering funds for a disabled or handicapped person.

The range of potentially exempt transfers also includes certain transactions affecting settled property in which an individual or individuals retain a life interest in possession. Most transfers made by an individual to such a trust may be treated as potentially exempt transfers and the termination of an interest in possession during lifetime may usually receive similar treatment.

As the title suggests, potentially exempt transfers are potentially exempt from liability to inheritance tax and no tax will become payable at the time of the transfer. The absence of liability will be confirmed should the transferor survive throughout a period of seven years from the date of the gift or other disposition. However, if the transferor dies within the seven-year inter vivos period tax becomes payable at the full rate or rates in force at the time of death. The amount of tax due may then be reduced to the following percentages by applying a form of tapering relief, which is governed by the length of the period between the date of the gift and the date of death:

Period of years before death	Percentage
Not more than 3	100
More than 3 but not more than 4 . .	80
More than 4 but not more than 5 . .	60
More than 5 but not more than 6 . .	40
More than 6 but not more than 7 . .	20

Chargeable transfers

Finally, a limited range of lifetime transfers will incur liability to inheritance tax. These are restricted to transfers involving trusts, other than those falling within the exempt and potentially exempt transfer rules, transfers to non-individuals and transfers affecting close companies. Tax is payable at one-half the full rate or rates but should the transferor die within a period of seven years from the date of the lifetime chargeable transfer additional tax may become payable by substituting the full rates, less a deduction for tapering relief.

GIFTS WITH RESERVATION

Troublesome rules apply where a lifetime gift is made but the transferor continues to enjoy some benefit in the subject matter of the gift. This will frequently arise where parents transfer the matrimonial home to children but continue to reside in the property without payment of a commercial rent. Where a gift with reservation is made it becomes necessary to establish the period throughout which the transferor continued to enjoy a benefit. If the benefit ceased to be enjoyed more than seven years before the date of the transferor's death no additional liability to inheritance tax will arise. A finding that the benefit was enjoyed immediately before the time of death will require that the value of the asset must be included when calculating the value of the deceased's estate on which inheritance tax becomes payable. Finally, if the transferor ceased to enjoy the benefit within a period of seven years before death he or she is treated as having made a potentially exempt transfer equal to the value of the asset at the time of cessation.

DEATH

Immediately before the time of death an individual is deemed to make a transfer of value equal to the value of his or her estate, representing assets less liabilities. However, exempt transfers involving transfers to a surviving spouse, charities, political organisations and national bodies will not incur inheritance tax liability, subject to limited exceptions. Inheritance tax payable is calculated by applying the full rates. In addition, death may trigger liability to tax on potentially exempt transfers, and also further liability for chargeable lifetime transfers made within a period of seven years before death.

VALUATION

The value transferred by lifetime transfers will usually reflect the fall in the value of the transferor's estate. Often this fall will be identical to the value of the asset transferred, but there are many exceptions, particularly where an individual transfers part only of his or her shareholding interest in a closely controlled company. Immediately before the time of death a person is treated as having transferred his or her entire estate for a consideration reflecting the value at that date. Therefore, the value transferred will represent the excess, if any, of the value attributable to assets, less liabilities.

BUSINESS ASSETS

In general, the value of property comprised in an individual's estate will reflect the price which that property might reasonably have been expected to fetch on a sale in the open market. However, where the transfer relates to certain assets the value transferred, both by lifetime transfers and on death, may be reduced by a percentage. When calculating this percentage a distinction must be drawn between dispositions, deaths and other events occurring:

a before March 10th, 1992; and

b after March 9th, 1992.

Events before March 10th, 1992

The percentage deductions available for transfers and other events taking place before March 10th, 1992 are shown by the following table:

Asset	Percentage deduction
Business or interest in a business	50
Controlling shareholding interest in any company	50
More than 25 per cent interest in an unquoted company	50
Not more than 25 per cent interest in an unquoted company	30
Land, buildings, machinery or plant used by a controlled company or partnership	30

Where a controlling shareholding interest exists it is immaterial whether the underlying company is quoted or unquoted when determining the availability of the 50 per cent deduction. However, the percentage deduction for minority shareholding interests cannot apply to shares in a quoted company or a company dealt in on the Unlisted Securities Market. For qualifying transfers of minority shareholding interests made before March 18th, 1987, the deduction was given at the rate of 30 per cent. This was increased to 50 per cent for events taking place subsequently if, throughout a minimum period of two years, the transferor retained more than 25 per cent of the company's issued share capital.

Events after March 9th, 1992

For transfers and events taking place after March 9th, 1992, most percentage deductions have increased considerably to the levels shown by the following table:

Asset	Percentage deduction
Business or interest in a business	100
More than 25 per cent holding in an unquoted company	100
More than 25 per cent holding in a USM company	100
Controlling shareholding interest in a quoted company	50
Not more than 25 per cent holding in an unquoted company	50
Not more than 25 per cent holding in a USM company	50
Land, buildings, machinery or plant used by a controlled company or partnership	50

91 *BUSINESS ASSETS RELIEF*

The issued share capital of A Ltd comprised 100 ordinary shares of £1 each. Mr B retained 65 shares at the time of his death on May 29th, 1991. It was agreed that these shares had a value of £150,000 and fully qualified for business assets relief.

The value to be included in the estate of Mr B for inheritance tax purposes is calculated as follows:

	£
Value of shares – as agreed	150,000
Less 50 per cent business assets relief	75,000
Value to be included	£75,000

The maximum 50 per cent relief can be obtained in this case as, at the time of his death, the deceased retained a controlling shareholding interest in A Ltd.

If Mr B had died one year later on May 29th, 1992, the value would be calculated in the following manner:

	£
Value of shares – as agreed	150,000
Less 100 per cent business assets relief	150,000
Value to be included	NIL

As a result of these changes, holdings in companies dealt in on the Unlisted Securities Market are now treated in the same manner as unquoted holdings. A more significant effect is that with the ability to obtain a 100 per cent deduction, many business assets may now be transferred without incurring any liability to inheritance tax.

Generally

It remains a general requirement in all cases that assets must have been owned for a minimum period of two years before the date of the lifetime disposition or death if the percentage deduction is to be forthcoming.

Only part of the value may qualify for the percentage deduction if not all assets of a business are used for a qualifying purpose.

AGRICULTURAL PROPERTY

The value of agricultural property transferred may also qualify for a percentage deduction. This is limited to the agricultural value and where, for example, property retains an "excessive" development value no deduction will be available for the excess.

To obtain this relief the property must either have been owned by the transferor for a period of seven years and used for agricultural purposes or occupied by the transferor for those purposes throughout a period of two years.

The percentage deductions for transfers and other events taking place before March 10th, 1992 are:

Asset	Percentage deduction
Owner occupied farmland	50
Farm tenancies	50
Land subject to a tenancy not terminating within twelve months	30

For events and transfers taking place after March 9th, 1992, the percentage deductions become:

Asset	Percentage deduction
Owner occupied farmland	100
Farm tenancies	100
Land subject to a tenancy not terminating within twelve months	50

CALCULATION OF TAX PAYABLE

The value of each non-exempt lifetime gift or disposition is added to the value of previous dispositions, if any, to establish the rate of tax on the current transfer. On death the value of the estate, after excluding any exempt transfers, will be added to the cumulative total of lifetime dispositions, if any, and tax calculated on the additional slice. This cumulative procedure affects only dispositions taking place within a period of seven years before the current transfer. Any dispositions made before the commencement of the seven-year period are ignored. When constructing the cumulative total, lifetime dispositions taking place before March 18th, 1986 and creating capital transfer tax liability must be included, if of course they fall within the seven-year period.

In those limited situations where inheritance tax becomes payable on a lifetime gift or disposition the value transferred must be "grossed up" by including tax payable, unless the obligation is discharged by the transferee.

92 *CALCULATION OF TAX PAYABLE – GIFTS WITHIN SEVEN YEARS BEFORE DEATH*

After making sufficient small gifts to exactly absorb the annual exemption, Mr R gifted freehold property to his son on December 18th, 1993. The value of the property at this time was £250,000 and it did not qualify for business assets or agricultural property relief. Mr R died on August 7th, 1997, without making any further gifts.

The gift was a potentially exempt transfer with no immediate liability to inheritance tax. However, as death occurred within the seven-year period, this will trigger liability. Assuming, for the purposes of illustration, that the rates of inheritance tax which apply from March 10th, 1992, remain unchanged, the tax payable will be calculated as follows:

	£	Cumulative total £
Value of gift		250,000
Tax payable		
On first £150,000	NIL	
On balance of £100,000 at 40 per cent	40,000	
	£40,000	£250,000

As death occurred more than 4 years and less than 5 years from the date of the gift, tax will be reduced to:

$$£40,000 \times 60\% = £24,000$$

RATE OF TAX

Rates of inheritance tax are usually amended annually, but an exception arose in 1993 when the existing rates remained completely unaltered. At the time of introduction on March 17th, 1986, an initial nil rate band of £71,000 was used, with six interim rate bands and a final 60 per cent top rate. Six years later the nil rate band had been increased to £150,000 with a single positive rate band of 40 per cent replacing all other bands.

Tables setting out the rates of inheritance tax which have applied since March 17th, 1986, appear on pages 205 and 206. These rates must be reduced by one-half when calculating tax on chargeable lifetime gifts.

93 *CALCULATION OF TAX PAYABLE ON DEATH*

Using the facts in Example 92, let it be assumed that the value of Mr R's estate at the time of death on August 7th, 1997, was £300,000, after subtracting all reliefs and exemptions.

The total inheritance tax then becoming due will be calculated as follows:

		Cumulative total £
Re gift within previous seven years . . .	£24,000	250,000
Re value on death		300,000
Tax payable		
On £300,000 at 40 per cent	£120,000	
		£550,000

Therefore the total inheritance tax payable, assuming rates which apply from March 10th, 1992, remain unchanged, is £144,000 (£24,000 + £120,000).

SETTLED PROPERTY

Complex rules apply when establishing inheritance tax liability for settled property held by trustees. In general, where a beneficiary retains an interest in possession the settled property to which that interest relates will be effectively treated as being in the ownership of the beneficiary. Property held by discretionary trusts is subject to a ten-year periodic charge, with interim charges where property leaves the trust before the first ten-year anniversary or between anniversaries. An accumulation and maintenance trust for the benefit of individuals below the age of 25 years will not be subject to the ten-year periodic charge, nor will liability to inheritance tax usually arise on the removal of property from such a trust.

These brief comments provide no more than a summary of the rules to be applied and in all cases consideration must be given to the trust deed or other document governing the administration of settled property.

Rates of Inheritance Tax

Events after March 17th, 1986 but before March 17th, 1987

Portion of value	Rate per cent
£ £	
0 – 71,000	Nil
71,001 – 95,000	30
95,001 – 129,000	35
129,001 – 164,000	40
164,001 – 206,000	45
206,001 – 257,000	50
257,001 – 317,000	55
317,001 and above	60

Events after March 16th, 1987 but before March 15th, 1988

Portion of value	Rate per cent
£ £	
0 – 90,000	Nil
90,001 – 140,000	30
140,001 – 220,000	40
220,001 – 330,000	50
330,001 and above	60

Events after March 14th, 1988 but before April 6th, 1989

Portion of value	Rate per cent
£ £	
0 – 110,000	Nil
110,001 and above	40

Events after April 5th, 1989 but before April 6th, 1990

Portion of value	Rate per cent
£ £	
0 – 118,000	Nil
118,001 and above	40

Events after April 5th, 1990 but before April 6th, 1991

Portion of value	Rate per cent
£ £	
0 – 128,000	Nil
128,001 and above	40

Events after April 5th, 1991 but before March 10th, 1992

Portion of value	Rate per cent
£ £	
0 – 140,000	Nil
140,001 and above	40

Events after March 9th, 1992

Portion of value	Rate per cent
£ £	
0 – 150,000	Nil
150,001 and above	40

Independent taxation

Some practical considerations

INTRODUCED ON April 6th, 1990, independent taxation of husband and wife is now a well-established feature of the United Kingdom taxation code. However, problem areas do sometimes arise and it may be of interest to readers if a number of matters which occasionally create difficulty are examined. As this section affects only husband and wife "living together" the following comments are limited to a married couple retaining such a status.

SCHEDULE D – BASIS OF ASSESSMENT

Many forms of income assessable under Schedule D are chargeable on a preceding year basis, with special adjustments inserted where a new source is commenced or an existing source discontinued. The application of independent taxation does not, by itself, affect this principle but merely governs the identity of the spouse who must suffer tax on profits or income.

In those cases where a married woman commenced a new business in her capacity of a sole proprietor during 1988–89, any election for the 1989–90 and 1990–91 assessments to be based on the actual profits of the business for each year must be made by the wife and not by the husband. There is a time limit of seven years from the end of 1989–90 within which an election can be made or withdrawn.

SCHEDULE A – BASIS OF ASSESSMENT

The preceding year basis of assessment does not apply to income from land and buildings chargeable under Schedule A. However, where the income for a year of assessment is insufficient to discharge the costs of maintenance and other eligible outgoings, any surplus expenditure may be carried forward and offset against similar income in future years. Where a surplus of unused expenditure remained on April 5th, 1990, it must be carefully allocated between husband and wife in the proper proportions to ensure that only the spouse who incurred the surplus can benefit by offsetting that surplus against his or her future income.

DEEDS OF COVENANT

When making payments under a properly drawn charitable deed of covenant the payer will deduct income tax at the basic rate. Where the payments are made out of income chargeable to income tax at that rate the amount of tax deducted may be retained. It is also possible to offset the covenanted payments against income generally for the purpose of obtaining relief at the higher rate where income is sufficiently substantial. In those cases where the payer does not have sufficient income taxable at the basic rate to provide cover for the payment the tax deducted must be paid over to the Inland Revenue.

Husbands and wives "living together" should carefully consider which spouse will be making future covenanted payments. If payments are made by a wife who has little or no income she may be required to account to the Inland Revenue for basic rate income tax deducted. In addition, there will be no relief at the higher rate. Where her husband is liable at this rate there will be a substantial advantage if the husband, rather than the wife, makes covenanted payments. In some situations, and with the consent of the charity concerned, it may be thought advisable for a wife to discontinue future payments due under an existing covenant, with these payments being replaced by a new deed of covenant entered into by her husband. If the gross amount of the covenant remains unaltered this will not affect income reaching the charity but will provide the "household" with increased tax relief.

In the case of joint covenants the Inland Revenue will usually maintain that payments should be treated as made equally by husband and wife, unless there is evidence to support a different conclusion.

BUSINESS EXPANSION SCHEME

Both a husband and his wife may independently obtain relief on investments up to £40,000 made under business expansion scheme arrangements. It will generally be advisable for the investments to be undertaken by whichever spouse suffers income tax at the highest rate. No relief will be available for investments made after December 31st, 1993.

MORTGAGE INTEREST

Only interest on qualifying loans not exceeding £30,000 and applied to acquire an individual's residence qualify for tax relief, usually under the MIRAS deduction scheme. In the case of husband and wife "living together" £30,000 is the maximum amount of aggregate loans made to the couple on which relief will be forthcoming.

It remains possible for the couple to submit an "allocation of interest" election, which enables the interest paid to be apportioned between the couple in whatever proportions they consider advisable. The election must be submitted within a period of twelve months following the end of the year of assessment to which it relates. It will then continue in force until being revoked by either spouse.

The election would frequently be made for 1990–91 if only one spouse was liable to income tax at the higher rate. With the withdrawal of relief at that rate for future years the election has lost much of its former importance. This importance will diminish further after April 5th, 1994, when relief is limited to the lower rate of 20 per cent. However, there may be an advantage where interest is paid outside the MIRAS scheme or where one spouse is over the age of 64.

MARRIED COUPLE'S ALLOWANCE

Where a couple are "living together" a married couple's allowance may be obtained. In the absence of any election this allowance must be used by the husband and only where he has insufficient income can any unused balance be transferred to his wife. The decision whether to transfer is that of the husband only.

For 1993–94 and future years the wife may elect, as of right, to obtain one-half of the basic married couple's allowance, leaving the husband with the balance of that allowance. Alternatively, the couple may jointly elect that the entire basic allowance should be allocated to the wife only. Notwithstanding any election, if the spouse entitled to any part of the married couple's allowance is unable to utilise that part against taxable income the unused portion may be transferred to the other spouse.

An election must be submitted before the commencement of the year of assessment to which it is first to apply. An exception arises in the year of marriage where the election may be submitted at any time in that year. Disregarding matters of "fairness", an election will be beneficial, particularly for 1993–94, where the wife is liable to income tax at a rate higher than that suffered by her husband. This will become considerably less important from April 6th, 1994, when the married couple's allowance will attract maximum income tax relief at the lower rate of 20 per cent.

LIFE ASSURANCE RELIEF

Where substantial premiums are paid on life assurance and other policies taken out before March 14th, 1984, tax relief may be restricted by reference to the payer's income. Following the introduction of independent taxation the income of husband and wife cannot be merged for this purpose. Consideration must be confined to the income of the spouse paying premiums.

MEDICAL INSURANCE POLICIES

Where payments are made after April 5th, 1990, on a qualifying policy of medical insurance, income tax will be deducted at the basic rate, with further relief at the higher rate where the payer's income is sufficiently substantial. It may be worth considering whether premiums should be paid by a husband or by his wife, as there may well be an advantage from selecting the individual suffering tax at the higher rate.

JOINT CHEQUE ACCOUNTS

Many married couples maintain joint bank current or cheque accounts. Where a cheque is drawn on such an account to discharge a liability it may become doubtful whether the payment is being made by the husband or by his wife. Little difficulty emerges where the cheque is drawn to discharge a joint liability and in practice it is unlikely that the Inland Revenue would dispute the identity of the alleged drawer in other cases. However, for the avoidance of doubt, where a cheque is to be drawn to satisfy a payment attracting tax relief, perhaps a donation under the Gift Aid scheme, it may be considered advisable to open a separate account in the sole name of the drawer. This should place beyond doubt the identity of the person involved.

PARTNERSHIPS

Where the income of one party to a marriage substantially exceeds that of the other there is an obvious advantage from the transfer of future income by that party. One possible method of achieving this where a business is carried on by, say, a husband in his capacity as a sole trader, is to admit the wife as a partner. This will enable partnership profits to be shared between husband and wife. However, caution must be exercised to ensure that a "genuine" partnership exists between the parties and not merely a "paper" or "sham" arrangement which will fail to withstand detailed scrutiny.

DIRECTORSHIPS

A further method of providing one spouse, usually a wife, with income is for the wife to be appointed a director or employee of her husband's company. If this results in the earnings of the husband being reduced the Inland Revenue may decline to accept that income really has been derived by the wife. This rejection should be successfully opposed by the ability to demonstrate that real services have been provided in return for the remuneration paid.

JOINT INCOME

Some income-producing assets may be held jointly by a husband and his wife. The general rule is that any income arising from such assets must be apportioned equally between the couple. However, it is possible to submit a joint declaration requiring the income to be apportioned by reference to the beneficial interests held by the husband and by the wife. The declaration must be forwarded to the Inland Revenue within a period of 60 days from the date on which it has been made and will only apply to income arising subsequently.

Where husband and wife jointly retain income-producing assets the ability to submit an election, or indeed the ability to refrain from making any such election, is important. The election applies separately to each asset, and in some situations it will be advisable to submit an election for a number of assets only and to refrain from making any election for the remainder. Numerous cases will undoubtedly arise where wisdom indicates the inadvisability of submitting any election whatsoever.

TRANSFER OF ASSETS

Where a wife has little, if any, income and her spouse retains a range of income-producing assets, consideration may well be given to the transfer of an asset for the purpose of establishing future income accruing to the wife. If such a transfer is to be effective for income tax purposes it must comprise an "outright gift". Should any "strings" be attached to the gift, or the transferor be entitled to enjoy any benefit whatsoever from the asset transferred, the transaction is likely to be ineffective. All future income from an ineffective transfer will remain that of the transferor for income tax purposes.

LOSSES CARRIED FORWARD

Losses incurred by a husband or wife from the carrying on of a trade, profession or vocation may be carried forward and offset against future profits. Losses incurred by a spouse may only be carried forward and offset against future profits from the same business carried on by the same spouse. It is not possible for those losses to be carried forward and used by the other spouse.

In some situations business losses incurred in 1989–90 could be offset against any income for the following year. As independent taxation applies to the following year, 1990–91, it is only the spouse incurring the loss who can benefit from this arrangement. For 1989–90 and earlier years business losses of one spouse could be set against income of the other without restriction.

Finally, losses arising in the first four years of a new business may be carried back and set against profits, gains and income of earlier years. A married woman who incurs losses which are carried back to a date falling before April 6th, 1990, should be aware that the benefit of any loss relief will be enjoyed by her husband.

CAPITAL GAINS TAX

For capital gains tax purposes a husband and his wife each have an annual exemption of £5,800 for 1993–94. Unless each exemption limit is fully used annually it cannot be carried forward and will be lost. This may suggest a transfer of assets from one spouse to another before those assets are sold to a third party, thereby enabling the gain to be realised in the most tax efficient manner.

Problems may arise where gains or losses accrue from the disposal of a jointly owned asset. It will be necessary to allocate the gains or losses between the joint owners. No election is possible to determine the basis of allocation, which will probably proceed by an equal apportionment unless there is clear evidence that the beneficial interests support a different allocation. In some cases a husband and his wife may consider it advisable to adjust their interests to obtain the most tax efficient basis of apportionment.

Further hints on saving tax

ALL TAXPAYERS are understandably anxious to reduce their tax commitments. This can be achieved by:

a taking advantage of all available allowances and reliefs;

b carefully planning the dates on which transactions or events take place;

c taking steps to increase the reliefs which can be obtained; or

d refraining from action which will increase the amount of tax payable.

The requirements of one individual will differ from those of another, and there are often personal or business considerations which will outweigh possible tax savings. For example, ready access to savings may be more important than the amount of tax incurred on income arising. But few financial transactions can be safely carried out without considering the effect on tax liabilities. The following notes outline some areas where tax savings can be achieved, or additional obligations avoided. Other matters have been reviewed in the previous chapter dealing with the recently introduced system of independent taxation.

PERSONAL MATTERS

Allowances

All individuals are entitled to a personal allowance and should make sure that this is being claimed and used. Those approaching the age of 65 or 75 must advise the Tax Office if the increased personal allowances are to be forthcoming, and most other allowances will only be given where they are claimed.

Married Couple's Allowance

For 1993–94 and future years it is possible for a married woman "living with" her husband to obtain one-half, or all, of the married couple's allowance. This requires the submission of a claim before the commencement of a year of assessment and may be advantageous where the wife suffers a higher rate of tax. Any advantage is likely to become small after April 5th, 1994, when the allowance gives rise to relief at the lower rate of 20 per cent only.

Marriage

In the year of marriage the married couple's allowance reduces by £143 (at 1993–94 rates) for each complete month from May 5th to the date of the ceremony. For example, by postponing the wedding from, say, April 30th to May 15th, the allowance will fall by £143, which represents some £35.75 if tax is suffered at the basic rate of 25 per cent. This may justify advancing the ceremony by days, weeks, or even months.

Marriage breakdown

On the breakdown of a marriage leading to separation or divorce a great many tax considerations will arise. Where payments are made under a "new" Court order or maintenance agreement, the recipient will not suffer liability to taxation, nor can the payer obtain any substantial relief. Thus in some situations payments must be financed out of taxed income. This obligation must be recognised when the order or agreement is being proposed and it may be considered advisable to transfer the ownership of income-producing assets, rather than enter into a commitment for the payment of maintenance. Where there are children of the marriage the possible obligation of a parent to make child maintenance payments to the Child Support Agency is a further factor requiring detailed review.

Payments made under "old" orders or agreements may continue to obtain relief, but this is not to exceed the amount payable in 1988–89. It follows that where such an agreement or order is subsequently increased, the payer may obtain no tax relief for the amount of the increase.

Although the transfer of assets between husband and wife "living together" incurs no liability to capital gains tax, this exemption no longer applies once they are separated, or indeed divorced. Where the value of assets is substantial, this often creates considerable liability to capital gains tax. It is essential that parties to a marriage breakdown take professional advice on their tax commitments at an early stage.

Interest

Unless payments of interest can be deducted in calculating business profits, stringent requirements must be satisfied before the outgoing will qualify for relief in calculating income chargeable to tax. No relief is available for interest payable on a bank overdraft, and whenever possible a more permanent form of borrowing should be used.

Interest on a loan applied to acquire an individual's only or main residence will usually qualify for relief, subject to a maximum ceiling of £30,000 and with relief limited to the basic rate for 1993–94 and further limited to the lower rate for the following year. Some individuals may acquire a loan on the security of an existing dwelling but no relief can be obtained for the subsequent payment of interest, unless the loan is applied for a qualifying purpose. If the need to obtain additional finance can be anticipated, it may be advisable to obtain an increased mortgage when acquiring the property. This could enable interest to be relieved, unless the £30,000 ceiling is exceeded.

Relief may continue for interest paid on loans applied before April 6th, 1988 on the acquisition of a private residence for occupation by a separated spouse, divorced former spouse or a dependent relative. Relief may also be forthcoming where the loan was applied to improve the residence. However, if qualifying occupation is discontinued, or the old loan replaced by a new loan, future relief for interest paid will be lost.

There may be an attraction from borrowing funds overseas, where lower rates of interest can sometimes be obtained. However, the interest paid on these borrowings is unlikely to qualify for relief; thereby eroding the apparent advantage.

MIRAS

Income tax relief is obtained by deduction where MIRAS applies to interest payments. A number of conditions must be satisfactorily discharged before MIRAS can apply, and failure to observe those conditions may later have serious consequences. As a general rule, MIRAS is limited to interest paid on a loan applied to acquire a qualifying home. It cannot be obtained on property used for some other purpose or on property merely provided as security. Particular difficulties arise where two single individuals each have loans under MIRAS and subsequently marry. In the case of a husband and wife "living together" there can be only one recognised "only or main residence". Relief is limited to interest paid on a loan applied to acquire that residence and cannot extend to a loan on some other property. Nor can the couple obtain relief for interest on aggregate loans in excess of £30,000.

It is of great importance that when completing the initial MIRAS documents, or where some future change in circumstances takes place, the lender is made fully aware of the position. Subsequent detection that MIRAS has been applied to a non-qualifying loan may not only lead to a demand for the recovery of excessive relief but can result in demands for interest and penalties also.

Children

Minor children are entitled to the basic personal allowance of £3,445 for 1993–94. Many children have little, if any, income, unless they leave school or undertake a part-time job. This means that the personal allowance will be lost. To utilise the personal allowance, a grandparent, uncle or aunt would sometimes enter into a deed of covenant providing the child with income. Similar arrangements were used by parents having children over the age of 18 years and attending university or some other form of higher education establishment. On making payments under a deed of covenant the payer would usually deduct and retain income tax at the basic rate. The child could often obtain a repayment of the tax deducted from the Inland Revenue.

No payments made under such deeds of covenant entered into after March 14th, 1988, will be recognised for taxation purposes. Nor is it possible to backdate a deed executed on some later date.

However, covenants executed before March 15th, 1988, and inspected by H M Inspector of Taxes not later than June 30th in the same year remain valid and it is important that payments continue to be made where tax advantages are available.

Grandparents may contemplate placing funds in a building society account, bank deposit account or other income-producing investment as this can provide income absorbed by the annual allowance. Parents may undertake similar arrangements for their minor children but where income exceeds £100 it may be treated as that of the parent for income tax purposes. It is as well to take professional advice before parents transfer assets to, or for the benefit of, their minor children.

Charitable covenants

No income tax relief is available to individuals making modest voluntary gifts to charity unless those payments are made under an approved payroll deduction scheme. However, regular donors should contemplate using deeds of covenant. Payments made under charitable covenants enable the payer to obtain tax relief at the highest rate of tax suffered, without any limitation on the amount paid for 1993–94.

Single donations of £250 or more under the Gift Aid scheme will provide relief on a basis similar to that for payments under deed of covenant. Those contemplating substantial donations of an irregular amount may prefer the flexibility of Gift Aid to a formal deed of covenant.

DIRECTORS AND EMPLOYEES

Living accommodation

An additional taxable benefit arises where a director or employee is provided with expensive living accommodation. This benefit applies if the cost of the accommodation, together with the cost of carrying out improvements, exceeds £75,000. Those occupying property acquired at a cost falling below the £75,000 threshold should carefully consider the wisdom of moving to more expensive property where the threshold is to be exceeded. The move may create a taxable benefit which would not otherwise arise.

Car benefits

Directors and higher-paid employees provided with motor cars for private motoring suffer tax on a benefit calculated by reference to a scale charge which tends to be increased annually. The charge is further increased by 50 per cent where the vehicle is used for less than 2,500 miles of business motoring in a year, or reduced by 50 per cent if business motoring exceeds 18,000 miles annually. Wherever possible attempts should be made to exceed these thresholds and reduce the amount of the taxable benefit.

Those making little use of a motor vehicle may wish to consider whether the arrangement should continue. It could be cost efficient for an individual to provide his or her own motor vehicle for business travel and to receive a "tax free" mileage allowance under the Fixed Profit Car Scheme. This advantage may increase when a new code for taxing car benefits comes into operation on April 6th, 1994.

Loss of office

The first £30,000 received as compensation for the loss of an office or employment is usually tax-free. Where dismissal or redundancy is likely and negotiations are taking place between the parties, there may be an advantage in accepting a tax-free lump sum, rather than an extended period of notice with taxable earnings.

BUSINESS CONSIDERATIONS

Accounting date

Where a new business is commenced, special rules apply to determine the amount of profits chargeable to income tax in the opening years. Once the business has become established, profits assessable for a tax year are usually based on profits for the twelve-month accounting period ending in the previous year. For example, if accounts are prepared annually to March 31st, profits for the year ending on March 31st, 1993, will be assessable in 1993–94, with tax becoming payable by equal instalments on January 1st and July 1st, 1994. In contrast, where accounts are prepared to April 30th, the results for the year ending on April 30th, 1993, will be assessed for 1994–95 with tax becoming payable on January 1st and July 1st, 1995. Some deferment in the payment of tax may therefore be achieved by adopting an annual accounting date ending shortly after April 5th.

This strategy may cease to be tax efficient when details of provisions governing the new basis likely to be introduced in 1996–97 become available.

Capital allowances

Attractive first-year and initial allowances are available for expenditure incurred between November 1st, 1992, and October 31st, 1993. These allowances extend to expenditure on many items of plant and machinery, industrial buildings and hotels, together with agricultural buildings and works. In some situations it is a requirement that a newly constructed building should be brought into use for a qualifying purpose not later than December 31st, 1994. Adherence to these time limits is important if the first-year or initial allowances are to be forthcoming.

Where plant and machinery is anticipated to enjoy a relatively short life span there may be an advantage in removing expenditure from the normal "pool".

National insurance contributions

Class I national insurance contributions are based on the level of "earnings" paid to an employed individual. Primary contributions suffered by an employee are subject to a threshold. Once this threshold has been reached, contributions are not payable on the excess, although the rate at which contributions are imposed is due to increase on April 6th, 1994. No similar threshold applies to secondary contributions payable by the employer who must satisfy contributions at the rate of 10.4 per cent on all earnings of higher paid employees. Some employers may consider whether employees should be offered "perks" or "benefits", rather than an increase in salary. Many advantages of this nature, although creating taxable benefits in the hands of employees, are disregarded when determining the level of earnings on which contributions must be paid. The availability of a car for private motoring and the provision of fuel for a similar purpose will involve the employer, but not the employee, in a further liability to discharge contributions.

In the case of closely controlled family companies advantages may arise from the payment of dividends, or possibly rent for the use of assets, rather than remuneration. Before any steps of this nature are taken detailed consideration must be given to the possible effect on other forms of taxation. In particular it will not be overlooked that with the reduction in the rate of advance corporation tax to 22.5 per cent on April 6th 1993 and the further reduction to 20 per cent twelve months later, some of the advantages from paying dividends will be eroded.

INVESTMENT OPPORTUNITIES

Life assurance

No tax relief is available for premiums paid on new life assurance policies made after March 13th, 1984. However, relief continues for qualifying policies made on or before this date, unless the terms of the policy are altered. Relief reduces the cost of premiums by 12.5 per cent and this should be recognised before contemplating the surrender of older policies, or taking any steps which may terminate future relief.

Pensions for the employed

Employees who are members of a company, or other, occupational pension scheme obtain relief for contributions paid to secure benefits. The maximum relief is broadly limited to contributions not exceeding 15 per cent of earnings. Few schemes require contributions at this level but the employee may utilise the shortfall by paying additional voluntary contributions. The aggregate contributions paid must not result in the 15 per cent limit being exceeded, but subject to this the additional contributions may be paid to trustees administering the employer's scheme or to a "free-standing" approved financial institution. These contributions produce relief at the employee's highest rate of income tax. For example, an individual paying additional voluntary contributions of £1,000 and suffering tax at the higher rate of 40 per cent for 1993–94 will reduce his or her tax bill by £400, so that the true net outlay is only £600. Membership of an employer's pension scheme is no longer compulsory but before ceasing to participate in such a scheme employees should carefully review the available alternatives. It may be found that these alternatives do not justify removal from the scheme.

Pensions for the self-employed and others

Self-employed individuals and employees not covered by a pension scheme may contribute up to 17.5 per cent, or perhaps more for those aged over 35, of their earnings to a personal pension scheme or a retirement annuity scheme. Premiums paid may be set against taxable income. Where insufficient premiums have been paid in any year the balance of unused relief may be carried forward for a maximum six-year period. Any unused relief remaining at the end of this six-year period is lost. Those able to contribute should consider the advisability of paying maximum contributions, particularly where they are approaching retirement age. Although the purpose of paying contributions is to provide a pension or annuity in retirement, it is possible to obtain a tax-free lump sum, with reduced periodic payments in the future.

Business expansion scheme

Tax relief can be obtained on the cost of subscribing for shares in a qualifying company where the business expansion scheme requirements are satisfied. Maximum relief of £40,000 is available for shares issued in each year of assessment. If any part of the £40,000 relief available for 1992–93 remains unused it may be possible to utilise all or part of the balance by making investments in the first six months of 1993–94 which are related back to the previous year. Subject to this, any unused relief cannot be carried forward and will be lost.

It will not be overlooked that business expansion scheme relief is due to terminate on December 31st, 1993. Those seeking to achieve maximum relief for 1993–94 must therefore ensure that investments are made before this date.

Enterprise zones

Capital allowances up to a maximum of 100 per cent are available for the cost of constructing buildings, including commercial buildings, in an enterprise zone. It is possible for these allowances to be set against income generally and the year in which relief is to be obtained should be carefully selected.

Investment generally

A modest tax efficient investment is the purchase of National Savings certificates, as interest arising to the eventual date of realisation is not liable to income tax. An identical yield will be received by those who suffer tax at the higher rate and those who are not chargeable. This may prove a particular attraction for higher rate taxpayers as the tax free annual compound yield of 5.75 per cent which, for example, is available on the 40th issue held throughout the full five-year period, is equal to a gross yield of 9.58 per cent on which tax is suffered at 40 per cent.

Other tax efficient investments comprise TESSA accounts where interest is tax free and holdings of Personal Equity Plans where both dividends and capital gains avoid the inroads of taxation.

Interest received from building societies, banks and some other financial institutions suffers income tax by deduction at the basic rate. Investors not liable, or not fully liable, may obtain a repayment of any excessive tax deducted. Those of small means and not liable to tax may arrange for interest to be paid or credited gross. Interest on some government securities, with the addition of securities on the National Savings Stock Register and National Savings Income Bonds, is paid gross without deduction of income tax. Holdings of this nature also avoid the need to claim any repayment of tax, although where the investor is liable any tax due must be paid.

A note of caution

Newspaper advertisements sometimes list attractive opportunities for investment designed to secure tax advantages. Before taking advantage of the opportunities offered, potential investors should fully understand the working of the scheme and establish that it is not vulnerable to attack by the Inland Revenue. If substantial sums are involved, it may be worthwhile taking independent professional advice.

CAPITAL GAINS TAX

Annual exemption

The first £5,800 of gains, less losses, realised by an individual from the disposal of assets in the year ended April 5th, 1994, are exempt from capital gains tax. If the exemption is not fully used the excess cannot be carried forward to the following year. Attempts should therefore be made to fully utilise the exemption, perhaps by bringing forward disposals to a date falling before April 6th, 1994. In cases where the exemption limit has already been exceeded, disposals may well be deferred until the following year.

Losses

Where gains exceed the annual exemption of £5,800, it may be advisable to consider whether the excess gains can be reduced by creating losses. In some cases this may be achieved by bringing forward a disposal date which would otherwise fall after April 5th, or perhaps by arranging "bed and breakfast" transactions whereby shares are sold to produce a loss and subsequently reacquired.

Government securities

No capital gains tax will be payable on the disposal of Government securities and many securities (but not shares) issued by quoted and unquoted companies. Those retaining substantial holdings of securities should not overlook the accrued income scheme for calculating liability to income tax.

Deferment of tax

Liability to capital gains tax for disposals taking place in the year ended April 5th, 1994, requires satisfaction on December 1st, 1994. In some cases where the exemption of £5,800 has been used, it may be thought advisable to defer the contemplated disposal of assets until a date falling after April 5th, 1994. This will delay payment of tax for a further twelve-month period.

Rate of tax

The rate of capital gains tax due on chargeable gains will reflect an individual's marginal rate of income tax. Where income is expected to fluctuate considerably as between one year and another, this could become a factor governing the year in which a planned disposal should be made.

INHERITANCE TAX

Annual exemption

Few lifetime gifts and dispositions now incur liability to inheritance tax. If a lifetime transaction within the limited range producing liability is contemplated, the annual exemption of £3,000 should not be overlooked. This applies to gifts made in a year ending on April 5th, and if the exemption is not fully utilised in a particular year the excess can be carried forward and absorbed in the following year only. An aggregate exemption of £6,000 may therefore be obtained for 1993–94 if no part of the exemption has been used in the previous year. Failure to absorb the amount brought forward in the second year will result in the exemption being lost. Wherever possible the available exemption should be used.

Gifts with reservation

The making of a lifetime gift which reserves some benefit to the donor may create liability to inheritance tax on death, unless the reservation ceased to apply more than seven years before the time of death. Gifts made subject to reservation which do not fall within a list of exceptions are to be firmly avoided.

Potentially exempt transfers

Many lifetime gifts made by an individual to a second individual or to a limited range of trustees comprise potentially exempt transfers. No liability to inheritance tax will arise should the donor survive the seven year inter vivos period. There is an obvious attraction of making such gifts at the earliest possible date.

Gifts within seven years before death

Should the donor die within seven years of making a gift, liability to inheritance tax may arise on the value of the gift. Although this is mainly designed to frustrate "deathbed gifts", it will apply equally to all gifts within the seven-year period. The subsequent date of a donor's death cannot usually be anticipated with any measure of accuracy, except in the case of terminal illness, and an unexpected death within the seven-year period may create substantial liability to inheritance tax. In some situations it may be thought advisable to secure funds for the possible satisfaction of tax payable on gifts by means of a term assurance policy.

Reliefs

Certain reliefs, notably business asset relief and agricultural property relief, will only be available if assets have been owned throughout a required period of time ending on the date of a lifetime disposition or death. The need to establish a qualifying period should be recognised before transferring assets, particularly between members of a family, where ownership must inevitably change. Other requirements must be satisfied between the date of a gift comprising a potentially exempt transfer and the time of death if reliefs are to be preserved.

The need to satisfy these requirements is now of increased importance following the recent introduction of relief at the rate of 100 per cent for many business assets and a range of agricultural property.

Other considerations

Savings in inheritance tax and other tax considerations must never reflect the sole reason for making gifts. Once the ownership of assets has been transferred those assets will cease to be available to the donor, if the transaction is to secure the required tax advantages. Those contemplating substantial gifts must recognise the depletion in their available assets and perhaps a reduction in future income which the transfer will create.

GENERAL MATTERS

Claims and elections

Many tax advantages are only available if a written claim or election is made to the Inland Revenue. There is a very long list of time limits governing different elections and claims and it is essential that these limits are fully observed. If they are not, unexpected tax liabilities may arise.

Disclosure of information

The law requires that taxpayers should disclose details of income, profits or gains to the Inland Revenue, although this is of limited significance to those whose only income is derived from an employment and the PAYE deduction scheme applies. Failure to disclose details of a part-time job, the existence of a business, or details of chargeable gains assessable to capital gains tax, may have serious consequences. Not only will tax become payable but the individual may incur additional liabilities to interest and penalties.

Action before

APRIL 6th, 1994

AS THE END of the tax year approaches on April 5th, 1994, taxpayers should consider whether any action is needed to reduce tax payable. The Chancellor of the Exchequer is due to deliver his first Winter Budget Statement towards the end of November 1993. This should disclose details of any tax rate changes coming into operation on April 5th, 1994, and enable a comparison to be made with those in operation for the previous year. In addition, the following matters may be significant, among many others:

- Claims for repayment of income tax must be made within a period of six years from the end of the year of assessment to which those claims relate. The time limit for submitting claims in respect of 1987–88 expires on April 5th, 1994.
- Elections which may be of interest to a large number of taxpayers concern the married couple's allowance. A wife "living with" her husband can elect to receive one-half of the basic allowance for 1994–95 if action is taken not later than April 5th, 1994. It is also possible for the entire basic allowance to accrue for the benefit of the wife only, if a suitable claim is submitted by the same date. New elections will not be necessary if a suitable election has already been made for 1993–94, unless that election is to be varied.
- Many other claims and elections have time limits expiring on April 5th, 1994. For example, claims to relieve losses must usually be made within a period of two years from the end of the year of assessment in which those losses arose. An "interest allocation election", which apportions interest paid between husband and wife, must be submitted not later than April 5th, 1994, if it is to apply for 1992–93.
- Any additional voluntary pension contributions paid by an employed person must be satisfied by April 5th, 1994, if they are to reduce the tax bill for 1993–94.
- Personal pension scheme contributions and retirement annuity premiums paid during the year ending on April 5th, 1994 may be treated as satisfied in 1992–93, or perhaps earlier, if an election is made. The election may be particularly advantageous if the 17.5 per cent, or higher, maximum has not been fully used in the earlier year. Unused

relief for previous years can be carried forward for a maximum of six years. This enables unused relief for 1986–87 to be used in the year ended on April 5th, 1993, and that for 1987–38 to be utilised in the year ending on April 5th, 1994. These are matters which an individual should carefully consider when paying premiums not later than April 5th, 1994, which can, at his or her option, be allocated to the year ending on that date or to some previous year.

□ There may be an advantage in entering into a deed of covenant in favour of a charity before April 6th, 1994, to establish tax relief for a payment made under that deed in 1993–94. Those able to make substantial donations under the Gift Aid scheme may consider action before April 6th, 1994, if tax relief is to be obtained at the higher rate for 1993–94.

□ Employees earning £8,500 or more and directors provided with cars for private motoring should attempt to achieve 2,500 or 18,000 miles of business motoring before midnight on April 5th, 1994, is reached. The mileage travelled will govern the amount of taxable benefit.

These individuals should be aware that a new system for measuring taxable benefits arising from the availability of motor cars will come into operation on April 6th, 1994. The introduction of this new system may support a decision to change an existing model for the purpose of avoiding excessive liability to taxation.

□ If the full exemption of £5,800 is to be used for capital gains tax purposes in 1993–94, it may be necessary to undertake the disposal of additional assets not later than April 5th, 1994. Action may also be required to create losses which reduce that part of any gains which exceed the exemption limit.

□ Any part of the annual inheritance tax exemption amounting to £3,000 and which has not been used in the year ending on April 5th, 1993, will be lost unless it is utilised not later than April 5th, 1994.

□ There may be an advantage in making an unconditional gift of an asset between husband and wife, for the purpose of establishing the person on whom future income will be assessed for 1994–95.

Ready reckoner

BASED ON TAX AT 25 PER CENT

1p to 99p (to the nearest whole penny)

Amount	Tax	Amount	Tax	Amount	Tax
£	£	£	£	£	£
0.01	—	0.34	0.09	0.67	0.17
0.02	0.01	0.35	0.09	0.68	0.17
0.03	0.01	0.36	0.09	0.69	0.17
0.04	0.01	0.37	0.09	0.70	0.18
0.05	0.01	0.38	0.10	0.71	0.18
0.06	0.02	0.39	0.10	0.72	0.18
0.07	0.02	0.40	0.10	0.73	0.18
0.08	0.02	0.41	0.10	0.74	0.19
0.09	0.02	0.42	0.11	0.75	0.19
0.10	0.03	0.43	0.11	0.76	0.19
0.11	0.03	0.44	0.11	0.77	0.19
0.12	0.03	0.45	0.11	0.78	0.20
0.13	0.03	0.46	0.12	0.79	0.20
0.14	0.04	0.47	0.12	0.80	0.20
0.15	0.04	0.48	0.12	0.81	0.20
0.16	0.04	0.49	0.12	0.82	0.21
0.17	0.04	0.50	0.13	0.83	0.21
0.18	0.05	0.51	0.13	0.84	0.21
0.19	0.05	0.52	0.13	0.85	0.21
0.20	0.05	0.53	0.13	0.86	0.22
0.21	0.05	0.54	0.14	0.87	0.22
0.22	0.06	0.55	0.14	0.88	0.22
0.23	0.06	0.56	0.14	0.89	0.22
0.24	0.06	0.57	0.14	0.90	0.23
0.25	0.06	0.58	0.15	0.91	0.23
0.26	0.07	0.59	0.15	0.92	0.23
0.27	0.07	0.60	0.15	0.93	0.23
0.28	0.07	0.61	0.15	0.94	0.24
0.29	0.07	0.62	0.16	0.95	0.24
0.30	0.08	0.63	0.16	0.96	0.24
0.31	0.08	0.64	0.16	0.97	0.24
0.32	0.08	0.65	0.16	0.98	0.25
0.33	0.08	0.66	0.17	0.99	0.25

EXAMPLE
To find the tax payable on £1,420.80 proceed as follows:

	£
TAX ON £1,000.00	250.00
TAX ON £400.00	100.00
TAX ON £20.00	5.00
TAX ON £0.80	0.20
TOTAL TAX	£355.20

£1 to £100,000

Amount	Tax	Amount	Tax	Amount	Tax	Amount	Tax
£	£	£	£	£	£	£	£
1	0.25	46	11.50	91	22.75	136	34.00
2	0.50	47	11.75	92	23.00	137	34.25
3	0.75	48	12.00	93	23.25	138	34.50
4	1.00	49	12.25	94	23.50	139	34.75
5	1.25	50	12.50	95	23.75	140	35.00
6	1.50	51	12.75	96	24.00	141	35.25
7	1.75	52	13.00	97	24.25	142	35.50
8	2.00	53	13.25	98	24.50	143	35.75
9	2.25	54	13.50	99	24.75	144	36.00
10	2.50	55	13.75	100	25.00	145	36.25
11	2.75	56	14.00	101	25.25	146	36.50
12	3.00	57	14.25	102	25.50	147	36.75
13	3.25	58	14.50	103	25.75	148	37.00
14	3.50	59	14.75	104	26.00	149	37.25
15	3.75	60	15.00	105	26.25	150	37.50
16	4.00	61	15.25	106	26.50	200	50.00
17	4.25	62	15.50	107	26.75	250	62.50
18	4.50	63	15.75	108	27.00	300	75.00
19	4.75	64	16.00	109	27.25	350	87.50
20	5.00	65	16.25	110	27.50	400	100.00
21	5.25	66	16.50	111	27.75	450	112.50
22	5.50	67	16.75	112	28.00	500	125.00
23	5.75	68	17.00	113	28.25	550	137.50
24	6.00	69	17.25	114	28.50	600	150.00
25	6.25	70	17.50	115	28.75	650	162.50
26	6.50	71	17.75	116	29.00	700	175.00
27	6.75	72	18.00	117	29.25	750	187.50
28	7.00	73	18.25	118	29.50	800	200.00
29	7.25	74	18.50	119	29.75	850	212.50
30	7.50	75	18.75	120	30.00	900	225.00
31	7.75	76	19.00	121	30.25	950	237.50
32	8.00	77	19.25	122	30.50	1,000	250.00
33	8.25	78	19.50	123	30.75	1,500	375.00
34	8.50	79	19.75	124	31.00	2,000	500.00
35	8.75	80	20.00	125	31.25	2,500	625.00
36	9.00	81	20.25	126	31.50	3,000	750.00
37	9.25	82	20.50	127	31.75	3,500	875.00
38	9.50	83	20.75	128	32.00	4,000	1,000.00
39	9.75	84	21.00	129	32.25	4,500	1,125.00
40	10.00	85	21.25	130	32.50	5,000	1,250.00
41	10.25	86	21.50	131	32.75	7,500	1,875.00
42	10.50	87	21.75	132	33.00	10,000	2,500.00
43	10.75	88	22.00	133	33.25	25,000	6,250.00
44	11.00	89	22.25	134	33.50	50,000	12,500.00
45	11.25	90	22.50	135	33.75	100,000	25,000.00

Ready reckoner

BASED ON TAX AT 20 PER CENT

Amount	Tax	Amount	Tax	Amount	Tax	Amount	Tax
£	£	£	£	£	£	£	£
1	0.20	46	9.20	91	18.20	136	27.20
2	0.40	47	9.40	92	18.40	137	27.40
3	0.60	48	9.60	93	18.60	138	27.60
4	0.80	49	9.80	94	18.80	139	27.80
5	1.00	50	10.00	95	19.00	140	28.00
6	1.20	51	10.20	96	19.20	141	28.20
7	1.40	52	10.40	97	19.40	142	28.40
8	1.60	53	10.60	98	19.60	143	28.60
9	1.80	54	10.80	99	19.80	144	28.80
10	2.00	55	11.00	100	20.00	145	29.00
11	2.20	56	11.20	101	20.20	146	29.20
12	2.40	57	11.40	102	20.40	147	29.40
13	2.60	58	11.60	103	20.60	148	29.60
14	2.80	59	11.80	104	20.80	149	29.80
15	3.00	60	12.00	105	21.00	150	30.00
16	3.20	61	12.20	106	21.20	200	40.00
17	3.40	62	12.40	107	21.40	250	50.00
18	3.60	63	12.60	108	21.60	300	60.00
19	3.80	64	12.80	109	21.80	350	70.00
20	4.00	65	13.00	110	22.00	400	80.00
21	4.20	66	13.20	111	22.20	450	90.00
22	4.40	67	13.40	112	22.40	500	100.00
23	4.60	68	13.60	113	22.60	550	110.00
24	4.80	69	13.80	114	22.80	600	120.00
25	5.00	70	14.00	115	23.00	650	130.00
26	5.20	71	14.20	116	23.20	700	140.00
27	5.40	72	14.40	117	23.40	750	150.00
28	5.60	73	14.60	118	23.60	800	160.00
29	5.80	74	14.80	119	23.80	850	170.00
30	6.00	75	15.00	120	24.00	900	180.00
31	6.20	76	15.20	121	24.20	950	190.00
32	6.40	77	15.40	122	24.40	1,000	200.00
33	6.60	78	15.60	123	24.60	1,100	220.00
34	6.80	79	15.80	124	24.80	1,150	230.00
35	7.00	80	16.00	125	25.00	1,200	240.00
36	7.20	81	16.20	126	25.20	1,250	250.00
37	7.40	82	16.40	127	25.40	1,300	260.00
38	7.60	83	16.60	128	25.60	1,400	280.00
39	7.80	84	16.80	129	25.80	1,500	300.00
40	8.00	85	17.00	130	26.00	1,600	320.00
41	8.20	86	17.20	131	26.20	1,700	340.00
42	8.40	87	17.40	132	26.40	1,800	360.00
43	8.60	88	17.60	133	26.60	1,900	380.00
44	8.80	89	17.80	134	26.80	2,000	400.00
45	9.00	90	18.00	135	27.00	2,500	500.00

Ready reckoner

BASED ON TAX AT 40 PER CENT

Amount	Tax	Amount	Tax	Amount	Tax	Amount	Tax
£	£	£	£	£	£	£	£
1	0.40	46	18.40	91	36.40	136	54.40
2	0.80	47	18.80	92	36.80	137	54.80
3	1.20	48	19.20	93	37.20	138	55.20
4	1.60	49	19.60	94	37.60	139	55.60
5	2.00	50	20.00	95	38.00	140	56.00
6	2.40	51	20.40	96	38.40	141	56.40
7	2.80	52	20.80	97	38.80	142	56.80
8	3.20	53	21.20	98	39.20	143	57.20
9	3.60	54	21.60	99	39.60	144	57.60
10	4.00	55	22.00	100	40.00	145	58.00
11	4.40	56	22.40	101	40.40	146	58.40
12	4.80	57	22.80	102	40.80	147	58.80
13	5.20	58	23.20	103	41.20	148	59.20
14	5.60	59	23.60	104	41.60	149	59.60
15	6.00	60	24.00	105	42.00	150	60.00
16	6.40	61	24.40	106	42.40	200	80.00
17	6.80	62	24.80	107	42.80	250	100.00
18	7.20	63	25.20	108	43.20	300	120.00
19	7.60	64	25.60	109	43.60	350	140.00
20	8.00	65	26.00	110	44.00	400	160.00
21	8.40	66	26.40	111	44.40	450	180.00
22	8.80	67	26.80	112	44.80	500	200.00
23	9.20	68	27.20	113	45.20	550	220.00
24	9.60	69	27.60	114	45.60	600	240.00
25	10.00	70	28.00	115	46.00	650	260.00
26	10.40	71	28.40	116	46.40	700	280.00
27	10.80	72	28.80	117	46.80	750	300.00
28	11.20	73	29.20	118	47.20	800	320.00
29	11.60	74	29.60	119	47.60	850	340.00
30	12.00	75	30.00	120	48.00	900	360.00
31	12.40	76	30.40	121	48.40	950	380.00
32	12.80	77	30.80	122	48.80	1,000	400.00
33	13.20	78	31.20	123	49.20	1,500	600.00
34	13.60	79	31.60	124	49.60	2,000	800.00
35	14.00	80	32.00	125	50.00	2,500	1,000.00
36	14.40	81	32.40	126	50.40	3,000	1,200.00
37	14.80	82	32.80	127	50.80	3,500	1,400.00
38	15.20	83	33.20	128	51.20	4,000	1,600.00
39	15.60	84	33.60	129	51.60	4,500	1,800.00
40	16.00	85	34.00	130	52.00	5,000	2,000.00
41	16.40	86	34.40	131	52.40	7,500	3,000.00
42	16.80	87	34.80	132	52.80	10,000	4,000.00
43	17.20	88	35.20	133	53.20	25,000	10,000.00
44	17.60	89	35.60	134	53.60	50,000	20,000.00
45	18.00	90	36.00	135	54.00	100,000	40,000.00

Grossing-up tables

AT 25 PER CENT

1p to 99p (to the nearest whole penny)

Net	Tax Credit	Gross	Net	Tax Credit	Gross	Net	Tax Credit	Gross
£	£	£	£	£	£	£	£	£
0.01	—	0.01	0.34	0.11	0.45	0.67	0.22	0.89
0.02	0.01	0.03	0.35	0.12	0.47	0.68	0.23	0.91
0.03	0.01	0.04	0.36	0.12	0.48	0.69	0.23	0.92
0.04	0.01	0.05	0.37	0.12	0.49	0.70	0.23	0.93
0.05	0.02	0.07	0.38	0.13	0.51	0.71	0.24	0.95
0.06	0.02	0.08	0.39	0.13	0.52	0.72	0.24	0.96
0.07	0.02	0.09	0.40	0.13	0.53	0.73	0.24	0.97
0.08	0.03	0.11	0.41	0.14	0.55	0.74	0.25	0.99
0.09	0.03	0.12	0.42	0.14	0.56	0.75	0.25	1.00
0.10	0.03	0.13	0.43	0.14	0.57	0.76	0.25	1.01
0.11	0.04	0.15	0.44	0.15	0.59	0.77	0.26	1.03
0.12	0.04	0.16	0.45	0.15	0.60	0.78	0.26	1.04
0.13	0.04	0.17	0.46	0.15	0.61	0.79	0.26	1.05
0.14	0.05	0.19	0.47	0.16	0.63	0.80	0.27	1.07
0.15	0.05	0.20	0.48	0.16	0.64	0.81	0.27	1.08
0.16	0.05	0.21	0.49	0.16	0.65	0.82	0.27	1.09
0.17	0.06	0.23	0.50	0.17	0.67	0.83	0.28	1.11
0.18	0.06	0.24	0.51	0.17	0.68	0.84	0.28	1.12
0.19	0.06	0.25	0.52	0.17	0.69	0.85	0.28	1.13
0.20	0.07	0.27	0.53	0.18	0.71	0.86	0.29	1.15
0.21	0.07	0.28	0.54	0.18	0.72	0.87	0.29	1.16
0.22	0.07	0.29	0.55	0.18	0.73	0.88	0.29	1.17
0.23	0.08	0.31	0.56	0.19	0.75	0.89	0.30	1.19
0.24	0.08	0.32	0.57	0.19	0.76	0.90	0.30	1.20
0.25	0.08	0.33	0.58	0.19	0.77	0.91	0.30	1.21
0.26	0.09	0.35	0.59	0.20	0.79	0.92	0.31	1.23
0.27	0.09	0.36	0.60	0.20	0.80	0.93	0.31	1.24
0.28	0.09	0.37	0.61	0.20	0.81	0.94	0.31	1.25
0.29	0.10	0.39	0.62	0.21	0.83	0.95	0.32	1.27
0.30	0.10	0.40	0.63	0.21	0.84	0.96	0.32	1.28
0.31	0.10	0.41	0.64	0.21	0.85	0.97	0.32	1.29
0.32	0.11	0.43	0.65	0.22	0.87	0.98	0.33	1.31
0.33	0.11	0.44	0.66	0.22	0.88	0.99	0.33	1.32

Net column shows the actual income received less tax.

Tax credit column shows the amount of the tax deducted from other income.

Gross column shows the total income for tax purposes.

Note: These grossing-up tables do not apply to dividends received after April 5th, 1993.

£1 to £5,000

Net	Tax Credit	Gross	Net	Tax Credit	Gross	Net	Tax Credit	Gross
£	£	£	£	£	£	£	£	£
1	0.33	1.33	34	11.33	45.33	130	43.33	173.33
2	0.67	2.67	35	11.67	46.67	140	46.67	186.67
3	1.00	4.00	36	12.00	48.00	150	50.00	200.00
4	1.33	5.33	37	12.33	49.33	160	53.33	213.33
5	1.67	6.67	38	12.67	50.67	170	56.67	226.67
6	2.00	8.00	39	13.00	52.00	180	60.00	240.00
7	2.33	9.33	40	13.33	53.33	190	63.33	253.33
8	2.67	10.67	41	13.67	54.67	200	66.67	266.67
9	3.00	12.00	42	14.00	56.00	210	70.00	280.00
10	3.33	13.33	43	14.33	57.33	220	73.33	293.33
11	3.67	14.67	44	14.67	58.67	230	76.67	306.67
12	4.00	16.00	45	15.00	60.00	240	80.00	320.00
13	4.33	17.33	46	15.33	61.33	250	83.33	333.33
14	4.67	18.67	47	15.67	62.67	260	86.67	346.67
15	5.00	20.00	48	16.00	64.00	270	90.00	360.00
16	5.33	21.33	49	16.33	65.33	280	93.33	373.33
17	5.67	22.67	50	16.67	66.67	290	96.67	386.67
18	6.00	24.00	51	17.00	68.00	300	100.00	400.00
19	6.33	25.33	52	17.33	69.33	350	116.67	466.67
20	6.67	26.67	53	17.67	70.67	400	133.33	533.33
21	7.00	28.00	54	18.00	72.00	450	150.00	600.00
22	7.33	29.33	55	18.33	73.33	500	166.67	666.67
23	7.67	30.67	60	20.00	80.00	550	183.33	733.33
24	8.00	32.00	65	21.67	86.67	600	200.00	800.00
25	8.33	33.33	70	23.33	93.33	650	216.67	866.67
26	8.67	34.67	75	25.00	100.00	700	233.33	933.33
27	9.00	36.00	80	26.67	106.67	750	250.00	1,000.00
28	9.33	37.33	85	28.33	113.33	800	266.67	1,066.67
29	9.67	38.67	90	30.00	120.00	850	283.33	1,133.33
30	10.00	40.00	95	31.67	126.67	900	300.00	1,200.00
31	10.33	41.33	100	33.33	133.33	950	316.67	1,266.67
32	10.67	42.67	110	36.67	146.67	1,000	333.33	1,333.33
33	11.00	44.00	120	40.00	160.00	5,000	1,666.67	6,666.67

Tax payable on specimen incomes[1]

SINGLE PERSON OR MARRIED WOMAN[4]				MARRIED MAN[4]	
On total income of	Persons under 65 years of age		Persons over 65[2]	Persons under 65 years of age[2]	Persons over 65[2]
	One person[2]	One parent family[3]			
£	£	£	£	£	£
4,000	111.00	—	—	—	—
4,500	211.00	—	60.00	—	—
5,000	311.00	—	160.00	—	—
5,500	411.00	67.00	260.00	67.00	—
6,000	513.75	167.00	360.00	167.00	—
6,500	638.75	267.00	460.00	267.00	—
7,000	763.75	367.00	575.00	367.00	67.00
8,000	1,013.75	583.75	825.00	583.75	267.00
9,000	1,263.75	833.75	1,075.00	833.75	467.00
10,000	1,513.75	1,083.75	1,325.00	1,083.75	708.75
12,000	2,013.75	1,583.75	1,825.00	1,583.75	1,208.75
14,000	2,513.75	2,083.75	2,325.00	2,083.75	1,708.75
16,000	3,013.75	2,583.75	3,013.75	2,583.75	2,433.75
18,000	3,513.75	3,083.75	3,513.75	3,083.75	3,083.75
20,000	4,013.75	3,583.75	4,013.75	3,583.75	3,583.75
25,000	5,263.75	4,833.75	5,263.75	4,833.75	4,833.75
30,000	6,942.00	6,254.00	6,942.00	6,254.00	6,254.00
35,000	8,942.00	8,254.00	8,942.00	8,254.00	8,254.00
40,000	10,942.00	10,254.00	10,942.00	10,254.00	10,254.00
45,000	12,942.00	12,254.00	12,942.00	12,254.00	12,254.00
50,000	14,942.00	14,254.00	14,942.00	14,254.00	14,254.00
75,000	24,942.00	24,254.00	24,942.00	24,254.00	24,254.00
100,000	34,942.00	34,254.00	34,942.00	34,254.00	34,254.00
150,000	54,942.00	54,254.00	54,942.00	54,254.00	54,254.00

NOTES

1 The same amount of tax becomes payable whether income is earned or unearned.

2 The tax shown is that due where there are no allowances other than the personal allowance and the married couple's allowance, as appropriate. Rather less tax will be payable by elderly persons aged 75 or over.

3 A single person with a qualifying child receives both the personal allowance and an additional personal allowance of £1,720.

4 The entire married couple's allowance has been allocated to the husband only.

Index

A
accommodation
  job-related 40–1
  office 69
  provision of living 73–5, 215
  rent-free 6
  see also private residences
accounts
  adjusting 99
  dates of 90, 216
action before April 6th, 1994 222–3
administration 158–66
  date tax payable 162–6
  how to appeal 166
  repayment of tax 158–60
  schedules and cases 161–2
  VAT 196
agricultural
  buildings 111–13
  property 202
allowances 6, 8–24
  blind person's vii, 4, 18–19, 25
  capital 104, 216
  death and superannuation benefits 25
  enterprise 100
  how to obtain 25
  indexation 24, 174–7
  married couples vii, 2, 4, 8, 9–15, 25, 148–50, 150, 157, 209, 212–13, 222
  personal *see* personal allowance
  transitional 4, 19–24
  widow's bereavement vii, 2, 4, 17–18, 150
  writing down 105
annual returns 3, 25, 182, 183–6
annuities 6, 7
  life 41, 131
  retirement 28–30
appeals 166
assessments 64, 161
  basis of 65, 207–8
  tolerance 64–5

B
back pay 65
bad debts and VAT 194
bank interest 6, 127–8, 158
basis of assessment
  employment 64–5
  Schedule A 207–8
  Schedule D 207
benefits in kind 6, 72–86
  all employees 72–5
  assessment of 76–7
  directors' benefits 76–86, 215–16
  employees earning £8,500 or more 76–86, 215–16
  fuel benefits 81–2
  living accommodation 73–5, 215
  loan facilities 84–5
  mobile telephones 83
  motor cars 78–82, 215
  scholarship awards 77
  use of assets 77–8
  workplace nurseries 77
bereavement allowance *see* widow's bereavement allowance
blind person's allowance vii, 4, 18–19, 25
bonuses 6–7
books, cost of 69
bounty payments 7
bridging loans 39–40
building society interest 6, 43, 126–7, 128, 158

buildings
agricultural 111–13
forestry 113
hotels 110
industrial 107–9
workshops 109–10
business expansion scheme 51–4, 208, 218
businesses and professions 90–103, 216–17
accounts 90, 99, 216
assets 200–202
capital allowances 216
closing businesses 91–2
enterprise allowance 100
expenditure allowed 97–8
expenditure not allowed 97
expenses 43, 68–9
losses 93–5, 179
National Insurance contributions 216–17
new businesses 90–1, 94–5
professional fees 69
profit 6, 90, 96
remuneration to employees 98–100
small businesses 100
sub-contractors 101–2
trading stock 98
work in progress 90
see also companies; partnerships

C
capital expenditure 104–14, 216
agricultural buildings 111–13
allowances 104, 216
companies 114
enterprise zones 110–11, 218
forestry land and buildings 113
hotels 110
industrial buildings 107–9
motor cars 106–7
non-traders 114
partnerships 114
plant and machinery 104–6
pooling 105–6
small industrial workshops 109–10
capital gains tax 3, 4–5, 168–82, 211, 219
annual exemption 179–80, 219
calculation of gains and losses 177–9
calculation of tax payable 180–2
deferment of tax 219
disposal of assets 168
exemptions and reliefs 168–9, 179–80, 219
gifts and hold-over relief 173–4
government securities 219
husband and wife 152, 169, 180, 180–2
indexation allowance 174–7
private residences 169–70
rates 219
retirement relief 170–2
returns 182
roll-over relief 172–3
trusts 182
cars *see* motor cars
Cases 161–2
changing jobs 62–3
charities 143–7
company donations 144, 190
covenants 138–40, 143–4, 208, 215
general exemption 143
Gift Aid scheme 145, 146
gifts of business equipment 145–7
inducements for funding 143–7
payroll deduction scheme 144
cheque accounts, joint 209–10
Child Support Agency 157
Children's Bonus Bonds 7, 122
children vii, 4, 214–15
income 150–2
Christmas boxes 6
claims 221
allowances 25
for interest paid 44–9
repayment of tax 158–60, 222
clergy, expenses and 69
close companies 42
closing business 91–2
clothing 69
code numbers 58–60

commission 6–7
companies 187–91
  business expansion
    scheme 51–4, 208, 218
  capital expenditure 114, 216
  chargeable gains 189
  charitable donations 144, 190
  close 42
  corporation tax 103, 187–90
  distributions 190–1
  employee-controlled 42
  interest payments 42, 44, 190
  pay and file 191
  small companies rate 187–9
  see also businesses and
    professions
compensation for loss of office 7,
  215–16
corporation tax 103, 187
  rates 187–90
covenanted payments 7, 138–42,
  208
  charitable 138–40, 143–4, 208,
    215

D
dates of payment of tax 162–6
death
  bereavement allowance *see*
    widow's bereavement
    allowance
  inheritance tax 200
  of spouse 150–2
death and superannuation
  benefits 25
deductions
  accounting for 62–3
  from business profits 96
  omission to deduct tax 63
  working sheets 60
deeds of covenant *see* covenanted
  payments
directorships 210
  benefits 76–86, 215–16
disclosure of information 221
distributions 190–1
dividends 1, 6, 7, 123–6
divorce and separation 23–4,
  152–7
  Child Support Agency 157
  maintenance payments 2, 7,
    152–7, 213
  marriage breakdown 213
  reconciliation 157
  year of separation 152

E
elections 221
employee-controlled
  companies 42
employments 58–71
  changing 62–3
  loss of 7, 87–9, 215–16
  overseas 66–7
enterprise allowance 100
enterprise zones 110–11, 218
entertainers, overseas 100–101
exemptions
  capital gains tax 168–9,
    179–80, 219
  inheritance tax 198–9, 219–20
  VAT 193–4
expenses, business 43, 68–9

F
farmers 96, 121, 195–6
Fixed Profit Car Scheme 70–1
forestry 121–2
  land and buildings 113
fuel benefits 81–2
furnished lettings 6, 118
  holiday accommodation
    119–21
  rent a room scheme 7, 118–19,
    120

G
Gift Aid scheme 144–5, 146
gifts
  business equipment 145
  capital gains tax 173–4
  charitable 143–7
  inheritance tax 199, 203, 220
government and other
  securities 129–31, 158, 219
grossing-up tables 228–9
Gulf War 66–7

H
hints on saving tax 212–21
hire-purchase interest 43
hold-over relief 173–4

holiday accommodation 119–21
home improvement loans 37
hotels
  capital expenditure 110
  expenses 69
how to obtain
  allowances 25
  relief for interest paid 44–9
  repayment of tax 158–60
husbands and wives 148–57
  allowances vii, 2, 4, 8, 9–15, 25, 148–50, 150, 157, 209, 212–13, 222
  business expansion scheme 54, 208
  capital gains tax 152, 169, 180, 180–2
  children's income 150–2
  death of spouse 150–2
  divorce and separation 23–4, 152–7, 213
  husbands with low income 19–21, 22
  husbands with older wives 21–3
  joint assets 134–5, 209–10
  joint income 210
  marriage 148–50, 212–13
  mortgage interest 47–9, 208–9
  pensioners and elderly persons 150
  pensions 35
  transfer of assets 135–6, 169, 210–11
  see also independent taxation

I

improvement loans 37
income
  assessable 6–7, 161
  disclosure of 221
  from abroad 134, 161–2
  investment 122–36, 217–18
  non-assessable 7
  property 115–22
  specimen 230
  treatment of 115–37
income tax
  grossing-up tables 228–9
  liability 6–7
  rates vii, 167
  ready reckoner 224–7
  returns 3, 25, 182, 183–6
  specimen tables 230
independent taxation 1, 3–5, 197, 207–11
  business expansion scheme 208, 218
  capital gains tax 211
  deeds of covenant 208
  directorships 210
  joint cheque accounts 209–10
  joint income 210
  life assurance relief 209
  losses carried forward 211
  married couple's allowance 209
  medical insurance policies 209
  mortgage interest 208–9
  partnerships 210
  Schedules A & D 207–8
  transfer of assets 210–11
  transitional allowances 4, 19–24
indexation allowance 24, 174–7
industrial
  buildings 107–9
  co-operatives 42
  workshops 109–10
inheritance tax 3, 197–206, 219–20
  agricultural property 202
  annual exemption 219–20
  business assets 200–202
  calculation of tax payable 202–3
  death 200
  gifts with reservation 199, 220
  gifts within seven years before death 220
  lifetime transfers 197–9, 220
  potentially exempt transfers 220
  rates 203–4, 205–6
  reliefs 220
  settled property 204
  valuation 200
instruction fees 69
interest 213–14
  bank deposit 127–8, 158
  building society 6, 43, 126–7,

128, 158
Children's Bonus Bonds 7
Government and other
securities 129–31, 158
hire-purchase 43
job-related
accommodation 40–1
let property 42–3, 48, 49
mortgage 2, 36–40, 47–9,
208–9
National Savings Bank 7, 128,
130
National Savings Capital
Bonds 129
National Savings Certificates 7
overseas 43
paid 36–49
partnerships 41
Save As You Earn Schemes 7,
131–2
short 43
on overdue tax 164–6
TESSA deposit schemes 7,
122, 133–4
see also loans
investment
income 122–36
opportunities 217–18
relief for 52–4

J
job-related accommodation 40–1
jobs *see* employments
joint
assets 134–5, 209–10
cheque accounts 209–10
income 210
owners of residence 38–9

K
'K' code 61–2

L
liability to income tax 6–7
life assurance
premiums 55
relief 209, 217
lifetime transfers 197–9
living accommodation 73–5, 215
loans
bridging 39–40
close companies 42
commercial property 42–3
employee-controlled
companies 42
facilities 84–5
home improvement 37
industrial co-operatives 42
interest free 84–5
mortgage 2, 36–40, 47–9,
208–9
personal representatives 42
plant and machinery 42
to purchase life annuity 41
see also interest
losses
business 93–5, 179
capital gains tax 177–9
carried forward 211
of office 7, 87–9, 215–16

M
maintenance payments 2, 7,
152–7, 213
market gardeners 96
married couples *see* husbands and
wives
medical insurance
premiums 55 6, 209
mileage allowances 70–1, 102–3
MIRAS scheme 2, 44–7, 214
mobile telephones 83
mortgage interest 2, 36–40, 47–9,
208–9
motor cars 78–82, 215
fuel benefits 81–2
future charges (1994–95)
79–81
insubstantial use 80
mobile telephones 83
motor mileage allowances
70–1, 83
scale benefits 79–82
substantial business use 78, 80
volunteer drivers – mileage
allowances 102–3
writing down allowances 106–7

N
National Insurance
contributions 50–1, 82–3,
216–17

National Savings Bank interest 7, 128, 130
National Savings Capital Bonds 129
National Savings Certificates 7, 122, 218
new businesses 90–1, 94–5
non-traders 114

O

office, loss of 7, 87–9, 215–16
office accommodation 69
overalls and clothing 69
overdue tax 164
overseas
  employments 66–7
  entertainers and sportsmen 100–101
  income from abroad 134, 161–2
  interest 43

P

partnerships 100
  capital expenditure 114
  changes 92–3
  husband and wife 210
  independent taxation 210
  interest paid to finance 41
pay and file 191
Pay As You Earn 2, 58–71
  accounting for deductions 62–3
  assessing tolerance 64–5
  assessments 64
  basis of assessment and back pay 65
  changing jobs and new employments 62
  code numbers 58–60
  date earnings received 65–6
  deductions working sheets 60
  expenses 68–9
  'K' code 61–2
  motor mileage allowances 70–1
  omission to deduct tax 63
  overseas employments 66–7
  pensions 68
  profit-related pay 67–8
  recovery of tax 63–4
  repayment of tax 60–1
  unemployment 61
payments in kind 7
payroll deduction scheme 144
penalties 164–6
pensioners and elderly persons 150
pensions 6, 68, 217–18
  contributions 26–35
  occupational schemes 27–8
  personal schemes 30–5
  relief 31–5, 217
  retirement annuities 28–30
  self-employed 217
  state 26
personal allowance vii, 3–4, 8–9, 25, 212
  additional 2, 15–16, 25
  basic 9
  increased 8, 9
  marginal 10
  special 23
personal equity plans 122, 132–3
personal representatives 42
personal tax system 1–2
plant and machinery 42, 104–6
pooling 105–6
premiums
  leases 6, 117–18
  life assurance 55, 209, 217
  medical insurance 55–6, 209
private residences
  bridging loans 39–40
  capital gains tax 169–70
  improvement loans 37
  joint owners 38–9
  limitations of relief 37–8
  mortgage interest 2, 36–40, 47–9, 208–9
  occupation by borrower 36–7
  occupation by dependent relatives 37
professions *see* business and professions
profit-related pay 67–8
profits 6, 90, 96
property income 115–22
  assessment 116–17
  calculation of liability 115–16
  commercial 42–3
  excess expenditure 116

inheritance tax 204
let property 42–3, 48, 49
see also rents
purchased life annuities 131

R

rates
capital gains tax 219
corporation tax 187–90
income tax vii, 167
inheritance tax 203–4, 205–6
VAT 194
ready reckoner 224–7
recovery of tax 63–4
redundancy payments 7, 87–9, 215–16
registration for VAT 192–3
reliefs
business expansion scheme 52–4, 208, 218
capital gains tax 168–74, 219
for interest paid 44–9
hold-over 173–4
inheritance tax 220
life assurance premiums 55, 209, 217
medical insurance premiums 55–6, 209
National Insurance contributions 50–1, 216–17
retirement 170–2
roll over 172–3
transitional *see* transitional reliefs
unused 33–5
vocational training 56–7
rent-free accommodation 6
rents 6, 7, 48–9, 69
assessment 116–17
for clergy 69
furnished 6, 118–21
lost 117
premiums from letting 117–18
property let commercially 42–3
relief for interest paid 46–8
repayment of tax 60–1, 158–60, 222
residence 161–2
residence, private *see* private residences
retail prices index 24, 175
retirement
annuities 28–30
relief 170–2
see also pensions
roll-over relief 172–3

S

salaries 6–7
sand and gravel quarries 121
Save As You Earn schemes 7, 131–2
saving tax 212–21
scale benefits, cars 79–82
Schedules 161–2, 207–8
scholarship
awards 77
income 7
securities, government 129–31, 219
separated couples *see* divorce and separation
settled property 204
short interest 43
small businesses 100
see also businesses and professions
small companies rate 187–9
small industrial workshops 109–10
social security benefits 7, 136–7
specimen incomes, tax payable on 224
sportsmen, overseas 100–101
sub-contractors 101–2
subscriptions 69
superannuation benefits 25

T

tax 1–2
administration 158–66
annual returns 3, 25, 182, 183–6
appeals 166
dates of payment 162–6
interest and penalties 164–6
interest attributable to offences 165
omission to deduct 63
on investment income 122–3
on profits 6, 90, 96

overdue 164
rates *see* rates
ready reckoner 224–7
recovery 63–4
remission 163–4
repayment of 60–1, 158–60, 222
saving 212–21
Schedules and Cases 161–2
specimen incomes 230
see also names of taxes
Tax Exempt Special Savings Account (TESSA) 7, 122, 133–4
terminal payments 87–9
tips 7
tools 69
trading stock 98
transfer of assets
husband and wife 135–6, 169, 210–11
inheritance tax 197–9, 220
transitional allowances 4, 19–24
transitional reliefs 19–24, 33
husbands with low incomes 19–21, 22
husbands with older wives 21–3
separated couples 23–4
travel
expenses 69
vouchers, warrants, allowances 7
trusts 182

U
unemployment 61, 137

V
value added tax 192–6
administration 196
bad debts 194
exempt supplies 193–4
rates 194
registration 192–3
zero-rating 194–5
vocational training 56–7
volunteer drivers: mileage allowances 102–3

W
wages 6–7
widow's bereavement allowance vii, 2, 4, 17–18, 150
woodlands 113, 121–2
work in progress 98
workplace nurseries 77
workshops, small industrial 109–10

Z
zero rating (VAT) 194–5

Notes

25% 3 years vehicles

Notes

Notes

Notes

Notes

Notes

Notes

Notes

Notes

Notes